D0438548

Customer Relationship Management

A Strategic Imperative in the World of e-Business

Customer Relationship Management

A Strategic Imperative in the World of e-Business

Editor and Contributor

STANLEY A. BROWN

John Wiley & Sons Canada, Ltd

Toronto • New York • Chichester • Weinheim • Brisbane • Singapore

Copyright © 2000 by John Wiley & Sons Canada, Ltd

All rights reserved. No part of this work covered by the copyrights herein may be reproduced or used in any form or by any means—graphic, electronic or mechanical—without the prior writen permission of the publisher.

Any request for photocopying, recording, taping or information storage and retrieval systems of any part of this book shall be directed in writing to the Canadian Reprography Collective, 6 Adelaide Street East, Suite 900, Toronto, Ontario, M5A 1H6.

Care has been taken to trace ownership of copyright material contained in this text. The publishers will gladly receive any information that will enable them to rectify any reference or credit line in subsequent editions.

John Wiley & Sons Canada Limited
22 Worcester Road
Etobicoke, Ontario
M9W 1L1

Canadian Cataloguing in Publication Data

Brown, Stanley A., 1946-
    Customer relationship management: a strategic imperative
    in the world of e-business

ISBN 0-471-64409-9

1. Customer relations — Management. I. Title.

HF5415.5.B763 2000   658.8'12   C00-930953-9

Production Credits:
Cover & text design: Interrobang Graphic Design Inc.
Printer: Tri-Graphic Printing Ltd.

Printed in Canada
10 9 8 7 6 5 4 3 2

C O N T E N T S

I t is called customer management, customer information systems, customer value management, customer care and sometimes customer centricity or customer-centric management.

But clearly, now, the term Customer Relationship Management has overtaken the market. eCRM is the management of customer relationships, and it is revolutionizing marketing and reshaping entire business models.

THE CUSTOMER IS THE CORE OF eCRM

More than ever, businesses are subjected to stronger, more rapidly changing forces: globalization, deregulation, convergence of industries, to name a few. These changes have been with us for quite a while, but now a well-established newcomer is providing even more fuel to this bonfire of change: e-business, the Internet and the Web, and electronic commerce are the new kids that are causing more disruptive changes on the business block.

New entrants invade old industries. Look at Travelocity in the travel industry, Autobytel in auto retailing, eSteel in steel products or eBay in auctions. Entirely new industries are created, such as AOL-Time Warner or Vodaphone, Mannesmann or Vivendi, and new marketing channels for traditional industries such as banking, insurance, telecom or retailing appear.

With all of these changes, businesses have rediscovered that, more than ever, in the face of increasing competition, mature markets and the ever-demanding customer, treating existing customers well is the best source of profitable and sustainable revenue growth. In other words: once we have a customer, let's do everything we can to keep them and develop our business with them. It is a lot cheaper than trying to look for some new ones—by a ratio of one to three in terms of marketing and sales expenditures.

Indeed it has always been the marketers' deepest aspirations to be able to:

- Target and serve customers on an individual basis (one-to-one rather than mass marketing)
- Establish long-term relationships with them (relationship rather than transaction marketing)
- Get rid of all these barriers and distortions created by the non-value adding intermediaries placed between the supplier and the customer (disintermediation or selling directly to the customer).

CRM is nothing more than one-to-one relationship marketing and disintermediation, but that is a lot. Over the past decade, we have gone from a situation where we used to sell products or services on a transaction basis and behaved as if we were constantly in a customer acquisition mode to a situation where we tried to retain our customers to make sure they would spend more on our products and services. We are now driving toward establishing a dialog with our customers, to understand and anticipate their evolving, individual needs and maximize the lifetime value of this relationship.

Customer Relationship Management as has just been described, is old hat in a sense—it is the way the corner grocer used to treat his customers. What is new is that we now can do it on an "industrialized" basis for tens of thousands, even millions of customers. That's what is entirely new. We have gone back to the old way of doing business, a customer at a time but for millions of customers. That is Customer Relationship Management today. The customer is back at the core of business strategies.

TECHNOLOGIES ARE REVOLUTIONIZING MARKETING: eCRM

As marketers, we are finally able to realize our aspirations to successfully execute these CRM strategies on a mass basis through the availability of technologies that allow us to establish individual relationships with customers like never before. The foundation for all this are PCs, telecom networks and especially Internet, multimedia contact centers, data warehouses and data-mining tools and marketing automation systems.

NOT ALL eCRM INVESTMENTS ARE EQUAL

Businesses have seen the opportunities offered by Customer Relationship Management enabled by technology, as evidenced by the investments they are making and plan to make in the future. Globally, businesses invested about $8 billion in hardware, software and external services in 1999 to design and implement eCRM solutions. And these investments will grow to over $38 billion by 2003. We also see that it is happening everywhere from New York City to Sydney and Frankfurt to Seoul and Rio de Janeiro.

Thirty-five percent of all eCRM investments are made first and foremost to reengineer or upgrade significantly customer care. Customer satisfaction is no longer a differentiator, it is a minimum requirement: customers today no longer tolerate poor service. With more choices than ever, they simply leave if not fully satisfied.

The major eCRM technologies used for customer care are contact centers and Internet sites and channels. Especially Web multimedia contact centers, in which the customer in self-service mode on an Internet site (for example, configuring his or her own insurance contract) can, if he or she needs help, be immediately connected to a contact center in which an agent in web chat, voice over IP or regular phone talk sees the same page as the customer and can help him or her on-line.

The second area of investments (about 20 percent) is in relationship marketing—loyalty management, target marketing, marketing automation—using a data warehouse and data-mining tools for segmentation, profiling, profitability analysis and targeting and some campaign management tools to manage the marketing campaigns.

The third area of investments (15 percent) is in implementing a multichannel strategy and the various sales automation tools associated with it (mobile offices, kiosks, agent's counters and so on). And finally at about

30 percent and growing very quickly is the deployment on the Internet of all the tools of Customer Relationship Management in marketing, sales and service (product information, configuration, pricing, product support, help desk and more and more often, orders on-line).

But a final and important point: More than implementing one point solution (a contact center, or a marketing automation tool), the true value of eCRM, the payback, comes from the integration of the various eCRM technology solutions. Integration, to ensure that the same customer information and customer intelligence is available at all customer touch points in all channels, is the basis for obtaining the complete benefits of eCRM investments. The customer today wants to choose the channel with which he will do business, and he expects that he will be known, understood and served in the same manner on each channel at each customer touch point.

BENEFITS: REDUCTION IN THE COST OF CUSTOMER CONTACTS

The first type of benefits from the successful execution of a eCRM strategy is reduced cost of a customer contact. That cost in a call center is about one-tenth of a contact through a distributor and one-twentieth of a direct face-to-face contact. And the cost of a self-service Internet contact is again one-twentieth of a call center contact. Knowing this, the direction is obvious.

And these companies get the customers to use the proper channel for the right transactions by using the right incentive. But the Internet does not solve everything. New Internet operators such as e-banks and e-brokers have learned that their self-service Internet channels are not sufficient. They need to add integrated contact centers as a complement to Internet, and in some cases some old-fashioned bricks and mortar branches, because some customers still like to see someone face-to-face in some situations.

In fact, it has been shown that about 20 to 30 percent of sales initiated on Internet required human intervention to be successfully completed. Best-in-class companies develop a multichannel strategy that gives them the right mix. For example, a retail bank keeps brick and mortar branches but at the same time develops contact centers and Internet channels. Successful eCRM clearly involves the integration of multiple channels to serve multiple markets at the optimal cost.

BENEFITS: PROFITABLE AND SUSTAINABLE REVENUE GROWTH

Reduction in cost of customer contacts is one dimension, but most of the benefits come from revenue from additional sales and margins leading to profitable and sustainable revenue growth. Improved customer satisfaction due to better customer care has a major impact on customer loyalty and retention. This leads to improved margins (higher prices) and less marketing and sales expenditures for acquisition of new customers to replace defections.

The second side of profitable revenue growth covers three major areas: up-selling and cross-selling to existing customers, targeting of more profitable customers and of products and services with better margins and an improved conversion rate of prospects with greater potential. These benefits are the basis of the development of the lifetime value of the relationships with the customers from acquisition through development and retention. Sustainable and profitable revenue growth through the development of lifetime value is the largest benefit of eCRM.

THE INTEGRATION CHALLENGES: MARKETING, TECHNOLOGY AND PEOPLE

There are major challenges to extract all the benefits of eCRM, which relate to integration in marketing, technology and people. The central challenge in marketing integration in CRM is the difficulty of implementing a multichannel strategy that has always been difficult, even without technology solutions, and it is even more complicated with Internet. It raises a number of questions:

- How do you integrate the new Internet channels with the existing ones?
- How do you prevent conflicts with the existing channel partners?
- How do you make sure that this is not simply cannibalizing traditional channels, rather than really winning new customers, when new Internet channels are created?

Today about 200 million people regularly connect to the Internet, and by 2003 that figure will be at least 500 million. Obviously everyone is anxious to reach 500 million potential customers and if one business doesn't do it, its competitors will. But in the meantime, what happens to the existing channels and customers? Barnes & Noble is a good example. If they had not entered the e-business, Amazon.com would have kept on taking away their customers. But now that they have entered ebusiness, it has become obvious that:

- It is not that easy for a chain of bricks and mortar bookstores, even one as innovative as Barnes & Noble, to become a successful Internet bookstore.

- When they are eventually successful (because they will be), will they actually attract new customers or simply transfer existing ones from their stores to the Internet? If only this happened, it would have a negative impact on their profitability, as it would only add costs, in which case they would have to start closing branches.

So marketing-wise, the CRM challenge today centers around the implementation of a multichannel strategy—the integration of multiple channels.

There is also a major challenge in integrating the various eCRM technologies. It is not easy to get all the front- and back-office technologies working together. For example, a bank customer wants the branch, the contact center, the Internet site and the ATM all to have the same up-to-date view of her accounts and transactions. And she wants her bank to make her personalized offers that are timely and relevant. She does not want her bank to inundate her with offers for savings accounts or credit cards for her children, when the bank knows quite well that she doesn't have any kids. At least it should know it, because as she gave all these details when she applied for her mortgage loan.

PwC just completed a survey showing that businesses experience a 70 percent success rate at implementing one eCRM technology (for example, Internet or Call Center), but the success rate drops quickly when several eCRM technologies have to be integrated, especially when more than three technologies are involved. With five technologies, there is less than a 40 percent chance of success, unless major precautionary measures are taken.

It is also clear, from lessons learned, that successful eCRM projects happen when people are integrated into the process of change from day one. Change management is fundamental to achieve the expected project benefits because people—from employees to channel partners and customers—are the ones generating the benefits by using the eCRM technologies to implement the eCRM strategies.

Change management has four major dimensions: training, communication, involvement and sponsorship. The fundamental importance of training is universally acknowledged, but the need for communication, the second dimension, is often overlooked. It is essential to have good communication with all concerned parties to avoid the tunnel effect. Good communication is the right message to the right audience, in the right medium, at the right time. It is not easy to do well.

Involvement is the third dimension. All parties concerned must be involved in the project to develop a sense of ownership, to give empowerment and eventually to generate enthusiasm. And finally there is sponsorship. The project must be sponsored by key decision makers from the business side (not just IT) who want to do the project because they need and want to produce the benefits. Only when this sponsorship is in place will the barriers be removed, the right priorities applied and the resources made available to make the project successful.

CONCLUSION

eCRM is revolutionizing marketing, and customer-centric marketing and technologies are driving this revolution. The benefits and the payback of eCRM projects are well worth the investments and the integration challenges. And this is why eCRM is so important today and is not just a fad. It delivers profitable and sustainable revenue growth, and this is why it is revolutionizing marketing.

DENIS COLLART
Global Leader
CRM Consulting
PricewaterhouseCoopers
Paris, April 2000

Customer Relationship Management: A Strategic Imperative in the World of e-Business

Survey after survey has shown that the key to success lies in focusing on customers' needs, providing products and services that meet those needs and then managing the customer relationship to ensure that customer satisfaction and repeat purchases occur. However, in the past, too many organizations have assumed that their products or services are so superior that customers would continuously come back simply on the basis of that. The myth about building a better mousetrap has been shattered. Customers have become increasingly bold and aggressive in their demands not only for superior quality but also for responsive service. The only way this can be provided is through customer relationship management. But what is customer relationship management? That is not an easy question to answer, but it is what we will set out to do in this book, through the collective wisdom and thought leadership of those who operate in this rapidly changing marketplace.

Customer Relationship Management (CRM) is neither a concept nor a project. Instead, it's a business strategy that aims to understand, anticipate and manage the needs of an organization's current and potential customers. It is a journey of strategic, process, organizational and technical change whereby a company seeks to better manage its own enterprise around customer behaviors. It entails acquiring and deploying knowledge about one's customers and using this information across the various touch points to balance revenue and profits with maximum customer satisfaction.

However, CRM is a strategy that must be tailored to each market segment and therein lies the challenge and the opportunity. To be effective in managing the customer relationship, an organization must:

a) Define its customer strategy. To do that there must be an understanding of customer segments and their needs. This is a mandatory requirement if one is to understand which products and services to offer and if that offering will be identical for each segment.

b) Create a channel and product strategy. This defines how the organization will deliver its products and services efficiently and effectively, ensuring sales productivity and effective channel management.

c) Understand the importance of a robust and integrated infrastructure strategy. This entails creating an environment to enable a relationship with the customer that satisfies the customer's needs. It requires an ability to achieve proactive customer management and reactive customer care.

Sound complicated? It's not. Perhaps the best way to explain the synergies and efficiencies of this approach is by way of a case study.

Recently, PricewaterhouseCoopers worked with a large North American financial service organization that faced some interesting challenges—challenges common to many others. Simply put, the company lacked a customer-focused service culture. It failed to respond to multiple and rapidly evolving constituent and customer needs. Moreover, its technology infrastructure (the hardware and software that allowed it to respond to the customer and its needs) was insufficient to support a customer care strategy. As a result, customers and the agents who sold its products and services were defecting, retention rates were falling and operating costs were escalating.

The organization had an immediate need to:

- Identify and understand customer needs. (It had to conduct interviews with its customers,)
- Effectively deliver products and services to meet those needs.
- Enhance revenue by attracting new high-value customers and improving the retention rate of existing customers.
- Improve the cost efficiency of services.

In short, it had to establish a customer relationship management culture within the organization and it had to ensure that that culture would take hold and translate into changed behaviors. What the organization failed to recognize was the following:

- There is a strong correlation between customer satisfaction and customer retention. For example, a recent study determined that 95 percent of customers who rate service as "excellent" will repurchase from an organization and are unlikely to switch to another product or service provider. For those customers who rate service as "good," the number drops significantly—to 60 percent.
- The key to enhancing revenue opportunities is linking particular products and services to particular customer segments.

From these facts the basic tenet of the recommended strategy was formulated: Improve revenues through increased customer satisfaction and retention by better aligning products and services to customer needs and then improving customers' access to those products and services through improved delivery channels (Part One of this book).

IMPLEMENTING A CRM STRATEGY

As highlighted earlier, implementing a CRM strategy requires focusing on three areas that affect customer care: customer strategy, channel and product management strategy and infrastructure strategy. (These are discussed in Parts Two, Three, Four and Five.)

What questions must be addressed in each area to implement such a strategy effectively? Consider the following:

Customer Strategy (Part Two)

- What are your key customer segments based on current and future customer needs?
- Are there distinct customer groups that have unique needs?
- Are there certain customer groups that should be offered unique products and services?
- Do you have unique strategies in place to ensure customer loyalty and retention?
- Have you established a win-win relationship with the customer?

Channel and Product Management Strategy (Part Three)

- Do customers prefer to receive the products or services through a particular channel of distribution such as the Internet, fax, mail or the telephone?
- What are the preferred channels through which to interface with the customer from an organizational perspective?
- What are the costs per channel?
- Which products and services should be directed through which channels to the various customer segments?
- What channel conflicts can possibly occur, and how do you plan to address them?

Infrastructure Strategy (Parts Four and Five)

- What common technology infrastructure is required?
- What technology will be required to create a learning organization?
- What new CRM practices, processes and tools are required?
- What new organizational and people competencies are needed in order to successfully implement the CRM strategy?

Once these questions are addressed, a set of synergies may emerge. Let's return to our case study to see how that organization addressed these questions on its way to forming a strategy.

Customer Strategy: First, the financial service organization segmented its customers into four key customer groups. Coincident with this, it reviewed its product offering to these groups. It then estimated the revenue, profitability and potential against these key segments.

Product and Channel Strategy: Next, it identified the channels of distribution through which its various products and services could be provided, including kiosks (ATMs), the Internet, customer care centers, faxes and mail. Then, the organization identified the most appropriate channel for distributing each service to the respective customer segment.

Infrastructure Strategy: Finally, the organization ensured that the technology, systems and organizational structure to support a dedicated channel strategy was developed. This allowed management to place the service responsibility in the most efficient channel of distribution. This strategy allowed the organization to channel particular products and services to particular customer segments in an efficient and cost-effective manner.

The result? Customer satisfaction increased 15 percent; operating costs decreased by 10 percent as a result of a streamlined distribution system and retention rates improved by over 18 percent. This translated into a net profit improvement of 25 percent.

CAN THESE LESSONS APPLY TO MY ORGANIZATION?

What we have tried to highlight is a process or route map to success that may in fact have a number of paths to get you to a destination that we call Customer Relationship Management. The chapters that follow will provide important insights on:

- Leading trends and best practices in customer relationship management (CRM).

- The successes and failures of organizations around the globe in trying to implement CRM.

- The role of people, processes and technology to enable it.

The foundation of this book is an exploration of these three strategies (customer strategy, product and channel strategy, and infrastructure strategy) and a discussion of the critical steps to creating the framework that we call Customer Relationship Management. As you read the materials in this book, I offer up a challenge to you. The chapters that follow provide examples from a number of industries such as financial services, automotive and telecommunications. But the principles discussed are applicable to all industry sectors, and to large multinational corporations or small domestic enterprises. Push the envelope and accept the fact that there is much to be learned from industries other than your own. Accept the ideas and concepts presented, look at them from different angles and dissect them further. The challenge is to discover the key principles that are real winners, and adapt them within your organization.

The first section of this book (Part One—First Principles in Customer Relationship Management) will explore the concept of CRM and how organizations actually achieve it. This is not theory but practical examples related to the people, process and technology issues that must be addressed.

The second section (Part Two—Building and Implementing the Customer Strategy) discusses two primary goals—customer loyalty and customer dependency—and the options available to organizations for achieving a robust and successful customer strategy.

Part Three (The Need for Effective Channel and Product Strategies) covers the fundamentals of channel and product strategy from the role of new product development, channel management and the e-channel to what processes must change and what technology must be embraced. Part Four (The Infrastructure Strategy) addresses infrastructure strategy and the role to be played by database management and marketing. It also addresses the issue of organization structure and competencies as well as methodologies to implement CRM. Part Five (Enabling the CRM Strategy) provides an overview of best practices in customer care, culture and performance measurement.

This book has been compiled through contributions from partners and senior practitioners at PricewaterhouseCoopers who will provide discussions of leading approaches and trends. Leaders in our Customer Relationship Management consulting practice have contributed ideas, models and case studies. This book contains a complete package for anyone seeking to leverage the strategic advantage to be gained from Customer Relationship Management.

WHAT MAKES THIS BOOK DIFFERENT

This book does not confine itself to a discussion of the theory of CRM, rather it focuses on actual practice, leading technology and proprietary research. The practices described have been used by some of the major global organizations in CRM. This emphasis on the practical makes this book an excellent source for those looking for real solutions to actual challenges. Here are some of the ways in which the book will emphasize the practical:

- A proven best-practice approach to achieving a CRM enterprise (which we call the Market Intelligent Enterprise—MIE), together with work steps, templates and best practices
- Case studies from organizations that PricewaterhouseCoopers has worked with that explain how to implement the various stages of CRM
- Case studies from those organizations that have implemented or exhibited best practices in the key principles and technology of CRM.

- White papers, proprietary research and best practices.

By seeing where organizations started and how they realized their customer management goals, readers will not only learn the practices but also see them in real action, moving organizations into more prosperous futures.

A C K N O W L E D G M E N T S

This is my sixth book on customer care and when I sit back to consider how this ever came to be, I recognize that each and every time, it was only made possible by the collective support of many. In this case the cast has once again changed slightly, but the feature players have remained almost in tack.

In the role of director, special credit goes to Mike Stoneham, the leader of PricewaterhouseCoopers' Management Consulting Services in Canada. My thanks for your continued encouragement over the years. Your leadership and insight have been a guiding light for me.

In the role of producers, are my colleagues in the Customer Relationship Management practice around the globe, the contributors to this work. Special appreciation goes to Denis Collart, the Global Leader of the Customer Relationship Management practice at PricewaterhouseCoopers.

The executive producer honours go to my publisher, John Wiley & Sons. This is now our fourth book together. Special thanks to Karen, Elizabeth and Ron. Each time we get better and challenge each other to raise the bar.

The supporting cast, but perhaps the most critical players, is my family, who once again have forgiven me for breaking the promise that this is my last book. Without the consideration and support of my wife

Rhonda and children Lowell, Brian, Cynthia and Neil this would not have been possible. Thank you for your continued patience, and help in the research and edits for this book.

Thanks to all of you and a special wish to the "little princess," Elena Rachelle, and those that follow her—may we all enjoy life, sunshine, love and good health together.

Stanley Brown
April, 2000

Part One

First Principles in CRM: Overview

What exactly is CRM and why is everybody so concerned about it? The basic problem appears to be that many organizations do not truly understand what CRM is, how it must be used, and who is the beneficiary of this new focus on the customer. They believe that CRM can be achieved through investment in new technology; the more expensive the hardware or software, the greater customer satisfaction and revenue growth that can be achieved. Look at this headline from a respected technology research group, META Group:

> META Group Predicts "Serious Risk of Failure" for Leading Companies Implementing Customer Relationship Management (CRM) Initiatives

The study, which was based on interviews with Global 2000 companies, including Sprint, Nortel Networks, Eastman Kodak and PNC Bank, found that most enterprises do not have adequate CRM business plans in place and are not spending nearly enough on their CRM projects. The study revealed that most CRM projects are highly fragmented and lack customer focus. It was also revealed that most companies underestimate the value of customer information, purchase disparate CRM products and services, focus too heavily on the electronic channel, and fail to employ meaningful measurement techniques.

Other findings from the META Group/IMT study include:

- 64 percent of respondents lack techniques to measure the business value of CRM.

- Less than 10 percent of companies are able to measure a tangible return on investment (ROI).

- Less than 30 percent have begun to take steps to integrate operational and analytical CRM environments.

- In spite of marketplace perceptions of the Web—e-channel—as a dominant customer contact point, traditional methods such as face-to-face selling, business partners, and tele-channels continue to account for more than 95 percent of revenues.

- Respondents provided multiple, conflicting and often incomplete definitions of CRM.

- While 78 percent describe CRM primarily as a customer imperative, the other 22 percent of respondents define CRM largely as a set of tools and technologies.

Let's not stop there. While a proper definition of CRM and its purpose (goals and objectives) is required, there is no one product on the market that will create optimal CRM. CRM requires an enterprise approach to customer care. It involves an integration of the front and back office. It requires a focus on the customer and an ability to learn from each customer interaction. Another highly respected Information Technology research organization, the Gartner Group, stated in a research report:

> Competitively differentiating applications for managing prospects, customers, partners and suppliers are becoming increasingly hot areas. Revamping business processes around selling, servicing, marketing, e-commerce and supply chain planning and scheduling will be on the agendas of every CEO and CIO.
>
> The key to achieving success will be to achieve integration end-to-end, front office to back office. This entails enterprise workflow, purchased applications, in-house legacy applications, telephony infrastructure and the Internet. All these products, hardware and software applications must be integrated into one seamless solution that interacts with the customer and the organization.

Times are obviously becoming more complicated.

To bring order to this chaos, our first chapter, "Putting CRM to Work: The Rise of the Relationship," starts with what we believe to be the fundamentals of CRM. It is based on the principle that mass-media advertising is on the decline as a tool, and that focusing on customer relationship management (CRM) may be the best way to win, retain and increase business. Organizations are finding that they must use more select methods and channels to reach their varied customer segments. To be successful they must turn to CRM, learning what their customers want and tailoring their marketing accordingly. The chapter provides a framework to succeed and gives examples from the telecommunications field.

Our next chapter—"The Need for Market Intelligent Enterprise (MIE[1]): Laying the Foundation"—provides a framework. The chapter highlights the six somewhat overlapping characteristics that define the market intelligent enterprise:

- Strategic use of customer and prospect information
- Transactional focus
- Operational use of information
- Enterprise-wide approach
- Strategic channel management
- Technology-enabled new business opportunities

As the chapter points out, some organizations have moved along the learning curve, but only a few have begun to pull together all the elements to become a true market intelligent enterprise.

We close the section with a chapter that is a case study in the financial services sector, one that will provide us with a substantial number of best practice examples in CRM. In this case the credit goes to Capital One. As you will see, Capital One's essence is not about status quo. It is about constantly reinventing itself and the way it does business. The organization believes that the only way companies can distinguish themselves in the eyes of the consumer is through customer service and customer relationship management.

What makes winners is not an emphasis on products, but on how you get out there and create the lasting relationship with the customer. That's what counts, and that means CRM.

---

[1] MIE is a (sm) of PricewaterhouseCoopers.

Putting CRM to Work:

THE RISE OF THE RELATIONSHIP

Lawrence Handen

With mass-media advertising on the decline as a tool, marketers are focused on customer relationship management (CRM) as the best way to win, retain and grow business. The mass-media ad campaigns of yesteryear, the ones that made people want to reach out and touch someone and that evoked warm feelings toward the phone company, are a relic of a much less complicated time and market. Today, with more and more services available, organizations can no longer expect results from broad advertising and marketing campaigns aimed at the broad mass of customer.

Increasingly, organizations are finding that they must use more select methods and channels to reach their varied customer segments. Some are turning to customer relationship management (CRM), learning what their customers want and tailoring their marketing accordingly.

CRM: WHY BOTHER?

Many organizations have been competing almost entirely on price, using advertising to assert that their products were significantly less expensive than their competitors'. Pricing strategy is still vital, but because of the fragmentation and commoditization of services, it is increasingly difficult to compete on the basis of price alone. As an example, in the telecommunications industry, since July 1997, margins on residential communications in the United States have declined 26 percent while the number of competitors has increased 14 percent, according to the Federal Communications Commission (FCC). Similar conditions exist for organizations in other countries with competitive telecom markets. This decline in margins and increase in competitors is unlike any other industry and thus has created unique challenges.

As the market becomes increasingly fragmented and commoditized, organizations are finding it difficult to use traditional mass-media marketing techniques to capture market share. Broad marketing and advertising campaigns are simply no longer as effective as they once were. One message does not fit all. Because of the proliferation of services and customer needs, organizations need to market to many more types of users. Further, customers' use of media has also fragmented, and the media used to reach them have proliferated.

In the past, organizations could be relatively confident that if they ran an advertisement they would be reaching a broad audience. Today, with the proliferation of cable TV channels (53 percent growth in 1999 vs. 1998, according to the Newspaper Association of America), decline in prime-time TV viewership (down 3 percent), and increased use of the Internet, organizations cannot reach the same number of people they did in the past through a single medium. More important, as with most mass-media campaigns, they cannot be sure that they are reaching the audience they are targeting.

To succeed in the future, organizations will need to better understand what customers want. Marketing will be more finely tuned and managing the relationship with the customer will be paramount. To counter the decline of mass media as a vehicle for effective advertising, communications organizations are moving quickly to embrace customer relationship management (CRM).

But what exactly is CRM? Simply defined, it is the process of acquiring, retaining and growing profitable customers. It requires a clear focus on the service attributes that represent value to the customer and that create loyalty.

Customer relationship management has several advantages over traditional mass-media marketing. It:

- Reduces advertising costs
- Makes it easier to target specific customers by focusing on their needs

- Makes it easier to track the effectiveness of a given campaign

- Allows organizations to compete for customers based on service, not prices

- Prevents overspending on low-value clients or underspending on high-value ones

- Speeds the time it takes to develop and market a product (the marketing cycle)

- Improves use of the customer channel, thus making the most of each contact with a customer

ANATOMY OF A CAMPAIGN

Customer relationship management begins with the development of a marketing strategy based on the critical forces that affect organizations, such as regulatory, societal, market, technological and business conditions. Part of the strategy is to determine how customer relationship management decisions will affect marketing behavior.

Using the marketing strategy as a foundation, the organization begins to define segments within its current and prospective customer base. Segmentation is a way of categorizing groups of customers with common characteristics for the purpose of delivering a targeted marketing message. Once the organization has defined its segments, it will develop a campaign targeted at one or more of these segments.

In building the campaign, a organization decides what type of products will be included, how they will be priced, what promotions will be extended, how long they will run and to whom they will be offered. Marketers also need to consider which sales channels are most appropriate, whether mass media, direct mail or outbound call centers. When this is done, the campaign is evaluated to assess the percentage of the target market that purchase the offer (potential take rates) and overall profitability. If the campaign is predicted to be profitable, the content—the message—of the campaign is created.

While the content is being created, the organization usually begins scoring its customer database to find potential candidates for the campaign. The customer database can contain a list of existing customers, customers who have recently defected, prospective customers, customers of affinity partners or a combination of all of these. The customers in this database have already been categorized in the earlier segmentation work. Scoring is a process of using the segments and other customer information to select the customers most likely to accept the offer. There are a number of software tools available to assist in this process; however each target market will have its own unique set of variables and weights assigned to these variables in developing a scoring pattern.

After scoring is completed, the campaign is tested on a small subset of selected customers. On the basis of the test results, the organization may adjust components of the campaign, such as price, promotion and features to increase yield. The organization will also use these tests to recalibrate its formula (known as a scoring algorithm) to determine how likely a customer is to buy a particular product and predictive acceptance models, which are used to predict the likelihood of a target market accepting an offer and thus estimate likely sales or purchases.

If the campaign is still deemed profitable after testing, it proceeds to sampling. The principle difference between testing and sampling is the size of the focus group and choice of sales channel. During the testing phase, the focus groups are small—often 5 percent of the target audience—and the contacts are usually made by the marketing organization. In the sampling phase, the focus group grows to 25 percent of the target audience, and the sales channels selected for the full campaign are used to contact the customers. The marketing organization will again consider revising its campaign and adjusting its predictive acceptance models and profitability calculations.

It should be noted that in several communications organizations, these testing and sampling processes are combined successfully. Unfortunately, in many more, these processes are either not performed adequately or are skipped entirely.

The final step before campaign execution is rollout. Lead lists are generated and sent to the sales channels, final promotional and advertising material is produced and distributed, the offering is entered into the billing and order entry systems and the channel representatives are trained in the specifics of the offer.

Once the campaign has been rolled out, it is up to the individual channels to execute it. From a customer relationship standpoint, the principal emphasis is on direct mail and telemarketing. Direct mail comes in two forms, "white mail" and e-mail, and telemarketing also has two components, outbound and inbound. Outbound telemarketing representatives call the prospects identified during the scoring process and use scripts to pitch the offering. Inbound telemarketers accept the calls generated by the mass media or direct mail portion of the campaign. The inbound customer service representatives may also be asked to promote the campaign while they are helping their existing base of customers with service problems or bill inquiries.

The final stage of the campaign is the treatment of the responses. Each prospect is evaluated. Ideally, a prospect accepts the offer and proceeds to have the service installed or activated. But evaluating the negative reactions is equally important. Did the customer not accept the offer because it was too expensive or did not fit their needs? Worse yet, was the organization simply unable to contact the customer because it lacked call center resources? All of this information is critical to continually refining and improving every step of the campaign process from segmentation through execution.

FOUR TYPES OF CUSTOMER RELATIONSHIP MANAGEMENT

CRM allows a company to address all of the types of customers it serves at different points in their life cycle and to choose the marketing program that best fits a customer's attitude toward the company and willingness to purchase its products and services. Four types of CRM programs enable the company to win back customers who have defected or are planning to, to create loyalty among existing customers, to up-sell or cross-sell services to these customers and to prospect for new customers.

Win Back or Save

This is the process of convincing a customer to stay with the organization at the point they are discontinuing service or convincing them to rejoin once they have left. Of the four categories of campaigns, win back is the most time-sensitive. Research indicates that a win-back campaign is four times more likely to succeed if contact is made within the first week following a defection than if it is made in the fourth week.

Selectivity is the other essential characteristic of a successful win-back campaign. Leading organizations often filter their prospects for contact to exclude customers who have frequently switched (churners), who have bad credit ratings or whose usage is low.

Most new selection techniques are allowing organizations to trim back their contact lists, but one trend is extending them. In years past, organizations would ignore customers who had a significant decline in usage or who had discontinued some services as long as they remained customers. The organizations assumed that such customers were merely switching to another product. Without good data and the ability to analyze it, there was no way to disprove this assumption. Recent work in this area has shown that many of these consumers are either reducing overall usage or, worse, migrating to a competitor's product. To preserve the revenue stream and prevent the customer from becoming a "traditional" win-back candidate, a few organizations are now including partial disconnects and reduced-usage customers in their win-back campaigns.

Prospecting

Prospecting is the effort to win new, first-time customers. Apart from the offer itself, the three most critical elements of a prospecting campaign are segmentation, selectivity and sources. It is essential to develop an effective needs-based segmentation model that allows the organization to effectively target the offer. Without this focused approach, the organization either fails to achieve an adequate acceptance or rate on the offer or spends too much on promotions, advertising and concessionary pricing. It is advisable to achieve a 95 percent confidence rate before embarking on a prospecting effort.

Selectivity is as important to prospecting as it is to win back. Needs-based segmentation defines what the customer wants from the organization and profit-based segmentation, defines how valuable the customer is and helps the organization decide how much it is willing to spend to get that customer. Pre-scoring a consumer credit rating is one of the techniques that organizations can use to determine the latter. Organizations have traditionally experienced rates of uncollectibles ranging from 4 to 8 percent. To reduce this figure, they are following an example set by the retail industry, which developed credit-scoring algorithms to apply to prospective consumers. Retail companies that do this have cut their uncollectibles in half—from 6 to 3 percent—on average. Today's organizations hope to meet with similar success.

Loyalty

Loyalty is the category in which it is most difficult to gain accurate measures. The organization is trying to prevent customers from leaving and uses three essential elements: value-based and needs-based segmentation and predictive churn models. Value-based segmentation allows the organization to determine how much it is willing to invest in retaining a customer's loyalty. It is possible that the organization will invest nothing in those customers it deems to be marginally profitable and will actively encourage unprofitable customers to leave (see Figure 1.1).

Figure 1.1: United States Long Distance Telephone Profit

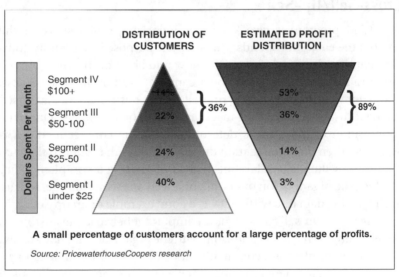

A small percentage of customers account for a large percentage of profits.

Source: PricewaterhouseCoopers research

Once the customer has passed the value-based segmentation screening, the organization can use needs-based segmentation to offer a customized loyalty program. Affinity programs, such as airline miles and hotel points, are some of the most popular. Besides affinity programs, organizations will often offer customized billing, special help lines or back-end loaded credits as a means of encouraging loyalty. It is important to note that most of these offers are based more on a customer's revenue level than tailored to their segments. However, as organizations focus more on the needs of individual customers, they find that they are able to achieve the same level of loyalty with less investment.

The final component of a successful loyalty campaign is the development of a predictive churn model. Using the vast amount of demographic data and usage history available for the existing base of customers, it is possible to predict customer attrition. Through the use of advanced data-mining tools, organizations can develop models that identify vulnerable customers, which can then be targeted for a loyalty campaign or offered alternative products. Organizations should achieve a confidence ratio of 70 percent or greater with their churn models before implementing campaigns. At levels lower than this the cost far outweighs the potential increase in gross profit.

Cross-Sell/Up-Sell

This CRM program is also known as increasing wallet share or the amount the customer spends with you. The purpose is to identify complementary offerings that a customer would like. For instance, a basic long-distance customer could be a candidate to buy Internet access. The nature of the offer is determined by the customer's needs-based segment, usage pattern and reaction to previous contacts. Once the composition of the offer is determined and the contact medium is agreed to, then the organization directly presents that offer to the customer. Up-selling is similar, but instead of offering a complementary product, the organization offers an enhanced one. For example, replacing an analog data line with ISDN is a good example of an up-sell.

Cross-sell/up-sell campaigns are important because the customers targeted already have a relationship with the organization. They are less likely to see the offer as a commodity and are thus more willing to pay a premium for it. In financial terms, when a customer accepts a cross-sell or up-sell offer, that customer begins to become much more profitable. At the outset of this relationship, the customer reduces gross margin by 3 percent (based on acquisition costs); within three years, this customer is enhancing gross margin by 7 percent (see Figure 1.2).

Figure 1.2: Retaining Customers Equals Profitability

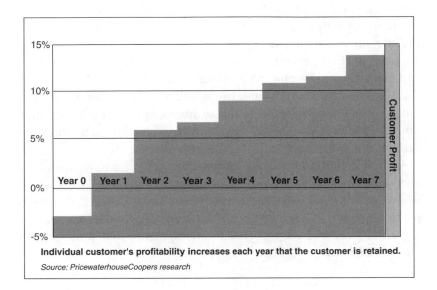

Individual customer's profitability increases each year that the customer is retained.

Source: PricewaterhouseCoopers research

IMPLEMENTING CRM

Five elements are required to implement a CRM program effectively: strategy, segmentation, technology, process and organization.

Strategy

Six types of strategy affect a CRM program: channel, segmentation, pricing, marketing, branding and advertising, and of these the first three—channel, pricing and segmentation—have the greatest impact. Segmentation will determine how clients, and ultimately the marketing organization, will be structured. Pricing strategy is the single greatest differentiator in a commoditized market and will determine more than half of the value of the offer. Channel strategy determines how the offer will be conveyed to the customer.

It is important to revisit all of these strategies frequently. Difficulties in implementation and evaluating campaign results may indicate the need for changes.

Segmentation

Historically, segmentation focused on a particular product or market, but more recently, organizations have used it to consider the value of the customer to their businesses. And today, some organizations are adopting a "third-generation" outlook for segmentation—categorizing and marketing to customers according to customers' needs.

The idea is straightforward, but developing an accurate picture of those needs can be difficult. To use segmentation effectively, organizations need to develop the right set of formulas (algorithms) for modeling the behavior of customers.

Often organizations begin with segments that are too nebulous, and sometimes they cannot fit customers to categories. This occurs when organizations rely too heavily on projected behavioral traits or psychographics, rather than on historical patterns and demographics. Algorithms need to be properly tested to ensure that prospects are appropriately categorized.

Technology

The CRM process depends on data. Concentrating on creating a single, operations-focused, integrated logical database is the most important technical consideration. Other essential elements to consider are the software for the database, data mining and decision support and campaign management tools, as well as call center software and hardware. Hardware, databases and decision support software are in use within the communications industry but campaign management, call center and data-mining tools are less well known.

The biggest technology problem for many organizations is the set up of their databases. Most organizations configure their databases to support data-warehousing functions, rendering them incapable of scaling up to support the order entry or billing process. Still more organizations create multiple separate databases to support data mining, campaign management and call centers. The process is not only time consuming and expensive, but it is often difficult to reconcile as well.

Process

Identifying the processes that need to be involved in implementing customer relationship management is not inherently difficult. The difficulty lies in gaining organizational buy-in, developing measurements to assess the effectiveness of new processes and implementing technology to support and enforce its use. The CRM process is the order and method by which the direct marketing activities are executed. It is not overly complicated, but it does emphasize speed to market. As a consequence, process reengineering efforts concentrate on minimizing the time it takes to execute a particular marketing activity and reducing the interdependencies, if not the total number of marketing tasks.

Given the importance of speed, it is interesting to note that problems that arise are most frequently attributable to the failure to measure and evaluate the process itself. Most organizations are so focused on tabulated "acceptance rates" of the service or product offering that they fail to consider continuous process improvement. The failure to capture and evaluate all of the data, both positive and negative, is another major contributor to implementation problems. Purging untreated records from the outbound call center without providing this information to the central database is a prime example. The organizations that are most effective in making these types of process improvements emphasize closed-end decision support: the process of tying your conclusion to an action and the action to a tracking mechanism so that the entire decision process can be evaluated and adjusted.

Organization

Organizational structure is often the most overlooked component of a customer relationship management implementation. As discussed above, most organizations' marketing is media-based. Consequently, making a transition to direct marketing is difficult, especially when it coincides with the introduction of needs-based segmentation. Creating cross-discipline segment teams is effective if they are formed for the purpose of learning and executing new styles of campaigns. Each segment team should take turns working through the four categories of campaigns—the win back or save, prospecting, loyalty and cross-selling/up-selling. Select members of each segment team should participate in the exercises to accelerate the transfer of knowledge and to coach their peers through the process. It is not advisable to pilot campaigns with a company's most-profitable segments first, except in the case of win-back campaigns to reacquire customers that have previously left.

Using the wrong performance measures can be another major organizational pitfall. Most of these are oriented toward the old process and reflect individual silos of achievement. The most common example is the practice of rewarding call centers according to the number of win-back accounts saved, without regard to the profitability of those accounts. It is essential that departments within the organization work together to form metrics that reflect the new process and the collaborative nature of customer relationship management.

CONCLUSION

How important has customer relationship management been? The answer can be found in two recent PricewaterhouseCoopers' (PwC) studies. The first shows a perfect correlation between revenue and stock price growth for publicly traded organizations. No other financial measure is so tightly correlated in this industry. A second study shows the impact of customer relationship management on profitability. Based on independent research, PwC estimates that bottom-line performance can be significantly increased in each of the four major categories of CRM campaigns: win-back, by 10 to 20 percent; loyalty (churn reduction), by 15 to 20 percent; cross-sell/up-sell, by 2 to 3 percentage points; and prospecting, by 3 to 4 percentage points. In essence, the market expects organizations to be able to manage down costs. What investors are skeptical about is the organizations' ability to attract and retain profitable customers. Customer relationship management allows them to do just that.

About the Author

LAWRENCE HANDEN

Lawrence Handen is a Partner in PricewaterhouseCoopers' America's CRM consulting practice. His primary focus is CRM in our Telecommunication, Information, Communication and Entertainment Consulting Practice.

The Need for a Market-Intelligent Enterprise (MIE)^{Sm}

LAYING THE FOUNDATION

Harris Gordon
Steven Roth

A REGIONAL PHONE COMPANY lost 27 percent of its intrastate long-distance customers' business to other long-distance providers. Using its information on the profitability of those customers, the company segmented its defectors and tailored strategies to win back its most profitable customers—7 percent of those who left. Result: the company won back close to 50 percent of its profitable customers within 48 hours of their defection, leaving unprofitable customers with the competition. In addition, through additional research the firm gained important information from those customers, including how the competition lured them away and how those customers rated its own service quality. The company learned, for instance, that service was not up to par in one region, a problem it quickly rectified. The competition's fate: left with unprofitable customers, it was out of the marketplace one year after the provider described above began its information-rich campaign.

Generally, a small percentage of the customer base—about 20 percent or less—provides a significantly higher percentage of revenues and profits. (This relationship is known as the Pareto Principle.)

Figure 2.1

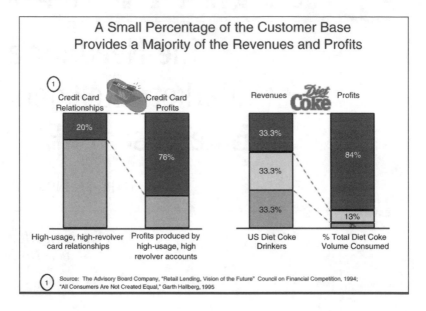

In Figure 2.1 above, a financial institution found that 20 percent of its credit card customers represented 75 percent of its profit from credit card operations. In another research study, the Coca-Cola company found that one-third of its Diet Coke drinkers consumed 84 percent of the total sold.

Leading-edge companies are driving to increase profits from high-yield customers. They aim to acquire and retain profitable customers and get them to spend more. But with competitors seeking the same customers, companies that take an enterprise-wide focus, looking across the organization to share and leverage information and processes, are the ones positioned for long-term profitability. The goal of those trailblazers is to transform themselves into market-intelligent enterprises that are connected, responsive and fluid.

The Market-Intelligent Enterprise looks dramatically different than companies built on the earlier "we make it, you take it" model of business. In the old model, products and communication moved mostly one way, from production to customers, through limited channels. Senior management dictated what, when and how to sell. Not any more. As the marketplace matures, consumers receive more voluminous information faster and through more channels. Swift and shrewd entrepreneurs enjoy higher gross margins in the early stages by being first to market and can capitalize on limited competition.

Figure 2.2: The Market-Intelligent Enterprise Business Model

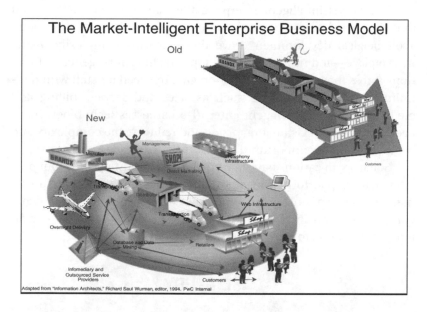

The key to prolonging the competitive lead is using customer information at a granular level—the more detail, the better. The history of a company's relationship with its customer—gleaned from each transaction, its preferences and service needs—is not easily available to competitors. The market-intelligent enterprise embraces a more evolved vision of its customer relationship. The current military metaphor of the marketing lexicon—"targeting" and "capturing" markets, for instance—suggests a win-lose relationship. But what company wants to destroy its customer? A more apt description is one of the market-intelligent enterprise partnering in a dance between an organization and its customers. The customer swings one way, and the company follows. The market-intelligent enterprise begins to anticipate the moves of its partner—the customer—and refines its response so efficiently that it's difficult to discern who is leading. It's a win-win relationship with greater profitability for the company and improved satisfaction for the customer.

The market-intelligent enterprise begins with a customer-centric vision, creates a strategy centered on that vision and builds processes and systems to support and implement that strategy throughout the organization. The organization develops new core competencies and new performance measures that guide continuous improvement and strategy.

The market-intelligent enterprise offers opportunities to hone and build business but also creates a more complex business environment. Technological development drove the increasing complexity of the marketplace—and now technology supports the convergence of functions across the organization, encouraging the need for staff with multidimensional competencies such as sales and service, billing and credit. The market-intelligent enterprise harnesses technology, management tools and vision, organizing and reducing the complexity and capitalizing on the opportunities it proffers.

Some organizations have moved down the learning curve, but only a few have begun to pull together all the elements to become a true market-intelligent enterprise. When that happens, here's what such a company—in this instance, in the financial services industry—might look like to the customer.

CASE STUDY

MIECO, a fictitious financial services company, tailors its products to each customer's needs. One particular customer's package includes a money market fund, a mutual fund, a credit card, a home mortgage, and home, life and auto insurance. MIECO knows the customer travels frequently for work and relays this information to its credit card partner to prevent unnecessary calls to the customer for authorization when there are periods of heavy use.

Having accumulated customer preferences by learning habits and trends through each transaction, MIECO sends offers that have a high degree of acceptance (for example, information on vacation home real estate opportunities and car lease changes). The company also provides information on the tax implications of owning a second home and reviews the customer's financial holdings, offering suggestions on how to finance a second mortgage. And when interest rates drop, MIECO e-mails the customer to see if he or she wants to speak with an MIECO representative about refinancing the first mortgage. Using family information from the insurance policy, the company sends timely information on college loan programs, something the customer has agreed to receive. This customer asked to be contacted by e-mail, never by phone, and MIECO makes sure that this happens.

A glance at the financial retail lending arena spotlights the dramatic success of companies leading the way. The Advisory Board found that "emerging winners" rely on statistical modeling based on voluminous data from internal and external sources to build their marketing and management strategies. According to its report, "The difference in performance between 'good' and elite organizations is not incremental but transformational—returns on assets and equity are double or triple industry norms."[1]

Companies that reengineer to become market intelligent can increase revenues 2.8 to 3.5 percent. In a study[2] of a nationwide chain store with more than $30 billion in US retail sales, more than $845 million in revenue opportunities were uncovered. A domestic airline with $2.6 billion in annual sales had $90 million in potential additional revenues.

Six somewhat overlapping characteristics define the market-intelligent enterprise:

1. *Strategic use of customer and prospect information:* Customer interaction data is collected and in some cases enhanced from external sources and made available across the enterprise.

2. *Transactional focus:* Every transaction and service contact is viewed as an investment in the customer relationship. Having an understanding of the customer enables the organization to influence the transaction as it occurs thereby turning every contact into a marketing event.

---

[1] The Advisory Board Company, *Retail Lending: Vision of the Future*, Washington, Council on Financial Competition, 1994.

[2] PwC Research, *The Market Intelligent Enterprise 2000*, January 2000.

3. ***Operational use of information:*** The process of gathering
   information during each transaction—in fact, during each contact with and about each customer—and operationalizing the
   use of that information is repeated across the organization.

4. ***Strategic channel management:*** Allowing the customer to
   use his or her preferred channels to reach the organization—
   whether by phone, Internet, mail, branch or other channel.

5. ***Technology-enabled new business opportunities:*** Technology supports the CRM infrastructure, systematizing the common business processes and strategic customer data capture
   across all customer touch points. It delivers common functionality to the different sales and service channels and supports
   the sharing of a common organization view of the customer.

6. ***Enterprise-wide approach:*** A common CRM infrastructure
   supporting common processes across the organization and
   customer touch points.

1. STRATEGIC USE OF CUSTOMER AND PROSPECT INFORMATION

Two questions drive the market-intelligent enterprise: What does my
customer value and what is the value of my customer? The market-
intelligent enterprise addresses these through its premier defining
characteristic: strategically using customer (and prospect) information
to segment customers—or, so to speak, finding the right dance music
for each partner. Information from various sources both within and
outside the organization flows into the organization's data repository.
Sources include customer information from transactions (such as purchase frequency or credit information), the sales force (competitive
information, corporate challenges and philosophy), call centers, sales
promotions (purchase habits), survey data (customer satisfaction), store

front interactions, the Internet, kiosks, demographic information, service bureaus, database marketing companies, other business partners and even motor vehicle registries.

The organization performs statistical analysis of a customer's industry value (its relative size and importance in the marketplace), company share (share of total market purchases), company affinity (likes and dislikes, share of purchases attributed to competitors), and lifetime value (estimating the customer's future value). Based on the results, the firm refines products and services to meet the needs of the most profitable segments and develops strategies for acquiring new customers, retaining and cross-selling to current customers and building customer loyalty.

FedEx analyzed its customer and prospect base and implemented a campaign management program that compressed its marketing campaign from 26 to eight weeks, effectively increasing the number of marketing campaigns the company can execute from two to six per year. That approach yielded a dramatic 8 to 1 return on investment and improved prospecting efforts 284 percent.

The MIE uses data and analyzes it to determine customers' long-term profitability. To do that they must take a long-term view of customers—looking at not just current spending but also projecting it over the life of the relationship with the customer. By identifying customers' life stage (see Figure 2.3) and life-event trigger points and linking with customers over the life of the relationship, companies maximize those consumers' spending and loyalty.

In the consumer electronics industry, for instance, young single adults are more likely to purchase a new car stereo; childless newlyweds want small appliances for new homes; new parents often seek camcorders; established families look for more televisions, VCRs and home computers; and retired adults buy electronics for second homes. In divorce, women generally inherit the household and the men begin spending to set up a new home. This sort of information is a goldmine to any company in the field.

Figure 2.3: Customers' Life Stage

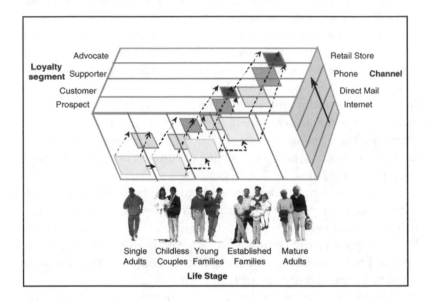

As Figure 2.3 suggests, there is a three-dimensional view that must be taken with every customer relationship. One dimension is the life stage; in the case of business to consumer (B2C) selling, it can grow from single adult to mature adult. At each life stage, one element of the second dimension, the channel, becomes more important than others. Lastly, loyalty, the third dimension, will vary depending on the channel being used, customers' propensity to use the channel and the stage in the life cycle.

Competitiveness hinges on centralizing and leveraging customer information. Witness General Motor's transformation from a vertically integrated company with internecine competition between divisions such as Chevrolet, Buick and Oldsmobile for customers and internal resources. GM is merging its customer databases into a single bank and using that information to create new models designed for particular subsegments and eliminate models with overlapping target markets across brands. The company also is compressing its 60 customer call centers to three to provide consistent, centralized customer service.

2. TRANSACTIONAL FOCUS

Every transaction—in fact, every contact—with a customer or prospect is an opportunity to gather data, invest in the customer relationship and build shareholder value. In addition, real-time communication enables the market-intelligent enterprise to influence each transaction while it occurs. Such just-in-time marketing dramatically expands opportunities for cross-selling and up-selling.

In the financial services industry, the ATM, already a so-called smart device, becomes a marketing agent if programmed with data and decision rules. Currently many ATMs feature marketing messages such as: "Call our toll-free number for information about such and such." But these companies are missing opportunities by sending customers elsewhere and forcing them to begin each inquiry afresh with a customer service representative who has little information about the customer's history or motivation for calling. Instead, the ATM could inform a customer, "We see that you have $5,000 over the required balance in your account. Would you like us to move that money into a higher interest-bearing money market account?" or "Interest rates have dropped one percent. Would you like to speak with a bank representative about refinancing your mortgage to save $2,000 annually in interest costs?" This type of seamless transfer of customer information improves customer satisfaction and spending.

During real-time communication, an organization also captures data beyond the transaction. For instance, the process can uncover what each customer actually wants, not just what the consumer purchases when a preferred item is unavailable. Then the company pushes that information throughout planning and production to cater to the reason for needing the product or service. Central to the market-intelligent enterprise, a transactional focus forces integrated functions across the organization.

Beyond the transactional focus, companies can gather data relating to the context of the interaction—when and through what channel the customer prefers to be contacted. Through so-called contextual marketing, a bank, could learn that a particular customer generally phones the bank on Sunday evenings. When the bank wants to communicate with that customer, that would be a good time and the telephone a good medium.

3. OPERATIONAL USE OF INFORMATION

The process of gathering information during each transaction—in fact, during each contact with and about each customer—and the use of that information is crucial to success. Consider the alternative—the "Three Stooges" scenario of one organization that has not operationalized its use of information.

CASE STUDY

The marketing agent of a long-distance phone service sells to a potentially high-usage customer wireless service on three cell phones and includes a bonus of 1,000 free minutes of service. First, the customer finds the wireless service does not work in his hometown, nor does it work in the first city to which he travels. After multiple calls to customer service, the customer finally obtains the full service for which he has contracted.

When the customer receives his first bill, it is wrong, providing the free hours of service on the first phone but then billing hundreds of dollars in charges for the other two. The customer calls billing and after long explanations is finally able to rectify the company's errors.

After two weeks, the company's fraud department shuts off the customer's phone service because his long-distance charges far exceed typical bills. Again the customer calls to explain, as he did in his first contact with the company's marketing agent, that he periodically amasses high phone charges due to high volume travel and relatives abroad. The company restores his service… until the fraud department cuts it off again in two weeks for the same reason.

And while this highly profitable customer is paying the highest service rate and receiving substandard service, the company tries to lure other less profitable customers away from the competition with bigger discounts. In fact, the company's most loyal customers are paying its highest rates, presumably staying with the provider out of inertia.

The marketing agent in this case aimed to make a sale rather than optimize the customer's relationship with the firm across multiple functions. Now consider the scenario if data were gathered and operationalized throughout all business silos.

CASE STUDY

A marketing agent sells wireless service to a potentially high-volume customer and cross-sells long-distance on the customer's home phones, bundling it to customize service and capitalize on several profit opportunities. The agent asks the customer what countries he calls most frequently and asks for a copy of his most recent bill. The billing information helps the agent design an attractive rate. The marketing agent feeds that information into a data repository that enables billing and credit, service fraud and other functions throughout the organization to see this customer's typical phone use. The attractive billing rate, seamless customer service and efficiency boost customer satisfaction and increase retention.

Companies are winning big by using information across business units to manage the supply chain; create customized pricing structures to heighten customer acquisition, retention and usage; improve quality assurance and restructure customer services for greater satisfaction and loyalty.

CASE STUDY

Dell Computer, manufacturer and direct marketer of computer systems, has electronically linked its front-end systems through which customers place orders with its back-end assembly, manufacturing and parts functions. A customer's order automatically sends information down the supply chain and Dell automatically sends e-mails to suppliers every two hours, for instance. By integrating its customer management system with its supply chain, Dell receives shipments from suppliers every two hours and maintains just eight days' worth of inventory.

CASE STUDY

Fingerhut, a catalog marketer of general merchandise such as electronics, household goods, apparel and jewelry, aimed to reduce overstocks. The company created an electronic catalog on the Internet, where it captures additional customer information and targets offers on a customer-by-customer basis. Prices on the site, named Andy's Garage Sale (www.andysgarage.com), change daily according to inventory, with the old price listed below the current price. Using these strategies, Fingerhut cut inventory costs and reduced overall costs by avoiding traditional liquidation channels. Fingerhut also strategically used another channel, the electric channel, to reach new customers and leverage its existing business systems such as transaction management and fulfillment.

Quality Assurance

The market-intelligent enterprise integrates customer information not only to grow sales and increase the efficacy of operations but also to promote quality assurance. Leading-edge firms enlist the customer in their quality assurance efforts, often by asking during a transaction, "how are we doing?" Organizations are designing creative approaches as well.

CASE STUDY

Software manufacturers aggressively solicit feedback. Intuit provides free prerelease software to some customers, then sends staff into those customers' homes to observe how they use the programs. Microsoft invites users into its usability lab to test the product while staff observe. Netscape gives away its software to a group of users who submit feedback. Both Intuit and Netscape sponsor Web pages that solicit feedback on problems and new features.

A leading confectionery manufacturer wanted to ensure that customer comments about product quality were rapidly incorporated into its processes. The candy maker charted each call to its

800 numbers according to symptoms and the potential cause of the complaint. The company then matched consumer feedback with candy batch and lot numbers, tracing the problem to specific suppliers. By integrating consumer feedback into manufacturing, logistics and quality assurance processes, the candy maker significantly reduced complaints by better managing the raw ingredients supply and the product's aging process.

A strong quality assurance program provides a barometer of customer satisfaction and a vehicle for continuous improvement.

Customer Service

Many senior executives consider customer service little more than complaint resolution, a costly function that seems to emphasize problems. Those companies build the infrastructure for customer service on the organization's capabilities rather than its management vision— what it currently is capable of rather than what the customer really needs. A bank that sends mailings trumpeting consumers as valued but then treats them poorly at teller windows has not operationalized service standards. Neither has the airline that boasts on-time departures but rushes passengers to board when a plane arrives late or forces them to check bags to speed departure. It is causing its customers inconvenience to maintain its schedule.

A market-intelligent enterprise, on the other hand, recognizes that customer service is the face the company presents to its market. That organization approaches the function more scientifically, first establishing its belief system, then designing a framework for customer service that reflects the vision the company wants to project. The company designs service so that at each touch point the customer experiences positive and consistent contact. Performance must meet customer expectations. A client who is informed that it may take one or two billing cycles before an address change appears on the bill will more likely accept that time lag graciously than one left guessing how long it will take.

Invariably, service improves in quality and consistency as technology, process and information support human interaction. Service with a smile but without technology to empower workers will soon lose its bite. Companies that pride themselves on personalized service as a point of differentiation will rely on technology-enabled information to improve marketplace penetration, and those businesses will far outpace their competitors. Information-imbued transactions will "rehumanize" the marketplace as organizations strive to create more effective, personal interactions.

In addition to raising the bar for service levels, many organizations are developing multi-tiered service levels, providing a base level of service to core customers and increasing it in proportion with customer value. This is known as treating your best customers best. However, differentiating between classes of customers based on economic profitability carries the risk of disenfranchising some and being branded elitist. Companies can maintain fairness by fully disclosing service policy and promoting customers to higher levels where it is warranted.

Firms with tiered service standards allocate scarce resources to their best customers—for instance, quick access to a customer service phone agent, or an airline's overhead space claimed by premier status passengers who board early. There's still room to expand that premise. For instance, an airline could quietly and efficiently provide its best customers with alternative flights before generally announcing a canceled or postponed flight.

These vignettes offer examples of how companies provide tiered service.

CASE STUDY

Customers who fly full fare more than 100,000 miles annually on American Airlines, an international passenger airline, earn American's Executive Platinum status. Passenger lists note key customers, and AA personnel can then offer early boarding, better seats and baggage space and improved meal choices. Executive Platinum status allows those customers guaranteed seats on any flight, any time. Almost all of the representatives at a priority customer call center know those customers by name.

CASE STUDY

A large computer manufacturer assessed customer profitability by analyzing process costs and benefits, then set out to increase satisfaction among highly profitable customers. Best customers receive priority in the queue for telephone service calls and less profitable ones get a 900 number to call for service. That cut service costs and increased customer retention.

Many companies trying to improve their service are revamping their call centers to provide better and faster problem solving or calling back customers at their convenience. Offering access through other channels also improves service.

CASE STUDY

Wells Fargo, a financial services institution, offers secure on-line access for customer transactions and routine inquiries. By implementing this customer service channel, Wells Fargo reduced customer service calls 40 percent and expects to expand on-line service to 2 million customers while holding customer service costs steady[3].

The best improvements in customer service derive, of course, from listening to customers and responding to their needs. An organization striving for world-class customer service can design meta-service—a higher level of service based on each customer's preferences. By creating service profiles for groups of customers, then modifying those profiles according to each subgroup's or even individual's preferences, an organization can provide customized service—with incremental costs to personalize service for each customer.

A direct marketer's customer might order more if offered volume discounts, while another customer would increase spending if assured that the company will arrange for free return shipping. When an

---

[3] The Direct Marketing Association, *CRM: Technology Enabled Marketing*, October, 1999.

upscale specialty chain launched a loyalty program, their best customers did not want discounts but rather a fashion show or lunch with the store manager. An upscale car dealership assigns each customer a specific service agent to personalize service. The problem is that if the particular agent is busy the customer waits, when all he or she wants is fast service. A bank client prefers to be contacted at a certain time of day. Another customer does not want her deceased mother's maiden name as verifying information with her credit card company—how about her college alma mater instead? Small concessions such as these can have a huge impact on customer loyalty.

To determine service levels, an organization needs to ascertain how to carry out its vision and decide what is important to its customers. Companies can apply conjoint analysis, an analytical tool used initially in product design, to measure how much service is worth to customers. The company asks respondents to rank or trade off their preferences for price, product characteristics and service and then tries to match these.

Organizations need new ways to measure their performance as customer-centric companies. For businesses that manage information as a strategic asset measuring customer satisfaction, assessing and managing customers by profitability and measuring return on marketing and sales investment are important indices for organizational direction and improvement.

To achieve balance and sustain both short- and long-term growth, a company needs a mix of customers, including those who provide profitability in the short term and the long term. Some are profitable to the finance division and others to the merchandising unit. For instance, in a retail environment merchants focus on the good merchandising customer, one who spends a lot while paying bills on time, while the credit department sees profitability in a good credit customer, who may not buy as much but doesn't pay off the balance every month thereby accruing interest charges on those smaller purchases.

4. STRATEGIC CHANNEL MANAGEMENT

Good service also allows the customer to use his or her preferred channels to reach the company—whether by phone, Internet, mail, store or other channel.

CASE STUDY

For instance, at Talbots, a specialty women's clothing chain, when an item is not available in the store, a sales clerk can order it with the store's red phone to the catalog call center. Orders placed in this fashion pay a flat $4 shipping charge rather than the $5 to $14 charge for regular catalog orders—incentive for the customer to place that order on the spot. In addition, the store earns credit for the catalog sale. This process motivates personnel to use the most effective channel to serve customers and eliminates conflict between channels.

Leading-edge firms are building synergy between channels and capitalizing on the advantages of each channel to form seamless, efficient organizations.

CASE STUDY

iMarket, Inc. is a privately held leading provider of desktop direct marketing and database software and services. Its primary products are a CD-ROM version of the 11 million-record Dun & Bradstreet business file and a market matching and analysis product. iMarket generates sales leads on the Internet with business-to-business banner ads and a Web page. After a prospect has registered on iMarket's Web site, a sales representative contacts them. iMarket cut costs by acquiring customer leads online, which incurs smaller and less variable costs than finding customers through most traditional channels. And those leads are qualified, more solid than cold calls. The sales force earns commission on sales from any source, ensuring that sales staff pursue Internet-based leads as vigorously as prospects targeted through other channels. The company created a specific purpose for the Web site (in this case, driving customer acquisition) and created incentives so all channels work toward uniform goals.

More companies are offering customers incentives to move to more cost-effective channels.

CASE STUDY

Columbia House, a music CD and tape manufacturer and distributor, offered customers a 10 percent discount on orders placed on the Internet or by phone rather than by mail.

CASE STUDY

Several airlines including American, Delta and United award customers 1,000 bonus frequent flier miles for ordering tickets on the Internet rather than other ways. Some offer 500 bonus miles for the electronic order and 500 for using a Web-purchased e-ticket—in which you present a reservation and identification code rather than an actual ticket at the boarding gate.

5. TECHNOLOGY-ENABLED BUSINESS OPPORTUNITIES

Technology supports the new business model and makes it capable of developing a strategic, information-efficient infrastructure. The technology provides a platform to turn data into knowledge. Here's how it works: An organization collects internal data on customer demographics, billing, summarized transactions, and customer satisfaction and service, to name a few, and external data available from service bureaus, vehicle registries, syndicated data from organizations such as Nielsen or Claritas or mailing list rentals. That data flows into a central database called a data warehouse, which stores, manages and analyzes the information through a technique called data mining.

The trend toward "disintermediation," in which companies forge direct links with customers, closes a window for some organizations—forcing them to seek new avenues to profitability—while it opens up doors for others. Companies are leveraging technology so information itself becomes a primary product. And they're delivering that information on the Internet.

CASE STUDY

Auto-By-Tel is an Internet marketing and information service that sells, leases and insures cars and trucks at low cost. On the Auto-By-Tel Web site—www.autobytel.com—consumers select their vehicles of choice and submit free purchase or lease requests, which are routed to local Auto-By-Tel accredited dealers. Those dealers call customers within 48 hours with low, no-haggle prices. Auto-By-Tel pre-qualifies and trains its more than 2,700 subscribing dealers to ensure quality and consistency.

6. ENTERPRISE-WIDE APPROACH

The infrastructure for the customer-aligned organization must extend throughout the enterprise and beyond to customers, manufacturers, outsourced services, distributors and retailers. Consider the case of a major US car manufacturer and its vendors that have failed to take an enterprise-wide approach. With little coordination, they end up contacting most customers 14 times during their first year of car ownership. The customer wonders, "Did I buy a car or join a cult?" The organization that has built an enterprise-wide infrastructure reaps substantial benefits.

CASE STUDY

Heineken USA, a subsidiary of Heineken NV, the world's second-largest brewer, needed to communicate with its large distribution network to manufacture and stock from current trends in customer demand, rather than forecasts based on historical trends. It built an intranet that provided: company-wide, instantaneous access to inventory and sales data; instant, accessible information for simultaneous collaboration among manufacturing, warehousing, finance, logistics, sales and marketing; access of marketing data for Heineken management in the US and Europe; a system through which distributors can place orders, adjust depletion figures, and replenish orders; and encrypted data to ensure security. The results: Heineken USA halved the time—from 10 or 12 weeks to six weeks—from brewery to retail shelves and enhanced manufacturing, planning, scheduling and inventory management. More timely data improves brand management, forecasting volume trends and analysis of promotional effectiveness. Distributors and manufacturers provide better service by using the same current data. And sales representatives are able to devote increased time to sales rather than administrative and forecasting work.

BECOMING MARKET INTELLIGENT

The checklist that follows can help organizations begin to assess their market-intelligent enterprise quotient.

Assess Your Organization's Market-Intelligence Quotient

- Do your customer service representatives have easy access to customer service, customer delivery and customer history information?

- Does your organization quantify the profitability of each customer?

- Does your organization use customer information for sales and marketing?

- Does your organization integrate campaign results—the promotions and offers it provides to customers and the acceptance levels of these offers—into forecasting and planning?

- Does your company have programs to reward loyal customers?

- Do you have quantitative methods for measuring the effectiveness of marketing programs?

- Is customer information access and analysis software deployed across all functions of your organization?

- Does your company know how your customers prefer to communicate with you (such as fax, Internet, person-to-person or not at all)?

- Is your corporate culture customer-based versus product-based?

- Does your company segment existing and potential customers on multiple dimensions?
- Does your company's senior management support the organization-wide goal of being customer-centric?

Most competitive companies are in the process of defining the vision, processes and technology they need to become customer-centric. The growing efficiency and effectiveness of those businesses in a marketplace covered with multitudes of channels and powerful emerging technology has far-reaching implications for every organization. While companies that fail to become market intelligent trip over each other in their effort to woo customers, market-intelligent enterprises will step lightly and gracefully into the global economy with plenty of dance partners.

About the Authors

HARRIS GORDON

Harris Gordon is the Global CRM Partner responsible for Relationship Marketing at PricewaterhouseCoopers' Management Consulting. He specializes in developing strategy for direct and database marketing.

STEVEN ROTH

Steven Roth is a Principal Consultant at PricewaterhouseCoopers' America's CRM consulting practice. He specializes in direct and database marketing.

A Case Study on CRM and Mass Customization:

CAPITAL ONE

Stanley A. Brown

IN THE PREVIOUS chapters, we have provided you with the first principles in creating CRM and an understanding of the foundation upon which it must be built. As you might imagine, some organizations are further ahead than others and they are great examples of CRM in action. One of those is Capital One, a formidable force in the credit card industry.

THE COMPANY

In 1994, a spin-off of Signet Banking Corp. was created by employees Nigel Morris and Rich Fairbank under the name Capital One Financial Corp. Headquartered in Falls Church, Virginia, the organization began offering financial products and services to consumers and in just five short years ranked in the top-10 issuers of credit cards in the US. From simple beginnings, the organization now employs 11,000, services 19.2 million customers (as of June 1999—five million of them were acquired in the previous year alone) and has total balances of $17.4 billion. So powerful is this company today that many have said that it was singularly responsible for having pushed down interest rates in the US and passing value onto the customer.

THE CHALLENGE

In 1997, Capital One became aware of serious dissatisfaction with their service when customers complained about the time it took to have problems handled. This had implications on both customer retention and the company payroll. The customer was annoyed with not getting connected to the right person right away and having to go through too many transfers and waiting periods in the process. At the same time, all the seconds that ticked away during this lengthy period cost the company money in employee wages. Capital One employs a large number of people in its call center and research has shown that 65–70 percent of call center costs are labor. Thus saving seconds per call translates into millions of dollars. This can have a serious effect on a company's bottom line particularly when it takes 2.5 million live calls a month. Thus arose the challenge stated by Jim Donehey, Capital One's Chief Information Officer, "How can we minimize all that?"

Capital One was not alone in facing this challenge. A quality survey of the credit card industry, conducted by J.D. Power and Associates in March and April 1998, interviewed 10,420 consumers about 35 products from the 17 largest credit card issuers and found that pricing isn't everything.

While "teaser" rates—a low initial interest rate given to new card holders for the first few months—may attract consumers in the first place, that is no guarantee that they will remain once the rate returns to normal. The study found that service was the key differentiator. Call center contact and satisfaction with billing, payment processing and the reputation of the issuer were the most important elements in customer satisfaction.

In 1998 credit card companies sent out 3.45 billion offers for credit cards. Consumers sent back 41 million credit card applications. The winners were the organizations that had the best combined offering and high customer relationship management. Capital One was not getting its fair share.

By itself, that would have been enough to work on, but market dynamics issued a few more challenges. They included market saturation (thus heavy competitive pricing), customer empowerment (customers wanted more choice in the way they would do business with the financial institution of choice), and effective implementation of technology (more and better technology was required, and it had to be implemented with minimal disruption to the customer and the organization). Customers wanted change, and they wanted flexibility and value for money, something that they were not getting from their credit card company. And they wanted to be able to deal with this company in a friendly, informed and facilitated manner—in short, they wanted to do business with a business that was easy to do business with. That was the challenge before Capital One, and the CRM strategy began to unfold.

As was stated at the beginning of this book, for an organization to be effective in implementing CRM Strategy, three sub-strategies must be considered: the customer strategy, the channel and product strategy and the infrastructure strategy. Here's how Capital One went about it: At the heart of its success is customer knowledge, allowing it to clearly define the most valuable customer groups and their needs—its customer strategy. While its primary channel is the telephone, over the years it has opened up new channels, including the e-channel, to selected customer groups and tailored its product offering, by channel, to each of its customer groups—its channel and product strategy. Its technology investments and its strategic alliances have helped create a highly competitive innovative organization in support of its customer and channel and product strategies.

Action Taken

Capital One realized that they would lose their customers quickly if they couldn't get them to the right agent to meet their needs as quickly and effectively as possible. That is why they developed their "infrastructure"-based strategy which combined information technology (data warehousing) and analysis (data mining) that helped them to identify, manage and execute new ways of doing business. They began to analyze customer calling patterns to determine why customers would pick up the phone and make a call. New technology (intelligent call routing) was implemented that essentially predicted why the call was being made and who would be the best agent to service the request. High-speed computers that gather background information on US households and typical Capital One customer behavior, took just milliseconds to identify who was calling and why, picked the best person to notify and forwarded essential information about the person calling. In turn, information was also acquired as to what this customer would be likely to buy (once their original problem had been resolved) even though that would be far from the reason for their call.

In its 1998 annual report, cofounder Richard Fairbank stated, "Our goal: to leapfrog high-priced, one-size-fits-all marketing with 'mass customization, delivering the right product to the right consumer at the right time and at the right price…" This "customer, channel and product strategy" required a revitalization of the product offering (a single credit card offer was no longer acceptable), a need to excite the customer base (there had to be more reasons to be associated with Capital One other than price) and improved productivity (more effectively route the customer to the appropriate agent).

To combat the problem of "product fatigue syndrome," they introduced new attributes to their credit cards. Along with their low interest rates and annual fee, they introduced value-added elements such as cashback programs (a rebate or credit based on actual purchases on the card) and loyalty rewards (points that could be redeemed in related affinity programs). Affinity cards, teaming with a partner that has a customized appeal to a particular customer segment, were implemented. The result enticed those who desired an affiliation based on rewards with such organizations as Mercedes Benz, World Wrestling Federation or Thomson Holidays.

Capital One was not alone. Other organizations faced similar challenges. Citibank met its challenges through different value offerings to specific customer segments. American Express, GE and Discover implemented rewards programs, based on the amount of customer spending. MBNA and Bank One/First USA were among the first to introduce the affinity card. MBNA's primary target market was members of clubs, organizations and alumni groups. And all got involved in the cross-selling of products such as loan and insurance products. But all learned one important lesson: To be effective in CRM, customer service responsiveness is a key differentiator, and the more one knows about the customer, the greater the advantage for the company.

Benefits Achieved

As indicated earlier, at the heart of Capital One's success was a powerful database, one that kept information on one in seven households, calling habits of its customers, profitability, likely purchase habits and the probability of selling new products based on previous history and customers with similar profiles.

As a result of the data warehousing and data-mining, questions can be answered before they are even asked, calls last a third of the time they used to, customers are satisfied and the cost of the call is reduced. "This started as such a simple problem," says CIO Donehey, "but IT enabled us to go back to the business side with a solution that went beyond solving that problem."

That solution that went beyond—termed "intelligent call routing"—led to Capital One's innovative strategy "inbound cross-selling." Through much research and numerous tests—which are now part of Capital One's culture—the company discovered that people were more likely to purchase something if they called rather than the company calling them, the traditional telemarketing way. Therefore, while the customer called to complain about a problem or ask for some other information it was easier to sell them other products when they were already on the phone and satisfied with the response to their request. A Capital One agent, armed with information from the company's data warehouse could offer the customer an opportunity to purchase products ranging from auto insurance to loans, mortgages and long-distance services. These are special offers to preferred Capital One customers. In 1998, half of all their new customers bought another product from them within a year of signing up for their credit card. Capital One currently makes more than one million in sales (and millions more dollars) a year through customer service marketing, which costs them nothing.

According to cofounders Fairbank and Morris, Capital One's real capital lies in the data on behavior of its current and potential customers and the analysts who interpret what really matters to their customers. This information has allowed them to enter new business markets beyond the issuing of credit cards. One example is a new subsidiary, America One, which sells cell phone services in much the same manner as Capital One sells credit cards—they utilize the valuable computer data to determine what should be offered to which customer.

Capital One became the company that people could turn to for just about anything. When you were ready to buy a car, the company wanted to be the first thing the consumer thought of—the first and last choice.

CRM Lessons Learned

Capital One put its CRM strategy together in a unique way. Rather than look at the three principles of customer strategy, channel or product

strategy and infrastructure strategy as separate yet fundamental components, it wove them together in a unique manner. Its keys to success
are listed below.

Testing and Innovation (Product Strategy)

Capital One has become so successful because of its ability to recognize
the fact that innovation is the answer to their continued growth. But
innovation cannot stop with one product or one solution to one problem. The company must constantly test and reassess, learn and apply,
invent and then outmode their own invention. In 1998, the company
performed 28,000 experiments—tests of new products, new advertising
approaches, new markets and new business models. Every person in
the company was encouraged to participate and contribute, regardless
of job title or the division in which they worked.

Capital One's innovative "teaser" rate won the company tremendous numbers of customers, but it worked so well, however, that it was
quickly copied by their competitors, which resulted in lost customers.
The solution was to offer flexible rates to different groups of people
based on their credit history and group affiliation. But the competitive
game didn't end there. The lesson learned; innovate, but be the first to
implement and the first to reinvent.

Data Mastery
(Infrastructure and Customer Strategy)

Capital One uses its database for everything, and doesn't just jump in feet
first. Every idea is an experiment; it is tested and a learning curve is
applied. They don't just track what they sell to their customers, they also
track whether it is used in the end. As stated earlier, in 1998, for instance,
they conducted 28,000 tests of products, features, prices, packages, marketing channels and credit policies. The company uses testing to learn
how to customize products and services to the individual consumer; they
also used testing to build an innovation laboratory capable of creating a
steady stream of new ideas to stay ahead of the competition.

And this testing isn't just applied to their product lines. It is also
used in analyzing their human resources practices—in how they hire
employees for instance. This has resulted in them reducing the time
commitment to meet and interview potential candidates. Capital One

now meets them only after candidates are hired because testing showed they did not have the ability to predict their future job performance anyway. As well, 10 new pre-employment tests have been created.

New Product Development (Product and Channel Strategy)

At Capital One, everyone is involved in product development regardless of their occupation. In the words of Capital One's marketing manager, "Even if they don't work in the marketing department, everyone is a consumer. Everyone has a credit card and has a view on it. New ideas are important in terms of the evolution of products and strategies."

Capital One is now preparing for its next technological challenge. By announcing partnerships with Internet service providers such as X-Stream network in the UK and online advertising agency Double Click Inc. in the US, they are jumping into the field of e-commerce. Ads are placed on certain clients' Web sites and Capital One becomes the preferred credit card issuer on the partner's sites. A plan to enhance Capital One's Web site will allow them to introduce on-line customer service and instant decisions for on-line card applications. This plan comes well after other large credit card companies have made Internet-related deals. For example, First USA has more than 50 partnerships with Internet companies already. It has employed a more mass-marketing approach in contrast to Capital One's target-marketing.

Matt Cooper, Capital One's UK senior vice president, says, "The Internet is a natural way to deliver the best value to customers on an individual basis. This exciting partnership will enable us to target and acquire new customers...and learn more about the interests of the growing number of consumers who use the Internet."

SUMMARY

Capital One is not about the status quo, it is about constantly reinventing itself and the way it does business. It is about creating a unique CRM strategy that creates true value in the eyes of its target customers. That said, Capital One has taken it a step further. Differentiation in the marketplace starts with a CRM strategy, a recognition that there is a need to tailor products and services to the needs of its defined target markets and to invest in the infrastructure/technology to enable it to learn, grow and constantly reinvent itself. It has learned that successful CRM may not necessarily mean just improved customer satisfaction but improved customer value profitability, and that means the status quo is not enough. Gavin Shreeve, chief executive of the Chartered Institute of Bankers, believes the only way companies can distinguish themselves in the eyes of the consumer is through customer service and customer relationship management. "In the past five years it has become difficult to differentiate on product. It is how you get out there and sell your products that counts."

About the Author

STANLEY A. BROWN

> Stanley Brown is a Partner in PricewaterhouseCoopers' America's CRM consulting practice and leader of its Center of Excellence in Customer Care. His primary focus is CRM in the Financial, Government and Business Services Sectors.

Part Two

Step One: Building and Implementing the Customer Strategy: Overview

Who exactly is the customer and what must we do to keep them? And do we need to keep all of them? True, customers are the lifeblood of every organization—the simple fact is that without them we will not survive. For years now the traditional pundits of customer care have expounded over and over again the virtues of exceptional customer service. You've heard the slogans—"The customer is always right", "We put our customers first" and several others along similar lines. Are they right?

Well, yes… and no. The fact is that you simply cannot afford to give exceptional customer service to all your customers. But does that mean you should give poor service to some customers? Absolutely not. What it does mean is that you need to learn to be more selective in your choice of customers, and that is what this chapter is about—first, how to create loyalty and then how to be more selective in which customer you want to create a longer more strategic relationship.

You must differentiate customers first by their value to you and then by their needs. You don't want to waste time on the needs of low-value customers, because there is no point in creating a high-cost relationship with a low-value customer. Organizations that have well-developed customer strategies understand this principle: the longer a customer stays with a company, the more the customer is worth. Long-term customers buy more, take up less company time, express less sensitivity to price and bring in other customers. But then remember that these customers were not always that way and that getting them to this state was often an extremely long, hard haul.

As we will discuss further in this chapter, organizations go through an evolutionary process in their customer relationship management strategy. There are three key stages. In Stage I, organizations consider all customers to be important and continuous customer acquisition is the goal. At Stage II, the primary focus is on customer retention and loyalty. By Stage III the focus switches to differentiated service for their select, crown jewel customers and the mutual benefits of partnership with these key customers. This is covered in more detail in my previous book, *Strategic Customer Care*, John Wiley & Sons Canada, 1999.

Organizations with well-developed customer strategies obsess about maximizing their customer relationships and are most concerned about customer retention and loyalty, the topic of Chapter 4, "Creating Loyalty: Its Strategic Importance in Your Customer Strategy." Their concern stems from a renewed respect for the customer, motivated by a number of factors:

- Intensifying global competition
- The transition from a manufacturing to a service economy
- Shorter product cycles and saturated markets
- Less opportunity for product differentiation
- An increasing sensitivity toward service on the part of the consumer

As your customer strategy further evolves, you become more concerned with those strategic customers that are or will be the lifeblood of your organization, and thus moving customers from loyalty to dependency, the topic of Chapter 5, "From Customer Loyalty to Customer Dependency: A Case for Strategic Customer Care." After all, certain customers require special treatment and, rather than having just an individual salesperson responsible for them, perhaps a more focused team approach is warranted. This team hones in on customer needs to create a win-win relationship with them. If the customer can improve their profitability by working with your organization, they will be more loyal and dependent on you, and you will, in turn, achieve increased profitability.

After all, if a small portion of your customers represent a significantly higher portion of your potential, you need to find a way to form strategic partnerships with those select customers in order to further nurture the relationship for mutual benefit.

We close with Chapter 6, "Customer Acquisition and CRM: A Financial Services Perspective." While the focus is on best practices examples from the financial services sector, its message applies to all areas of our economy. The chapter is based on a major research paper produced by PricewaterhouseCoopers—*Tomorrow's Leading Retail Bank*. We all know that when it comes to new-client acquisition and customer relationship management (CRM), large retail banks are investing a great deal of time and money to improve their strategy and capability. Today the goal is to enhance the bank's growth and profitability by acting on fresh and deep insights into the individual, whether a prospective or a current customer.

Tomorrow's successful organizations should learn from these examples. They must use what is learned about individuals—not just segments or even micro-segments—to determine the product configurations, promotion tactics, pricing, service levels and channel mix that make sense for each individual. The ultimate goal is to offer unprecedented value to individual customers and maximize profitability from each customer relationship.

Creating Loyalty:

ITS STRATEGIC IMPORTANCE IN YOUR CUSTOMER STRATEGY

Henrik Anderson
Per Ø. Jacobsen

THE CONCEPT OF LOYALTY

Normally, we understand loyalty to be a positive word. Everyone expects loyalty from a good friend, spouse or colleague. We apply it to people who understand problems and who always make themselves available. In most cases, loyalty can be given to people, enterprises and products and is normally characterized by equality and mutual cooperation.

However, when it comes to customer loyalty, traditional definitions no longer hold up. Theories about customer loyalty are relatively new in the literature of international management. Richard L. Oliver defined the concept of loyalty in this way: *"A deeply held commitment to re-buy or re-patronize a preferred product or service consistently in the future despite situational influences and marketing efforts having the potential to cause switching behaviour."*[1]

But this definition may be too limiting. Customer loyalty is actually the result of an organization creating a benefit for a customer so that they will maintain or increase their purchases from the organization. True customer loyalty is created when the customer becomes an advocate for the organization, without incentive.

---

[1] Richard L. Oliver, *Satisfaction: A Behavioral Perspective on the Consumer*, New York: McGraw Hill, 1997.

In the last 10 years, interest in the subject has risen considerably, and today customer loyalty is regarded as the recipe for increasing revenue but perhaps it is only one stage in the evolution of customer care, to be replaced, as we will see later (and in Chapter 5), by customer dependency (or Strategic Customer Relationship Management).

Of course, there are those who jokingly say, "If the enterprise wants loyalty it can buy a dog" because it is fleeting and never attainable in today's market environment. This rather defeatist attitude is today being replaced by a more pragmatic one. Loyalty can be attained, but the organization has to work at it, continuously, and it will not be possible with all customers. A win-win relationship must be established, and this cannot be accomplished if both parties cannot realize benefit. The two poles must be attracted to each other.

Figure 4.1 shows the correlation between loyalty and value according to what we will refer to as the "fried egg" model. The yoke stands for the enterprise's selected customers and the egg white for the CRM strategy, because like an egg white, it forms a protective and nurturing layer around them. Certain customers need to be protected and shielded from the elements of competitive offerings (pricing options, performance enhancements or promotions to name a few). Without this protection, leakage may occur, starting with a trickle and ending in a full-scale flood.

Figure 4.1: The Value Process

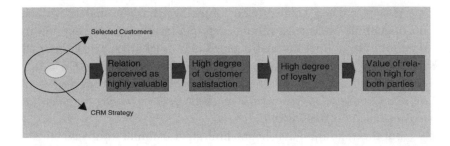

The yolk may get stronger over time, and the desire to "leak" may abate, but only if it remains in this protective mode. The goal is for the relationship between customer and enterprise to get stronger as it passes through different CRM stages on the journey. In this way, customer satisfaction grows, as does the perception of value in the relationship. This, in turn, leads to an increase in loyalty. If the enterprise continues to satisfy customer needs and keeps its services in demand, a mutual creation of value emerges and the final goal of customer dependency or Strategic Customer Relationship Management (S-CRM) is achieved.

Defining Loyalty

Before you can achieve loyalty, an organization has to define it, in a manner that the organization as a whole can accept and rally behind. Here are some questions that must be asked and issues that must be addressed:

- How does the enterprise define loyalty?
- How does the enterprise measure loyalty?
- How loyal are your customers?
- How many customers does the enterprise lose each year?
- How many customers does it keep?

As a start, an organization must realize that its relationship with its customers must evolve just like a courtship. Mutual loyalty and trust must be built gradually and selectively. The enterprise that builds relationships wins the battle for customers.

Figure 4.2. The Path to Strategic Customer Care

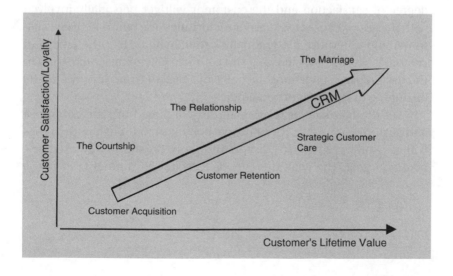

The Courtship

The enterprise must first get to know the customer. In this phase, loyalty is considered very weak because it is not based on relationships but solely on "look and feel"—products and prices. In fact, the customer may switch to a competitor if their products and prices are better. The attitude is summed up as, "what have you done for me lately?" A good example of this is the fierce price competition in the mobile telephone market.

The Relationship

Affection grows and a solid relationship is created. The enterprise engages with customer attitudes both before and after the purchase. It listens to the customer who is gradually getting to know the enterprise. Loyalty is no longer based on price and product alone. The relationship is also becoming a factor, even though there is no guarantee the customer will not seek new pastures. But the relationship is solid enough for loyalty to no longer be seen as fleeting. A mutual desire exists, and both parties begin to see benefit in continuing to grow the relationship.

The Marriage

A long-lasting relationship is mutually agreeable, and both parties become inextricibly linked. At this stage, loyalty is based on a high degree of satisfaction and the customer will get personally involved with the enterprise. As the marriage continues, the bonds between customer and enterprise are gradually strengthened. Here the feeling of customer satisfaction increases and with it loyalty to the enterprise. On the basis of such a relationship, one can speak of "true" loyalty and the beginning of customer dependency.

For the marriage or relationship to continue both the enterprise and customer must receive a positive benefit even though both parties will inevitably experience disappointments on the journey to their common goal. The goal, however, is a feeling of mutual trust and a desire to continue the relationship. Consider the CRM strategy to be one of evolution and personal growth. Some customers do not have the maturity or capacity to evolve to the marriage stage and will never achieve a lasting relationship with any one organization. Others do have this capacity and desire but it is the organization that must create the reason for maintaining and maturing the relationship.

A solid marriage translates into advocates—customers that are living advertisements for the enterprise, praising it and recommending it to others. The prerequisites for this are, of course, that all the basic conditions of service, quality, price, and so on are in order. It is impossible to build loyalty if products or services are poor.

The opposite situation can be analagous to a jealous or jilted lover, sometimes also referred to as the "terrorist," who will use every opportunity to publicize negative experiences with the enterprise. It takes the praises of many advocates to offset the negative criticisms of just one terrorist.

CRITICAL MEASUREMENT TO GUIDE YOUR CRM STRATEGY

Loyalty

Loyalty will be measured differently depending on where one is in the CRM process. In the *customer acquisition* phase (1), loyalty measurement will relate to transactions, such as turnover. Measurement of profitability will be product related, such as the product's profit margin. In the *customer retention* phase (2), measurement of loyalty changes to being relationship-oriented using, for example, the customer satisfaction index. Measurement of profitability changes to being directed at share of wallet—the proportion of potential spending by the customer.

Figure 4.3: Measuring Loyalty in the CRM Process

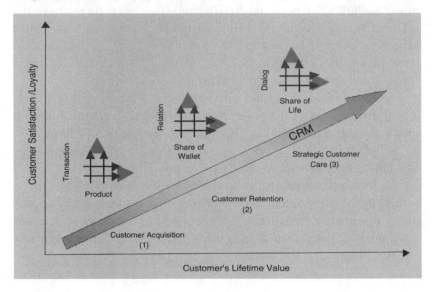

When we discuss the *Strategic Customer Care* phase (3), the norms for customer value merge with those of the enterprise and the measurement of loyalty will be tied to these. The profitability measurement will be based on share of life discussed in the section that follows. The complexity of these measurements varies considerably depending on what one desires. Is it information on customer satisfaction or economic analyses of earning per individual customer? Experience shows that loyalty measurements should include, at the very least, a consumption-related measurement and a customer satisfaction measurement.

Share of wallet is often used as the consumption-related measurement of loyalty. It expresses the relation between the customer's actual purchases from the enterprise and the purchasing potential. This loyalty indicator, however, fails to take into account whether one is dealing with true or false loyalty. When we speak of false loyalty, we mean that there can be situations where the customer is "forced" to use a particular product or specific service benefit. It may be a car repair shop that you have to use according to the warranty, or an airline company with the monopoly on a particular route. If the market offers only a limited number of choices, it is easy to give a large part of one's business to the enterprise without necessarily being its advocate. For this reason, "share of wallet" measurements are often complemented by measurements of customer satisfaction.

Lifetime Value

Ask yourself this question, what is the overall length of the relationship (retention) and how much will the customer buy in his or her lifetime? Figure 4.4 provides a viewpoint on this critical dilemma.

Instead of focusing on customer retention and maintaining the relationship, many enterprises lose focus and concentrate almost exclusively on attracting new customers—keeping the numbers up. They are continuously in the courtship stage and cannot bring themselves to a meaningful relationship. Budgeting and goal setting are both based on this, and the same applies to marketing and setting prices. New customers get top priority because they supposedly compensate for those customers that leave the enterprise when, in reality, they only mask the organization's deficiency. Even though these new customers keep the total number at the same level, economic potential is weakened as growth within the existing customer base is limited.

As shown in Figure 4.4, it is more profitable to keep existing customers than acquire new ones. During the normal development of a customer relationship, the cost to market and sell to these customers gradually declines, and the potential for gross margin improvement increases.

The loyal customer rarely focuses on price alone but instead sees customer relationships in terms of "value for money." In this way, the customer acts as an advocate for the enterprise and thus helps attract new customers.

Figure 4.4. The Development of Lifetime Value

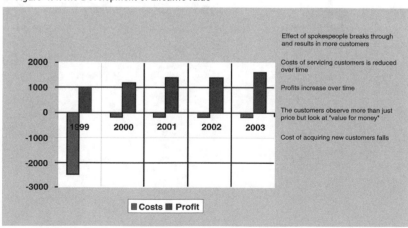

In year one of the customer acquisition, or courtship stage, costs of acquisition greatly exceed gross profit potential. Acquiring new customers costs a lot of money. Return on this investment depends to a great extent on how long the customer relationship lasts. Are we speaking of an isolated purchase or the beginning of a new 5, 10 or 70-year customer relationship? Over time, depending on the length of the relationship and the mutual benefit achieved, profit exceeds costs. In fact, cost per customer acquired is reduced, as existing customers become advocates and create positive word-of-mouth advertising.

From another perspective, a recognition and focus on lifetime value will have a positive impact on customer retention and that, in turn, will reduce customer acquisition cost. Retention rate is used to measure customer turnover. It shows how large a percentage of its customer portfolio the enterprise retains yearly. The churn rate, on the other hand, shows how large a percentage of its customer portfolio the enterprise loses every year.

When an enterprise operates with a churn rate of 20 percent—a retention rate of 80 percent—it means that it replaces one customer in five each year. In other words, it completely replaces all of its customers over a five-year period. In this case, the period over which the enterprise can generate income from the customer will be only five years—the so-called lifetime value.

Retention rate has great significance for the creation of value. Research has shown that when the enterprise increases the retention rate from 80 to 90 percent, it doubles customer lifetime from five to 10 years (Figure 4.5). Longevity creates value.

Figure 4.5. Retention Rate

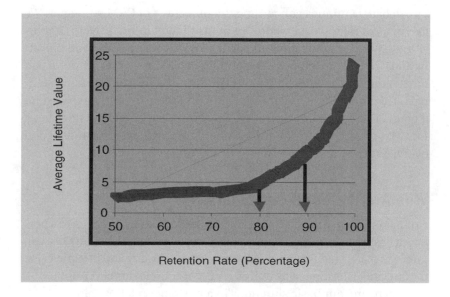

From Market Share to Customer Share

The transition from market share to customer share (share of pocket or share of wallet) is a prevalent theme in the CRM debate about customer loyalty and lifetime value. One result of the debate is a growing understanding that a large market share is not equivalent to having loyal customers. What you have today can be gone tomorrow, if the customer is not locked in or dependant.

What combination of offerings and communication suits the customer best? If one communicates in this way to both profitable and potential customers, are the enterprise's marketing resources utilized effectively? And does the message break through the noise of competitive offerings or advances? It is possible to have a dialog in a normal conversational tone of voice and increase the enterprise's share of wallet. When this happens, the relevance of the message ensures a creation of value for both parties.

From Share of Wallet to Share of Life

The debate continues concerning the objectives of CRM strategies. We live in a complex world where we do not function exclusively as individuals. We have many roles and diverse needs depending upon the situations we find ourselves in. Depending on their role, the customer can have numerous relationships and deal through many different channels. This situation makes it more difficult for the enterprise to sustain a good overview of the customer. This complexity highlights the need for CRM systems to ensure integration, knowledge-sharing and a good overview across all channels.

Who Are the Good Customers?

No matter where the enterprise is on its CRM journey, it needs to know about customer loyalty and profitability. Based on this, the enterprise can target its dialog and further the development of loyalty and lifetime value for individual customers as well as for the whole customer portfolio.

There are four basic situations in a customer relationship:

1. The customer is loyal and profitable—the enterprise focuses on deepening the relationship, strengthening loyalty and optimizing profitability through cross- and up-selling.

2. The customer is loyal but unprofitable—the enterprise should maintain the relationship and secure loyalty because the customer may still become profitable through cross- and up-selling. If not, the customer should be dropped.

3. The customer is profitable but not loyal—in this case the enterprise should focus completely on strengthening the relationship and building loyalty.

4. The customer is not loyal—and unprofitable—here it is probably worth considering giving the customer to the competitor.

Consider the four-quadrant model described in Figure 4.6. The Y axis is degree of loyalty, the X axis profitability. As you acquire customers, create customer loyalty, and, in turn, customer dependency, you will evolve to the top right quadrant. But when you start the process—the courtship—you are in the lower left quadrant. The customer is price sensitive and much more influenced by advertising, marketing and pro-motions. And as the relationship grows, there is movement towards improved loyalty and the creation of value. Mutual benefit is achieved and a reward mechanism is operational. (Movement to the top left and bottom right quadrants).

Figure 4.6: From Customer Acquisition to Strategic CRM

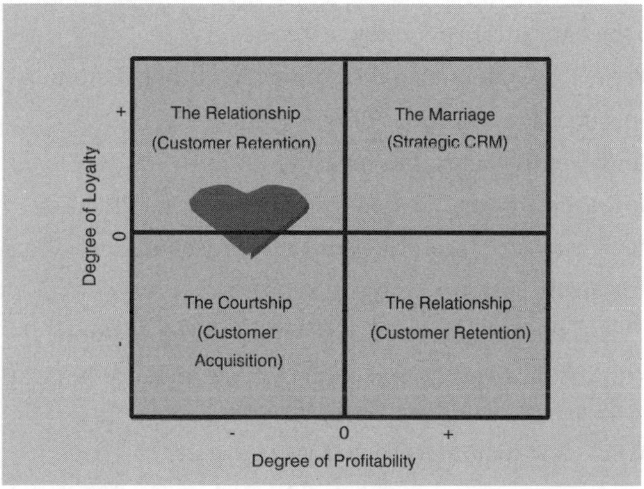

The segmentation model can be used throughout the CRM jour-ney. Loyalty and profitability are the names of axes for the entire process. But loyalty and profitability change on the way as, of course, does the character of the initiatives the enterprise takes up.

SUMMARY

In order to achieve customer loyalty you must start with a holistic pic-ture of the customer. Remember, the customer is a strategic asset, one that is in short supply, one that must be treated with care. Therefore, regard customer information as a strategic asset. Once you have a cus-tomer, surround him or her with care. Establishing team-based selling as the rule rather than the exception, and use each customer contact as an opportunity to create loyalty.

As you progress from customer loyalty to dependency, make sure that you can answer these questions:

- How deep is your enterprise's knowledge of the customers?
- How much does your enterprise earn from a new customer?
- How much does your enterprise earn from a current customer?
- Who is the enterprise's most profitable customer?
- Is the enterprise's potential utilized?
- What is the potential of the enterprise's other customers?
- How does the enterprise define loyalty?
- How does the enterprise measure loyalty?
- How loyal are your customers?
- How many customers does the enterprise lose each year?
- How many customers do you keep?
- What is the lifetime value of the enterprise's customers?
- Is it possible to catch a customer who is on his or her way out by means of an early warning system?
- Which new customers should you go after?
- Can the enterprise build an "ambassador effect"?
- How can you optimize the use of your resources?
- How can the enterprise ensure relevant and targeted communication with customers?
- What goals should your employees have?
- How do you ensure that the organization shares the knowledge there is about customers?

NOTES AND REFERENCES

1. Stanley A. Brown, PricewaterhouseCoopers describes the voice of customer concept and the stages of CRM in more detail in *Strategic Customer Care*, John Wiley & Sons Canada, Ltd, 1999.

About the Authors

HENRIK ANDERSON

Henrik Andersen is a Partner in PricewaterhouseCoopers Management Consulting and Nordic Group Leader of its CRM consulting practice.

PER Ø. JACOBSEN

Per Ø. Jacobsen is a Principal Consultant with PricewaterhouseCoopers Management Consultants, based in Copenhagen, Denmark. His primary focus has been CRM consulting encompassing Sales and Marketing.

From Customer Loyalty to Customer Dependency:

A CASE FOR STRATEGIC CUSTOMER CARE

Stanley A. Brown

THE THREE STAGES

Not all customers are created equal, nor are all organizations. There are three stages through which organizations evolve, and the one within which they operate has a significant impact on the way they treat their customers. The evolution starts at **Stage I**, where customer acquisition is the primary focus; it then evolves to **Stage II**, where the practice of customer retention takes center stage. Then it progresses to **Stage III**, where strategic customer care becomes the culture and practice, where customer dependency becomes reality. [1]

Stage I: Customer Acquisition

In Stage I, a company's main focus is customer acquisition. Attention is directed toward building a customer base through the use of technology and initiative-specific training to increase the effectiveness of salespeople. Stage I companies also spend a significant amount of time on best-practice benchmarking, analyzing customer care processes and conducting initial customer research.

---

[1] IDEAS research by PricewaterhouseCoopers LLP entitled The Route to Strategic Customer Care

Stage II: Customer Retention

When a company enters Stage II, the focus has shifted to maximizing the customer relationship. A Stage II company distinguishes itself from its Stage I colleagues by beginning to segment its customers into groups with similar needs in order to serve each client group more effectively.

Stage III: Strategic Customer Care

Stage III organizations have realized that they cannot be all things to all people. While most customers are potentially profitable, some hold more long-term promise than others. The ability to predict who these customers are is a necessary skill on the upward path to strategic customer care. By wisely applying the right technology and information tools (technology is not a solution on its own), companies at the stage of strategic customer care deliver a core level of service for all their customers and a distinctive, optimized level for their best customers. Equally important, Stage III businesses have orchestrated a winning situation for both their clients and for themselves: the clients are dependent on the business for their success and vice versa.

FIVE FOUNDATION PILLARS FOR STRATEGIC CUSTOMER CARE (STAGE III)

As the following Figure indicates, only eight percent of the North American organizations polled in 1998 considered themselves to be at the third stage in the evolution of their customer care practices. This represents a mere two-point increase over the previous year's total. Then (in 1997), the majority of the companies polled were preoccupied with either acquiring customers or dividing them into preliminary groupings. Most have been unable to realize the important connection between long-term promise and current value.

Figure 5.1: Three Stages of Customer Care

	% of respondents 1997	1998
Stage I: Customer acquisition	35	16
Stage II: Customer retention	59	76
Stage III: Strategic customer care	6	8

By analyzing the 1998 data and comparing it to the responses of previous years, several basic customer care practices were identified. To be exact, five practices or "pillars" are necessary to support a robust strategic customer care process. The sophistication with which an organization applies or has developed these practices, form the foundation of all organizations' success—is directly related to its upward ascent to strategic customer care.

Figure 5.2. The Five Pillars of Strategic Customer Care

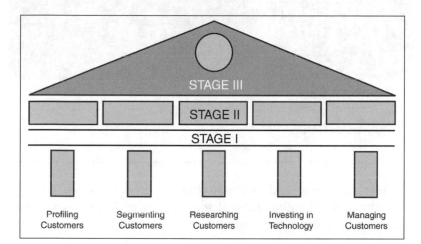

Pillar 1—Profiling Customers

One of the basic principles of strategic customer care is recognizing that some customers are more valuable than others. All businesses, on some level, are aware of certain customers' appeal over others. Stage III organizations, however, have profiled their customers in the most sophisticated way possible; they have focused on those that show the most promise and they have evolved their relationships with these customers to levels of mutual respect. Stage III organizations are in a position of mutual dependency with their strategic customers, offering a package of services or products the client depends upon while, at the same time, depending on the client for their business. In comparison, Stage II organizations may just be starting to identify their long-term clients. They are aware of the merits of profiling customers, but they have not yet maximized the information they are collecting or mastered the information management systems through which it can be collected. Of course, Stage I companies do neither of these things; they are primarily concerned with getting new customers.

Figure 5.3 shows how information retrieval and information management skills improve as organizations evolve through the stages. Stage III organizations, more than others, recognize the importance of using customer information to their advantage.

Figure 5.3: Pillar 1—Customer/Information Profiling			
	Stage I % of respondents	Stage II % of respondents	Stage III % of respondents
Maximizing advanced information management	25	31	32
Improved customer information retrieval systems	41	43	49

As you evolve towards Stage III, your customer profiles need more and more in-depth information. Here's what the evolving Stage II organization knows about its customers:

- Brief customer history, including innovations, milestones, myths, legends and folklore, mottoes and themes
- Key sales and marketing activities to date (What marketing and sales plans and promotions you have used in previous years and the relative success of each)
- Critical success factors for the customer's industry/market sector (The key challenges facing this industry or market sector)
- Critical success factors for the customer's organization

Once you reach Stage III, you will find that the extensive customer profiles you developed in Stage II simply do not contain enough information. You must now go into more detail, with a particular emphasis on the customer's buying patterns.

Consider the following crucial information you will require to successfully tackle Stage III customer care concepts. What is the size of your customer's budget or wallet? The customer's budget is a defined entity. With research, you can size it and report it within your customer profile. How much are they prepared to spend on product A or B become critical inputs for determining the worth and potential of this customer. What are the anticipated changes in the customer's wallet? Change is everywhere around us. Markets expand, contract and die. You must stay on top of the changes occurring within the product and service groups you sell, and you must properly analyze the impact of these changes on your customer's wallet.

What are your goals with regard to the customer's wallet? What do you want to achieve in terms of your customer's wallet? What issues do you currently "own" the way, say, Fedex owns next day delivery by 9:00AM? Which would you like to own? Are there areas in which you do not really want to compete? You also need to examine your current share of sales from the customer. Do you think your current share is sufficient? Is there potential to increase it? Do you want to take advantage of this potential or is it more worthwhile to pursue other customers? Finally, what is the potential of the opportunity? One important aspect of a customer's profitability centers on the expenses incurred in servicing them. Take a close look at the percentage of time and dollars spent on the account, categorized according to buying center and not simply by customer.

Pillar 2—Segmenting Customers into Natural Groupings

Segmentation is a key practice in an organization's evolution. Stage III companies—well grounded on the second foundation pillar—have recognized the need for differentiated service. This requires a robust segmentation strategy and tools that help to identify those customers that are deserving of this increased attention. In other words, Stage III organizations realized that by utilizing tools that can segment customers into proper customer care categories, the most important of which are identified as "crown jewels," they can differentiate the service provided.

Stage III customers are more concerned about providing differentiated service (35 percent of Stage III respondents versus 31 percent for the total research sample) and conducting profitability analysis of their customers.

But it's crucial that you can determine who exactly among your customers deserves the title crown jewel. These special, strategic customers have a number of distinguishing characteristics:

1. They contribute the highest proportion of gross profitability.

2. They have the potential to add further to the gross profit they already provide you.

3. They are quite profitable organizations themselves and financially sound.

4. They are customers who have permitted you to achieve a dominant share position in your product and service categories, and if you haven't yet, there's a very high likelihood that you will achieve a dominant position soon.

5. Savvy and intelligent, these customers are themselves aware of the continuous changes taking place in market conditions and are ready and eager to form strategic alliances.

6. Conscious of the need to be flexible and show adaptability, they are both market innovators and industry leaders.

Stage III organizations rank customers according to a list of critical criteria. They use a scoring template similar to rate each customer high, medium or low for each of the following criteria:

- willingness to become a partner
- trend of increased revenues generated for your organization
- your current share of customer's business
- potential for this customer to represent a significant share of your organization's business
- significance of your company's product or service to the customer's business
- current gross profit achieved from this customer
- customer's gross profit potential
- potential to cross-sell additional products and services
- customer's degree of innovation orientation

Pillar 3—Researching Customers' Industries and Concerns

Customer loyalty is not enough to ensure growth and success. To go beyond loyalty and achieve a mutually beneficial relationship, Stage III organizations have obtained a rich knowledge of their customers' worlds by asking and answering difficult questions. How satisfied are our clients with our performance? What can we do to increase contact and reduce complaints? Figure 5.4 illustrates that, as companies evolve to Stage III, they apply technology to continually uncover and respond to their customers' specific needs. In other words, Stage III companies know their customers so intimately they can anticipate their needs. The customers have no need to look elsewhere for products or service. A mutually beneficial situation has been created.

Figure 5.4: Pillar 3—Customer research				
	Stage I % of respondents	Stage II % of respondents	Stage III % of respondents	Average % of respondents
Measuring customer satisfaction and performance	63	64	58	64
Customer research through third-party telephone research	23	27	28	26
Proactive outbound telephone research	16	21	27	21
Contact/complaint management software	18	26	28	25

Stage III organizations recognize that research, sometimes termed voice of the customer (VOC) measurement, is broader than just asking customers to rate you on how satisfied they are on the quality of service you provided, the traditional approach to customer satisfaction measurement. VOC measurement is more probing and focused on both customer satisfiers—what makes the customer pleased to do business with you—and dissatisfiers—what may cause them to defect. It is focused on processes that touch the customer (after sales service, billing, order processing, delivery, etc.) and seeks to improve these points of contact. This form of research provides us with a broader method of measurement: an important point of differentiation when we all feel the driving need to measure, record and respond to what the customer is saying or thinking at each point of contact.

Pillar 4—Investing in Technology to Provide Solutions to Customers

Most Stage III organizations use some form of technology to gain information on their customers' needs. The fourth pillar necessary to support the strategic customer care process is technology, such as problem tracking software, call recording, sales force automation (SFA) or enterprise customer care technology. Remember, the objective is not to acquire the most expensive technology but to use the technology that best determines your customers' needs and delivers products and services at the appropriate time. Figure 5.5 indicates that Stage III companies have the highest rate of investment in this important foundation pillar for strategic customer care.

Figure 5.5: Pillar 4—Technology investment				
	Stage I % of respondents	Stage II % of respondents	Stage III % of respondents	Average 1997 % of respondents	Average 1998 % of respondents
Interactive voice response (IVR)	41	40	50	37	41
Intelligent call routing	38	40	42	29	40
Document imaging	26	31	50	23	32
Help desk/problem tracking software	44	43	62	31	45
Call recording	38	41	52	*	42
E-mail response Management System (ERMS)	26	24	33	*	25

* not tracked in 1997

Organizations operating within Stage III think within a new paradigm, one that is enterprise-wide and moves them beyond the concept of customer retention to that of strategic customer care. In other words, Stage III organizations understand that:

- Not all customers are the same and not all customers deserve the same level of service.
- Technology and efficiency will drive success.
- Internal competencies may not be sufficient and strategic alliances may have to be considered in order to provide the customer with a total solution.
- Customers become more valuable the longer they remain customers, but to reap the benefits of this requires customer profit maximization.
- Satisfied customers lead to higher profits.

At this stage, organizations focus on enterprise applications that share knowledge, react more responsively to their customers and permit the organization to be proactive. They recognize as well that one of the keys to success is customer longevity.

Some best practices in the use of technology among Stage III organizations include:

- Proactive database marketing systems that identify those accounts that should be most receptive to certain products and services and that leverage the organization's information sources.
- The ability to analyze profitability, a knowledge management system that captures, sorts and disseminates information related to commonly asked questions as problems or policies by customer and group of customers.
- The use of the "knowledge pipeline" as a key strategic tool for information-sharing across the organization.
- Executive information systems (EIS) that sort data and present it in a simplified manner are more robust than Stage I applications in that they allow the organization to be more responsive to changes and shifts in both market sectors and customer profitability performance.
- Applications tools specifically geared to support the functions of the organization's sales force, including sales, customer support, external help desk, field service, quality assurance and competitive and customer intelligence.

Restructuring undertaken by the Stage III organization usually results in a more centralized hub-and-spoke environment. By reengineering the sales process and empowering the sales representatives, sales management becomes free to focus on recruiting, hiring and training new representatives, a more efficient and productive use of time.

Pillar 5—Managing Customers Through Consistency of Treatment

The fifth foundation pillar necessary for successful customer care is customer management. As Figure 5.6 indicates, companies on their way to Stage III customer care have realized the merits of strategic account management (SAM). Applying the information they have gathered about their customers and their unique needs, they have created individualized action plans specific to each account or customer segment. The most sophisticated companies have created teams to deal with customers' different service needs, ensuring that the right people respond to customers' needs with the right information and support.

Figure 5.6: Pillar 5—Customer Management			
	Stage I % of respondents	Stage II % of respondents	Stage III % of respondents	Total % of respondents
Strategic account management (SAM)	27	31	37	31
Differentiated service	26	31	35	31
Web-enabled customer care	15	16	28	17

In Stage I organizations consider all customers to be important and continuous customer acquisition is the goal. At Stage II customer retention and limited differentiation becomes the goal. Stage III switches the focus to differentiated service for their select, crown jewel customers and the mutual benefits of partnership with these key customers. How does the Stage III organization meet the goals of differentiated service and strategic partnership? Consider the basic principles driving effective strategic account management.

- Revitalize, modify and systematically apply a streamlined account management process to all strategic customers. Strategic customers offer a very strong potential for the Stage III organization. After all, these are organizations within which you could potentially establish a dominant, if not exclusive, relationship with regard to the products and services you sell. And you cannot afford a haphazard approach.

- Create an environment where strategic account management receives priority through ongoing senior management sponsorship. You must ensure that your senior management plays an active part in this process. After all, they are part of the account team, champions of the cause and the individuals who ensure that the proper resources have been allocated to the strategic account teams.

- Give their strategic account teams objective measurement criteria to provide benchmarks for assessing success. As the Mad Hatter said to Alice in *Alice's Adventures in Wonderland*, "Any road will take you there if you don't know where you are going."

In Stage III the focus becomes differentiated strategic customer care through principles such as strategic account management, a team-based approach to the customer and individualized strategic account plans.

GETTING THE FOUNDATION RIGHT

To be strong and able to evolve to Stage III customer care, each of the five pillars must be built to the same height and fortified before you can raise the pillar to the next height. Most organizations don't fall completely within one stage or another. This is not an ideal situation, because if one pillar is more developed than another, stress occurs, and there is potential for disaster. Would you build a structure like that? Of course not, but it seems that some organizations choose to build their customer care that way. Would you construct the third floor before you built the second floor? Not likely, yet some organizations do just that by investing in technology that far outreaches their capabilities and needs. Would you make one pillar thinner than all the others? Hardly, that's inefficient. Yet some organizations gather too little information on their customers, only to have to build it up at a later date, at greater expense.

TWELVE STEPS TO SUCCESS

Organizations that have evolved to Stage III exhibit a number of best practices. Put together, they form a route map, a process that we call strategic customer care. By providing this 12-step, best-practice model (see route map below), we aim to ensure that the new heights you reach for are within your grasp. In time, you will no longer try to be all things to all people but concentrate on adding value to your most important customer relationships. Remember, when strategic customer care is achieved, it's a win-win situation for both you and your customers. The long-term relationships that result will, in turn, continue the cycle of profitability that will ensure your success.

The following map depicts the routes you can take through these 12 key steps.

Figure 5.7: Strategic Customer Care Route Map

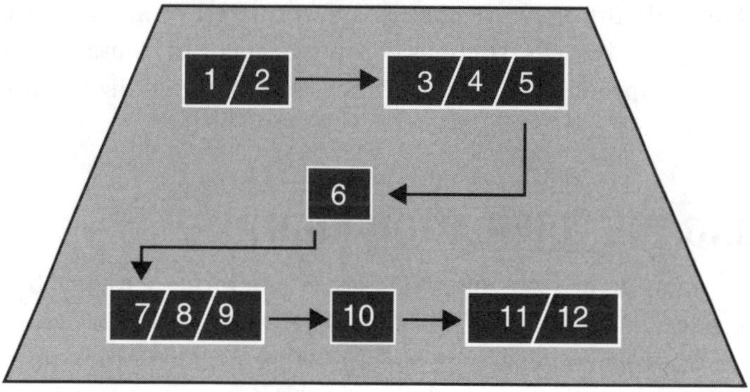

ARE YOU READY?

As you read through the sections that follow, consider:

- What stage are you in today and to what stage do you want to evolve? For some organizations, striving beyond Stage II customer care is inappropriate; for others, Stage III is a survival strategy.

- For those that are in Stage I and wish to evolve to Stage II or Stage III, the process that follows will guide you through this evolution.

- For those currently in Stage II who wish to remain there, the process will help strengthen those foundation pillars. In its present rate, the route map is overbuilt for Stage II organizations and must be streamlined a bit, although process steps should stay pretty much intact. Review the pillars described earlier and make adjustments. Your needs in the area of segmentation, customer research and technology are less demanding. As well, action planning/customer management will be done at a more general, market segment level, rather than at a strategic customer level.

- If your goal is to move to Stage III, the route map that follows will provide you with a proven blueprint.

Remember, you'll face a number of obstacles as you progress along the evolutionary route to Stage III customer care. With this route map as a guide, you *will* succeed, provided you meet the challenges ahead of you with resolve and commitment. If you're ready, let's start on the path to Stage III—*strategic customer care.*

The first two steps of the strategic customer care route map focus on ensuring that your management team and your entire organization are where they need to be in order to optimize your customer care process.

Step 1—Align your management team and mobilize it for action. Your senior management team must first buy into your vision, and then you must ensure that the rest of your organization is willing to follow. Without full support, your customer care process will not be built on a firm foundation.

Step 2—Assess your readiness for change. Determining whether your management team and organization are ready to support your plan and implement your program will help you identify—and then avoid—the issues that might become obstacles to success.

The next three steps are devoted to understanding your strategic customers in order to better focus your resources.

Step 3—Segment your customers. You have varied relationships with your customers. As previously described in Pillar 2, grouping customers according to the nature of those relationships allows you to isolate those customers who represent the greatest future potential. These are the ones who can derive the most value from what your organization has to offer.

Step 4—Profile your strategic customers. Depth and detail of knowledge of your best customers—crown jewels—is vital to strategic customer care, but no company can afford to waste too much time profiling. Quickly identify who your best customers are and then focus on them. In order to understand their needs and habits, you must understand the context in which your customers engage you as a provider. As described in Pillar 1, this involves collecting and analyzing a full range of information on your customers as well as the markets in which they do business.

Step 5—Listen to the voice of your customers. Through VOC (voice of the customer) intervention, which can take the form of one-on-one, telephone or written surveys, you will hear the needs—and complaints—of your customers. As explained in Pillar 3, make it easy for your customers to tell you what they need. The information you gain will help you concentrate your efforts in precisely the places they are needed. To achieve this, you must first establish a relationship of trust and confidence. Because of this, VOC represents a significant step toward reaching Stage III.

The next step ensures that your organization and your customers are operating within an effective relationship structure.

Step 6—Analyze the gaps. Going to market involves a series of people and events that operate as a linked chain. If there are weaknesses in these links—between, perhaps, your frontline staff and your decision makers—the process of delivering your product and satisfying your customers will be compromised. It is imperative to know where your weaknesses are by looking at your overall delivery chain, from senior and middle management to frontline support staff. How do you identify these weaknesses? Listen to the voice of your most promising customers and respond to the needs they express.

The next three steps entail putting your information to work by developing a strategic action plan.

Step 7—Mobilize your strategic account team. Using the information gathered from Steps 5 and 6, appoint a strategic account team to each of your top-tier customers. Stage III organizations clearly acknowledge the merits of strategic account management (SAM) as described in Pillar 5 and the need for differentiated service. But this requires a team, rather than an individual, that can focus on each customer's needs. Be prepared to manage all customers' needs to help them grow and, in turn, increase their dependence.

Figure 5.8: Importance (How important is each of the following activities)				
	Stage I % of respondents	Stage II % of respondents	Stage III % of respondents	Total % of respondents
Strategic account management (SAM)	27	31	37	31
Differentiated service	26	31	35	31

Step 8—Outline your strategic action program. This is one of the most important steps of the customer care process. Applying all that you have learned about your customers and their needs, as well as all that you have learned about your organization and its people, develop a strategic action program or programs for your top-tier customers. Your program should ensure that customers' needs are addressed by the most appropriate people. Why? Customer dependency. In order to achieve the successful relationship unique to Stage III strategic customer care, you must make your product or service indispensable to your customers.

Figure 5.9: Assessing your stage: Factors Adopted as Present Business Strategy				
	Stage I % of respondents	StageII % of respondents	Stage III % of respondents	Total % of respondents
Consolidation of operations	50	54	58	53
Outsourcing of operations	28	24	31	25
Integration of facilities and technology to provide "one-and-done" call handling	29	31	36	31
Call routing/workflow integration	31	36	40	35
Elimination of undifferentiated products	11	16	18	15

Step 9—Validate and assess the fit of your action plan. A further best practice exhibited by Stage III organizations is the ability to continually assess the appropriateness of the action plan created. Approach your customer and make sure that the program you have developed meets the concerns they are expressing today. Markets change—the most carefully crafted action plan and strategic account team is redundant if your customer's needs have shifted.

The next step may seem obvious, but it's important to remind yourself that no Stage III organization exists without a properly trained staff.

Step 10—Train your teams. The timing of employee training is different for every organization, but it is a best practice shared by all Stage III companies. Training, as well, is more than just lessons in customer service. Education on the merits of teamwork, the products of both your organization and those of your customers, and on communication skills (both internal and external), are key ingredients for strategic customer care. Each of these skills can be improved with training. Organizations' investments in training programs increase as they ascend the slope to Stage III.

The final two steps are devoted to putting all of the pieces of your program into place and then monitoring the program's implementation and effectiveness.

Step 11—Implement your strategies and activities. Taking all that you've learned from your customers—including the actions that you identified in Step 8—formulate concrete growth strategies. In the course of drafting these, you might find that some of the activities that are required are not supplied by your organization. That's where outsourcing and strategic alliances enter the picture. The most accomplished Stage III organizations surveyed have not been afraid to outsource selected services. They have recognized that they cannot be all things to all people, but they have also acknowledged that some clients (those who show the most long-term potential) may have certain needs to which it is worth responding in special ways. The most successful Stage III organizations, then, are not afraid to bundle their services with those of one or two outside organizations in order to better meet their clients' needs.

Step 12—Track your performance and adjust as necessary. Without being able to quantify the success of your program, you have no way of ensuring that you are on the right path. Stage III organizations conduct ongoing evaluations of their own performance to see if they have met the goals they set for themselves and to evaluate their own efficiency. They are aware, as well, that customers' expectations evolve, in the same way that a rock face changes as one climbs. An essential best practice of Stage III organizations is their ability to respond to their environment. They listen to the voice of their customers and they adjust their strategies as necessary. If they don't track their performance and adjust, evolving organizations might find themselves on the wrong customer care path and in danger of not getting to the top.

CONCLUSION

You now have in your hands a compilation of the five foundation pillars and a route map documenting 12 of the best practices employed by the most successful organizations. You know the five practices you must use in order to achieve new heights of strategic customer care (profiling, segmentation, research, technology and consistency), and you know how other organizations have made their way to the top.

Now it's time to prepare for your own climb or, perhaps, to adjust the route you're already on. What benefits can you expect for your efforts? Let's review.

- You and your customers will both win. When properly employed, strategic customer care enables you to develop strategic partnerships with your best customers. They depend on you to provide solutions as a business partner and, in return, your profits and theirs will increase.

- Your company will be able to better focus its resources. Using principles such as strategic outsourcing and the implementation of invaluable VOC research in the development of your customer care processes, you will effectively realign your organization and focus your limited resources on key market areas.

- You will gain technological leverage. With strategic customer care, the end result is an integrated technology used consistently throughout your organization. Rather than wasting financial resources on advanced technology inappropriate to your needs, you will be able to identify the best technology for your company and your premium customers.

But not all businesses will be up to the rigors of the climb. As all Stage III organizations know, the journey may be expensive, risky and tedious. The best-practices route map requires constant self-examination and a thorough knowledge of the surface on which you are climbing. Just as all Stage III organizations have realized that only some of their customers are worthy of the strategic customer care investment, a few Stage I and II organizations may realize that they have a long way to climb[2] before they can reach the third level of customer care.

In today's challenging business environment, only the strongest will survive. The success of the best-practices organizations indicates that the difficult climb to strategic customer care is well worth the effort. The question is are you and your business up to the challenge?

About the Author

STANLEY A. BROWN

Stanley Brown is a Partner in PricewaterhouseCoopers' America's CRM consulting practice and leader of its Center of Excellence in Customer Care. His primary focus is CRM in the Financial Services and Government Services consulting practice.

---

[2] Pricewaterhouse Coopers, IDEAS 98—The Route to Strategic Customer Care

Customer Acquisition and CRM:

A FINANCIAL SERVICES PERSPECTIVE

Christopher Formant

Wᴴᴇɴ ɪᴛ ᴄᴏᴍᴇs to acquiring new clients and customer relationship management (CRM), large retail banks are investing heavily in strategy and capability. Until recently the goal was to mine customer data to discover how to make retention and cross-selling efforts more cost effective. Today, the focus has shifted and the goal is to enhance the bank's growth and profitability by acting on fresh and deep insights into individuals, whether they are prospective or current customers. As Walter Shipley, chairman of the Chase Manhattan bank stated, "Technology allows you to recreate a relationship"[1].

The rationale is that banks have to evolve their marketing strategies, operating structures and systems to confront sophisticated, information-driven marketing models wielded by non traditional competitors such as monoline companies that sell only one product or service and Web-enabled financial services firms. As one observer puts it, "Large retail banks can no longer use their economies of scale and broad reach to compensate for strategic inelegance."

Tomorrow's leading retail bank must use what is learned about individuals—not just segments or even micro-segments—to determine

---

[1] "Survey on International Banking," *The Economist*, April 17, 1999.

the product configurations, promotion tactics, pricing, service levels
and channel mix that make sense for each person. The ultimate goal is
to offer unprecedented value to individual prospects or customers and
obtain the requisite level of profitability from each customer relationship. But many large retail banks worldwide have a lot of ground to
cover before they reach this new capability level. This is a point they
easily concede.

BUSINESS MODEL TRANSFORMATION

Many CEOs admit that more money, time and organizational change
will be required to make the needed transition from product- or chan-
nel-driven structures and tactics to an enterprise-wide growth strategy
that is truly customer-centric[2]. Most senior banking executives now say
that competitive customer acquisition and management involves much
more than data mining, even good data mining. They know it is silly to
claim you are customer driven if all you are doing is unearthing data on
customer segments and layering it on top of conventional product or
channel-oriented marketing campaigns. Ideally, they concede, no line of
business, product management group or distribution channel should be
laying claim to a customer relationship.

USING REAL-TIME INFORMATION ENTERPRISE-WIDE

The realm of information management is a particular concern: enterprise-wide data management capabilities are essential. For example,
any action initiated on behalf of any customer at any point of contact,
whether an airport kiosk, a Web site or a call center, should be able to
"travel" to any other access point that may be needed to conclude a
transaction. The customer should never be required to begin anew.
Then up-to-date information about customer account activity should
be consistent across all of the bank's access points. Moreover, segment
marketing managers should have access to real-time information that
allows them to understand individual needs, predict behavior and
design profitable promotions.

---

[2] Tomorrow's Leading Retail Bank, a 1999 PricewaterhouseCoopers study.

MOVING BEYOND DATA MINING

Most large retail banks have been heading towards information-driven customer acquisition and CRM, but at this stage few can demonstrate clear bottom-line rewards from this effort. By some accounts, since 1996 banks in the US alone have spent about $500 million on systems and services to identify which customers are profitable and to design marketing initiatives around that knowledge. In the near future, US banks are expected to spend that much each year in this manner.

Moreover, a number of large banks in the UK, Europe and Australia have invested in data warehouses and data-mining tools in the past few years. They have been diligently building models of consumer-segment profitability and behavior that help them target direct-marketing campaigns at the "right" groups of customers. They have been analyzing and classifying consumer needs, assessing the risk of loss and trying to predict demand and delivery methods for various types of customers. They have been leveraging information for cross-selling and for enhancing the effectiveness of new-customer marketing campaigns.

CREATING THE CUSTOMER-CENTRIC ENTERPRISE

But that is only half the battle. Tomorrow's leading retail banks will be those that will move across the three distinct stages of evolution and propel their growth with information-driven, strategic marketing and processes, structure and systems that are aligned with customer and prospect definitions of value. Figure 6.1 illustrates the three developmental stages of customer acquisition and management.

Figure 6.1: Customer Acquisition and Management

- Profitability-based segmentation and householding for current customers is the primary weapon
- Unrefined analyses of customers have some influence on the product, channel, pricings, retention, cross-selling and service mix offered
- Generally, the organization is internally focused

- Proactive prospect and customer management enabled by combining profitability and behavioral segmentation and analysis
- Information is delivered to customer touch points (e.g. branches or call centers) to influence customer activity and workflow management
- Intense internal conflicts erupt due to traditional silo organization structure

- Major transformation of strategies, processes, systems and structures
- Advanced predictive capability used for customer acquisition and cross-selling
- Bank gains influence over competitor strategies
- Testing, measuring and "retooling" of strategy and tactics are automatic; learning is continuous
- Traditional organization design is redrawn; IT infrastructure redesigned

Stage I: Broad Customer Segments Identified

The customer acquisition and relationship management activities of a bank in this stage are quite general, aimed at broadly drawn segments of prospects or customers. Analytical, organizational and technical constraints limit the bank's ability to create specific offerings targeted at individual customers. As a result, such a bank has no choice but to frame segments of its current customers based on rudimentary life-stage or profitability calculations. Meanwhile, prospects are segregated according to a simple calculation of potential profitability. If available, demographic and psychographic data may be appended for additional definition to the segmentation scheme. Such a bank will try to identify potential high-value and low-value customers and prospects and aim its marketing campaigns accordingly.

After completing its basic segmentation routine, the stage-one bank designs marketing programs that offer differentiated product, price, promotion and service levels to the members of each segment group. The primary goals of a stage-one bank are to obtain more value from high-value customers with targeted cross-selling while actively migrating low-value customers to lower-cost self-service channels and providing them with lower-cost service offerings.

Stage II: Customer Needs, Behaviors and Values Clarified

To improve the effectiveness of acquisition and customer management, the stage-two bank combines static, profitability-driven segmentation with some measure of insight on customer behavior. It then disseminates these relatively robust data sets to various distribution channels. The combination of customer behavior analyses, event data and static, profitability-based segmentation allows for the creation of dynamic statistical models that evaluate the causes and effects of marketing actions. Management can then try to predict the outcomes of acquisition, retention or cross-selling campaigns among various segments.

The delivery of this more sophisticated information to the distribution channels means more accurate advice is given to employees regarding the most appropriate selling or service steps. Visual prompts and pop-up menus on computer screens may supplement static customer information, providing staff with recommended actions that are most likely to be acceptable to a given type of customer. For example, a high-value customer may visit a branch to inquire about the payoff amount for a personal loan. Based on the customer's segment classification, a retention-alert may be triggered and delivered electronically to the call center. There, a staffer can review a series of appropriate customer management options such as calling the customer and offering another loan at a reduced interest rate or waiving fees to maintain the customer's business. In essence, the stage-two bank strives to manage and influence the work flow of its branches and call centers and generates more effective customer acquisition and management activities.

Stage III: Virtual Intimacy with Individuals Achieved

A bank that has truly reached stage three will be able to choose the customers that it wants while simultaneously reducing the universe of desirable customers available to its competitors. It will do this by creating virtual intimacy through Web-based technologies to capture individual customer data, immediately tailoring the offer to meet specific customer needs. In effect, the stage-three bank manages the strategy of its rivals. To reach this powerful position, such a bank will have completely transformed many elements of its customer acquisition and management strategies. Moving beyond the previous developmental stages, the stage-three bank relies on a comprehensive view of an individual customer that is constantly updated. Complementing this extensive information base will be:

- Clear strategies and goals for marketing to the individual customer
- Advanced customer acquisition and management technologies and processes that focus on testing new ideas against existing marketing programs and executing offers quickly and continuously
- The ability to generate information to support acquisition and relationship management activities and to produce information for senior management that illustrates the results of marketing activities; the goal is continuous feedback and learning
- Technical architecture that allows relatively easy acquisition and movement of customer information across the enterprise and that overcomes obstacles created by legacy systems created to support products rather than customers
- A new, customer-focused organizational structure and set of skills.

The stage-three bank constantly designs and tests product offerings tailored for specific micro-segments, even for individual customers. This is accomplished by running product-usage and behavioral data through rigorous decision models to identify the individuals most likely to respond favorably to a given promotion. A key, however, is making the offer quickly. The stage-three bank has completed the systems and process redesign work required to ensure that it can move fast and flexibly.

Another application is this bank's ability to provide customer service representatives with electronically delivered advice on how to make specific offers to individuals. The stage-two bank can make only specific offers to segment inhabitants. The advanced stage-three bank will be able to go even farther and use Web technologies to capture individual customer data and immediately configure product features, pricing and related services based on the information supplied by the individual prospect or customer. Using these techniques, the stage-three bank will be able to produce unusually high returns on its marketing and customer management activities and become one of tomorrow's leaders.

This may sound deceptively simple. As many capable and experienced senior banks can attest, however, the transformation that is required is complex, taxing and changeable. Success requires a clear vision, effective leadership, a reliable transformation process, middle-management acumen, sufficient capital and patience at the board level.

THE CURRENT STATE OF PLAY

When discussing customer acquisition and management strategy, most of the bankers interviewed said they try to emulate top-flight retailers. Whether it is Nike, Dell Computer, Pepsi, IKEA, British Airways or Wal-Mart, banks are aspiring to the superior service and detailed customer knowledge that these companies leverage so successfully.

A number of the banks in the study are struggling to emerge from stage one. Because of the transactions that pass through their systems, banks—in theory at least—know more about their customers' lives than anyone but the customers themselves. They know—or can deduce—a customer's income, net worth and creditworthiness; with more sophisticated systems, they can also track a customer's family relationships, lifestyle and interests. Historically, however, banks have allowed a huge stream of customer information to pass through their systems virtually untapped. Some have stored it in massive databases to which they have had almost no useful access.

One of the results of banks' backwardness in mining their huge reams of data was to allow monoline companies with a more sophisticated approach to overtake them in particular business lines. Banks have, for instance, had mixed success in the credit card business; many of those that jumped in enthusiastically in the 1980s suffered severe losses and even now look at it with deep caution. "Everyone thought that they could compete, and they tripped over themselves," says Robert Jones, group executive and former president of retail banking at KeyCorp. "We have all ventured into some stupidity with credit cards. It's a tough business."

Understanding Micro-Segments

Going a step farther is the bank that can tie the various types of data together and leverage that combination to segment its customer base in dynamic and multidimensional ways. Those that can manage this feat have identified segments that go considerably beyond the traditional model of going from A to Z without skipping a step in the sequence.

Broad insight into a customer segment is the first layer to be unveiled. For instance, the conventional wisdom is that the typical on-line banking customer is young and upwardly mobile. But two banks that have focused on Internet banking have found segments ignored by this common wisdom. While Citibank is pursuing the under-30 segment in its virtual banking model, it is also targeting consumers over 50, who are generally regarded as too old to learn new banking methods. "They are learning," says Ed Horowitz, corporate executive vice president at Citibank. "They're big Web browsers and big in on-line trading. They have a lot of money, and they're very cost conscious. What's more, they have a lot of time to worry about their money. And they have learned that e-mail lets them talk to their kids and their grandkids all around the globe for nothing."

Analyzing Profitability Drivers

In-depth segmentation can produce surprises when it comes to profitability. When First Union took a careful look at the drivers of profitability, it found that there was not as close a tie between wealth and profitability as it had expected. "Some of our most unprofitable customers are very affluent people who know how to optimize their own economic well-being and not ours," says Naras Eechambadi. Transaction volume is also an overrated driver of profitability First Union has discovered. "Yes, it matters at the margin," he says, "but what fundamentally matters is share of wallet—what are the depth and breadth and longevity of the relationship?" Careful analysis of customer data has also allowed First Union to design new products. When the bank realized that all its overdraft customers also had credit cards, it designed a product that tied the two together. "The interesting thing," Mr. Eechambadi says, "is that when we did it, these customers' balances went up by an order of magnitude, and some customers who formerly were unprofitable became profitable."

CASE STUDY

How Fleet Bank Matches Service Levels to Customer Profitability

Fleet has multiple, varying levels of customer service based on the strength, depth and profitability of customers. "We have built a very robust data-warehouse environment," says Robert Hedges, managing director of retail distribution. "We rate all our costs. We do profitability and revenue potential evaluations on all our customers, and then we run segmentation models using customer profitability algorithms, both actual and assessed potential."

Out of that process come scores that are used to determine everything from the way in which customers are greeted to the length of time they remain on hold, and the ease with which they can get charges waived. "Based on where you are along that spectrum," he says, "when you go into a branch or when you call on the phone, you get a differentiated level of service. It's all unseen—but clearly experienced by the customer."

In addition, the bank uses its segmentation data to determine which customers are good candidates for migration to a higher level of profitability. For those chosen—customers whose potential to move up is in the top 10 percent—the bank has an explicit high-service-level segment called preferred services. "You would know if you were in that program because you'd get different mailings and be given a different phone number to call. There are different call service standards, and the staff is trained differently."

The uses of data mining go beyond segmentation, however, to a bank's core strategy. A customer-driven strategy can hardly be carried out, after all, without a detailed knowledge of those customers. But beyond that, says First Union's Mr. Eechambadi, "Knowing your customers can give you tremendous insight in to what's going on in the marketplace." First Union has a group that concentrates on mining its data from a strategic perspective. "They look at trends, gaps, how people are changing and how pricing affects the way people behave."

Intelligent Data Mining

Bankers say that the goal is to move from segmentation to virtual customer intimacy; to get beyond groups of customers to develop a relationship with each one individually. "Ultimately," says Norris Tolliver, senior vice president at SunTrust, "it becomes a market of one. Right now, most of us broadcast out to everybody and see who bites, instead of saying, 'I've got a pretty good statistical chance that if I offer this product through this channel, that particular person will take advantage.' Over time, the intelligent data-mining companies are going to build incredible capacity to do that."

CASE STUDY

Royal Bank of Canada's Segmenting and Modeling Skills

In the area of segmentation and predictive modeling, the Royal Bank of Canada seems to be ahead of the pack. The bank has 1,300 branches, a large ATM network, point-of-sale capabilities and fast-growing phone and Internet banking services. Almost 90 percent of routine transactions are handled outside the bank. Products and services run the gamut from trust services and securities trading to personal financial planning and investing.

Royal also has a large mobile banking capability that originates about 40 percent of its residential mortgages. This sales force works on commission but is not allowed to take business away from branches. It is to develop its own sources of business that represent new customers to the bank. The push is now on at Royal to personalize and deliver advice to small micro-segments through the appropriate channel. James Rager, vice chairman of personal and commercial banking, believes the Internet will eventually dominate the banking business. So the bank is working hard to learn how to customize offerings via the Internet as well as its other electronic channels. At the same time, Royal wants to excel at target marketing.

"We will have strategies for each customer that will allow us to anticipate their needs and personalize all interactions that they have with us," says Mr. Rager. "Based on our segmentation knowledge, we will have pricing strategies and channel offerings for every single customer that are customized to the fullest possible extent." For example, an existing customer in good standing who visits the bank's Web site to investigate mortgages will be offered a pre-approval for a mortgage almost immediately.

Royal conducts extensive research on customers' channel preferences, current as well as anticipated. This allows marketing managers to include channel preferences when devising customized product offerings to micro-segments. The engine of all this activity is database technology that provides four key insights into customers:

- Likelihood of defection
- Current and expected value
- Credit-risk scoring at the client level
- Channel preferences

Segments are defined in terms of broad behavioral and attitudinal attributes that imply future profitability. In the past, the bank looked only at current profitability and the consequence was that the most profitable customers were seen as a homogeneous group. Today, Royal reports success with target marketing after studying channel preferences, combining external and internal data and applying modeling techniques to come up with clearer pictures of micro-segments.

Mr. Rager also says that this analytical capability provides a strong sense of where the bank needs to improve its management of the lower profitability segments—that is, the system helps to identify steps the bank can take to evolve the loss-makers or profit-neutral clients so that they generate value. The action may be simply directing a low-value customer to the direct phone bank. Salespeople are trained in how to find out what is behind channel preference and to address those issues in ways that will move customers to other channels. If the customer is uncomfortable with voice-response units, for instance, they may offer to demonstrate their use. "We migrate customers," Mr. Rager says, "but it's never forced."

The customer management system is currently being enhanced with contact management and campaign management software. The idea is that if a customer does a transaction in a branch, information about that transaction is immediately available in the call center or any other channel. Ideally, the information that is provided to the various channels about customers—and about strategies for managing the relationship with customers—will be consistent enterprise-wide.

Sound predictive modeling drives Royal's segment management strategies. But, Mr. Rager notes, "You have to constantly test the validity and the use of those models. You can't just develop them, put them to work and forget about them. You have to constantly look at changes in regional markets. And you have to constantly assess what kind of data you have and what you are doing with them."

In all, Royal is able to develop a unique offer for small microsegments that incorporates:

- Product needs and design
- Pricing that reflects current and future value
- A channel option that fits the customer's preference

This is the hallmark of a bank that has its evolutionary path clarified. In essence, it is the ability to leverage relationships with customers and give them the power to control their relationship with the bank. And that is, perhaps, the most powerful retention tool of all.

SUPPORTING SALES AND SERVICE STAFF WITH ADVANCED TECHNOLOGY

To reach stage three of the evolutionary path requires employees with strong sales skills and an unwavering commitment to high-quality customer service. Most crucial, however, are sophisticated systems that enable detailed analysis of customer information. If there is one point on which this study found unanimity among interviewees, it is that in today's difficult environment one of the retail banking industry's strongest weapons is its unparalleled access to a broad range of information about its customers. "We don't always use it as well as we might," says Michael Lilley, general manager of direct retailing and channel management at National Australia Bank. "Nevertheless, we have a lot of data. The nonbank competitors snapping around our heels don't have much data at all. They use what they do have quite well, but they just don't have the depths of understanding of the customers that we do."

Mr. Lilley believes that tomorrow's leading retail bank will be defined largely by its ability to delve into its customer data files and come up with value for the customer that cannot be obtained elsewhere. He makes the conceptual link between the need to get customers to use lower-cost channels and how a bank will retain its profitable clients once they are accustomed to electronic interfaces.

"Our view is that you have to provide superior service on the remote delivery channels to keep your customers on board. One way to do that is to perform an almost unheard of level of data analysis that ultimately becomes a service in itself," says Mr. Lilley. "Using all the data and data-mining capabilities at its disposal, the bank can conceivably offer the customer great insight into his personal balance sheet. This enables that customer to manage his financial affairs much more effectively. And that's a unique value." Put another way, the goal is to achieve virtual customer intimacy.

CASE STUDY

ABN AMRO'S SMART SYSTEMS FOR CUSTOMER MANAGEMENT

C. H. A. Collee, senior executive vice president of commercial development at ABN AMRO, a major global financial institution, says that a few years ago the bank recognized that it was doing a poor job of expanding its relationship with existing customers, not to mention holding on to them. "We were spending all this money on getting new accounts," he says, "but we were not nearly as good at keeping them from going right out the back door." That led to a decision to switch the emphasis to making sure the bank was doing as well as it possibly could with the accounts it already had. A major feature of that campaign, still under development, is a sophisticated middleware system that will not only connect all of the bank's channels but also organize and keep track of its customer-enhancement efforts as well.

The system will distinguish the customers with which ABN AMRO already has a strong wallet share from those with which it does not but could. For the customers it is cultivating, the system will establish a complete management system and direct each part of the work involved in building a relationship between an individual and the channel that best serves his or her needs.

Call-Center Intelligence

For many customers, the starting point will be the bank's award-winning call center. "The call center will call a customer, and if they need to make an appointment with a local customer representative, the call-center representative will have that schedule on the screen. They will make the appointment, and then call the representative to tell them about it," explains Mr. Collee. After the customer representative has met with the customer, the system will identify not just the next step but who needs to do it. "If we need to obtain complicated information from the customer, a reminder will be sent to the representative. But if it is simple information, let us say the person's salary, the system will tell the call center to ring up and get the information."

The system will also be able to target customer calls to the appropriate call center, which does not mean merely the one with the shortest, or longest, hold times. "It will be able to send a call, for instance, from the southern part of the country to representatives who are particularly skillful at dealing with people from that area," Mr. Collee says. The bank has also given increased authority to both call centers and branches to solve problems themselves, without having to seek approval from superiors.

This kind of sophistication does not come cheap. ABN AMRO's middleware system will cost more than £160 million to build, and it is expected to be created in the coming three years. But already, Mr. Collee says, the bank is not only doing a better job of retention; without even trying, it is getting more accounts as well.

THE ROLE OF SALES INCENTIVES

Incentive programs are another vexing subject: all banks have them, and few seem satisfied with what they have. The problem is that systems that are simple to understand do not have enough subtlety to influence employees, but as they become more complex they run the risk of losing their effectiveness, because employees have trouble figuring out exactly what behavior will benefit them most.

David Carroll, president of First Union—Florida, concedes that the complexities sometimes verge on the absurd. "It is challenging to amend our incentive plans to take into account all of these eventualities," he says. "A formula that would include every contingency would end up looking like the periodic table. You can't design incentive plans to totally direct behavior." Complexity can work, however, if it is done right. ABN AMRO has designed an incentive scheme that ties bonuses to, among other things, ambition. Managers who set their sights high have the chance of gaining higher bonuses than those who are more cautious. KeyCorp is moving towards rewarding salespeople for going after more difficult but profitable customers rather than concentrating on those who are easiest to sell.

Crédit Lyonnais has developed a cumbersome-looking but effective scheme for improving performance at its call centers: employees are expected to identify potential sales and direct those clients back to the branches. The Crédit Lyonnais call-center employees then put in claims for those referrals, and the bank tracks those that result in sales. The bank may even seek feedback from customers on the employee's performance. Bank of New York ties employee rewards to what John Hicks, senior vice president, calls a combination of incentives and piecework. "An incentive says that since you met a goal, you get a payment," he explains. "Piecework says you sold 30 accounts and you make 50 cents an account. You have to do both. Otherwise, people go for the big incentives and ignore the bread-and-butter business."

INNOVATIONS IN RECRUITMENT, TRAINING AND DEVELOPMENT

Banks have spent decades—in some cases, centuries—training their employees to process transactions. But the new retail bank model requires a different sales and service mentality that cannot be developed overnight. Banks surveyed for this report are trying all kinds of techniques. Abbey National requires new hires to visit not only conventional branches but its sales-oriented supermarket branches. Deutsche Bank tries to separate the sheep from the goats: sales-oriented employees are kept in branches, and those who cannot be weaned from transaction processing are moved to its centralized processing facilities. ABN AMRO uses a company that trains employees in the hotel/restaurant management business. And many banks have decided the only way to foster the employees of the future is to keep them out of the traditional bank model altogether; they have opened their direct banks as separate operations, hiring an entirely new staff and training it differently.

ENHANCE BRAND VALUE WITH SUPERIOR SERVICE

"More than anything else," says Barclays' John Varley, "customers are looking for the remorseless personalization of our offerings. In every letter I get from a happy or an unhappy customer, it starts with a name. Ms. X was just fantastic at sorting out my problem. Mr. Y is a pillar. And here's why. They want to be treated like individuals. They assume that we have this omniscience about our relationship with them. That's an assumption that we should deliver on."

Surely, virtual customer intimacy turns on the flawless utilization of customer data, but the most sophisticated banks recognize that they must be more than well-oiled sales machines. They are looking to enhance the quality of their service to individuals. They realize that one of the quickest ways to lose their customers is to give them the feeling that they are regarded primarily as fodder for a vast army of salespeople. "Helping our customers understand the choices that they face is different from just pushing product in their face day in and day out," says Karen Haefling, chief marketing officer at KeyCorp. "Our rallying cry is we want to do what's right for our customers. We take that very seriously, and it translates to our customers as well, hopefully, through our brand. If we don't do that, then forget the rest of it."

STRATEGIC IMPERATIVES

A bank's strategy around these crucial issues will, to a large extent, be defined by situational factors such as its size, its strategic investment portfolio, its base of skills, its present and potential customer base and its competitive position. Consider the diverging strategies of two of the largest banks in the world: BankAmerica and Citibank. BankAmerica has pursued an aggressive acquisition strategy geared to becoming one of the most formidable banks operating across the US. This was most recently seen in the merger of NationsBank and Bank of America.

Citibank (at least until its recent merger with Travelers, the insurance and investment banking company) followed a strategy of internal growth, which made it a global financial services powerhouse, but limited its retail banking to interregional spread. But now, aiming to build itself quickly into a national retail player, the bank has adopted a controversial strategy of becoming a virtual nationwide bank not a physical one. Through a combination of ATMs placed in retail outlets such as Kinko's (the copy shop chain) and Internet services, Citibank is trying to spread from coast to coast in the US at minimal cost.

Other points of strategic differentiation can be spotted across the retail banking spectrum. But setting aside unique situational factors, the research conducted for this report leads to the following conclusion: the large retail bank, regardless of location, will require new core operating capabilities.

OVERCOME OBSTACLES THAT IMPEDE PROGRESS

In their quest to evolve their marketing capabilities, banks will have to overcome several key obstacles, including:

- Customer-segmentation approaches that are based largely on demographic information or a simple profitability classification that limits the marketing staff's ability to gauge the outcomes of discrete marketing actions that are aimed at specific customer segments

- Constraints on information analysis and learning resulting from systems that were created to support product lines, not customer segments, and analytical constraints owing to the existence of multiple systems that cannot produce, without great difficulty, one comprehensive view of customer needs, behaviors, risks, preferences and propensity to buy

- Organizational units that are focused on products or geographic markets rather than customer segments and that have no incentive to share "ownership" of customers with other groups in the bank

- Weak analysis of the links between customer needs, behavior, product usage and profitability

Figure 6.2: Tranformation Involves Six Crucial Areas

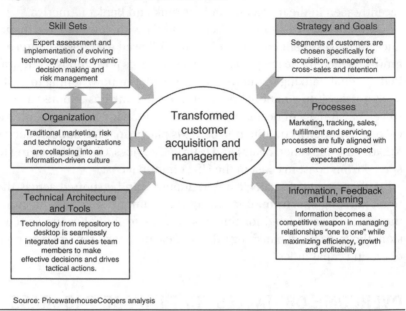

Source: PricewaterhouseCoopers analysis

Creating tomorrow's leading retail bank implies transformation in several areas (see Figure 6.2). Senior executives will need to focus on:

- **Skills Sets and Organization** The traditional organization units that are product- or channel-oriented are collapsed into a new marketing structure that combines elements of functional expertise such as marketing, risk, decision science and information technology. Such consolidation is necessary because many of the skills and processes that the bank will tap into to link customer information, perform statistical modeling, design unique value propositions and shorten cycle times will come from individuals who are traditionally located in function-specific work areas. Without such a functional consolidation, multiple hand-offs and lack of coordination will continue to preclude effective and timely value delivery.

- **Technical Architecture and Tools** A robust and well-planned systems infrastructure enables truly effective customer acquisition and management by overcoming product-oriented legacy systems to create a seamless environment through which information can be captured and shared. The stage-three bank will have the technical capability—including the right kind of information technology staff, hardware, software and networks—to process data on a vast customer and prospect population and deploy the more sophisticated inference-based models needed to create unique value propositions for prospects and customers.

- **Strategy and Goals** Specific markets, segments, products and channels are targeted based on the institution's strategic goals and operational strengths. This process of establishing strategies and goals will properly handle the less profitable individuals and focus on the most attractive prospects and customers.

- **Processes** Refined acquisition marketing and customer management processes leverage rich customer insights and eliminate organizational silos that increase cycle time. Instead, fast, flexible and continuous marketing is an operating hallmark.

- **Information, Feedback and Learning** Customer-centric information management drives planning and operations. Meanwhile, marketing processes are supported by systematic feedback on the results of discrete campaigns. Standardized management reports enhance performance management.

Completing a successful transformation of customer acquisition and management is essential to remaining competitive in tomorrow's marketplace. Leading institutions are already beginning the evolution and starting to manage the strategies of their competitors. Those banks that fully embrace the challenges will ultimately succeed in generating the levels of profitability that boards and owners demand.

Finally, the impact will extend beyond the individual firm and there will be ramifications for the industry as a whole. We are on the cusp of the most profound change in banking since the Great Depression, with the transformation of the financial services industry as a whole just now beginning. The momentum comes from the combination of advanced customer acquisition and management techniques with innovations in Web-enabled access and delivery. Overall, a new financial services paradigm, with new winners and losers, is about to emerge.

About the Author

CHRISTOPHER FORMANT

Christopher Formant is a Partner in PricewaterhouseCoopers' America's CRM consulting practice. Mr. Formant is PricewaterhouseCoopers' Theatre Leader in the America's Banking Group and also leads the Global Banking Consulting Practice.

Part Three

Step Two: The Need for Effective Channel and Product Strategies: Overview

OVERVIEW

Once the customer strategy is defined, it is now time to move on to articulating and planning which products or services will be offered to which customers through which channels—simply known as product and channel strategy. Surprisingly, this strategy appears to be more confused and misdirected within organizations, with the net result being channel conflict and suboptimized and misdirected efforts in new product development. What stimulates new product development—better yet, what *should* stimulate new product development? And once developed, to which customer groups should it be sold and through which channels of distribution?

Although no company has the ideal process, many have developed and are now revising time-tested approaches to new product development for use in today's markets. Based on a best practices study performed by PricewaterhouseCoopers during 1999, Chapter 7, "CRM Through New Product Development," describes how cutting-edge organizations are developing new products and services to meet the demands of these new environments. It addresses market strategy and customer strategy in the context of new product development and then discusses ways to include the customer in every step of the product development process—create, assess, test and implement. The concepts outlined herein are based on professional experience as well as best-practices interviews conducted with Fortune 500 companies on new product development. All names used in examples have been altered to maintain confidentiality for both our clients and our various study participants.

Chapter 8, "Channel Management and CRM," addresses channel management head-on. The sale and distribution of products from company to customer often happens through a number of intermediaries, each of whom performs part assignments within marketing, sales, distribution and service. These intermediaries constitute the sales and distribution channels of the company. Typically, these costs are 20 to 40 percent of the total retail price to the customer, and there is therefore great potential in optimizing the channel and maybe even pronounced restructuring it for the benefit of both company and customer. Furthermore, in connection with the optimization of the channel structure of the company, market and customer segments may appear that have not yet been considered.

We follow with two chapters related to the channel that will have the biggest impact on business in the twenty-first century—the e-channel. The first of these, Chapter 9, "Embracing the E-Channel," is based on a recently released PricewaterhouseCoopers study on e-business. In mid-1998, we asked executives and senior managers to describe their e-business progress to date and their outlook for the future. This survey of leading companies—all members of The Conference Board's Information Management Center—confirms that most firms have already begun the formative work of adopting such efficiency-driving technologies as e-mail, Web sites and intranets (and internal Web sites). The survey reveals that within three years, a majority of the companies surveyed intend to press forward into more advanced forms of e-business that will:

- Enable them to provide transaction processing over the Web.
- Target their customers more effectively through sophisticated data warehousing.
- Use extranets to link them with their suppliers and other key business partners.

Clearly, there is more at stake here than an automation of delivery channels or the codification of data on customers. Although each of these objectives has merit, the total force of the message from the survey is more profound. These executives have high expectations for e-business that point to a change in the very essence of how their companies earn revenue and grow market share. Their expectations concern the value their companies provide to their customers, how they must organize to do this in an increasingly dynamic world and how they can compete and win.

Executives' expectations are high as they look to e-business as an avenue for resolving some of the most illusive issues that they face. They understand that implementing e-business is no longer an issue of technology alone, even though there is still more to be done to make the technology effective for broad-based deployment. Consequently, they are prudently cautious about moving beyond their areas of greatest comfort but are preparing to do so in the near future nonetheless. Meanwhile, they are getting their internal houses in order, extending e-business capabilities where they can drive value today. Chapter 10, "E-Channel Management," addresses the question of which e-channels to use for which customers, and what other integrating issues must be considered.

We close with an industry perspective that has significant application across most industry sectors. Chapter 11, "The Customer-Centric Organization in the Automotive Industry." We review the current situation in the automotive industry and explore and map the forces that are driving the industry toward a consumer-centric entity. The views of the original equipment manufacturer (OEM), automotive suppliers, dealer/retailers and consumers are discussed. In closing, the chapter discusses the impact of transforming the enterprise to a consumer-centric view, the role e-business can play and the automotive industry services that will make it happen.

Customer Relationship Management through New Product Development

William M. Takis
Lorraine M.Cote
Catherine M. Stanmeyer

Iɴ ᴛᴏᴅᴀʏ'ꜱ ꜰᴀꜱᴛ-ᴘᴀᴄᴇᴅ, technology-driven marketplace, companies are struggling to maintain customer loyalty, generate new revenue and control costs while at the same time racing to beat their competitors to market. Customers are more knowledgeable about what they buy. Better educated, they are willing to pay for perceived value but no longer base allegiance to a single company solely on past results. The old loyalties are gone. Long-standing relationships are no longer relevant if customers do not feel that they are getting the highest quality product or service for their money. Companies are looking for ways to leverage their existing customer relationships to increase revenue. At the same time, mergers and acquisitions, consolidation and deregulation have increased competition to unprecedented levels and have accelerated efforts to increase efficiency and reduce costs.

Amid this turmoil, companies are turning toward new products and services to link them more closely to their customers and cement existing customer relationships. Thus, new product development is a critical part of customer relationship management; it involves providing customers with products and services they want and making them available and easy to use. New products and services include modifications of existing products and product line extensions as well as entirely new areas. Companies are also beginning to explore and use new channels such as the Internet to market both products.

"During 1998, we generated 31 percent of our sales from products new to the market within the past four years. We expect an even higher proportion of sales to come from new products in 1999."[1]

New product development is not new to these companies, but the changed environment in which customers reward speed above almost all else is. Pressure for speed to market can have unintended, negative results: Often new products and services arrive in the marketplace untested, overdue and over budget. These are some of the reasons companies are searching for new ways to do business.

These organizations are betting their futures on the choices they make today. Windows of opportunity may be limited, so companies need an effective new product development process to allow them to select only the best ideas that are targeted toward the customer and allocate scarce financial and human resources to develop them. Indeed, process is perhaps more important than ever.

Although no company has the ideal process, many have worked out their own ways to develop new products for today's markets. Some of the best ways to do this involve including the customer in every step of the product development process. The steps in that process are create, assess, test and implement.

Figure 7.1: The Product Development Process

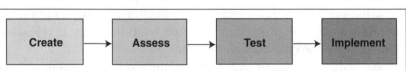

---

[1] The Chairman's Letter, 3M Annual Report, 1998.

CREATE

New technologies have transformed the traditional marketplace. Internet services, electronic commerce and increased global competition have changed the way companies think about their customers. Technological changes now play a considerable role in decisions that can alter or enhance an organization's overall service through new and existing channels. These advances in new technologies bring an increased opportunity for creative products and services to meet customer needs, many of which were previously unarticulated. In fact, they have changed customers' perceptions of their needs. New technologies also provide organizations with ways to reach out to these untapped customer markets.

The first step in developing a new product or service is identifying an idea or concept that has the potential to meet customer needs and increase revenue. Some companies have problems identifying ideas, while others have too many ideas and struggle to narrow the group down to a more viable subset. Often companies do not use all available resources to identify and capitalize on new ideas quickly and efficiently. To successfully develop new ideas, companies must have a strategic product development process that allows them to rapidly coalesce valuable human and financial resources around their highest potential concepts. Once such a process is in place, businesses can best take advantage of it by formalizing a program that constantly feeds ideas, options and opportunities into the development process and quickly performs a preliminary screen.

Creating the largest possible funnel for new ideas means tapping into all available resources, both internal and external. Although many organizations properly use ideas from customer feedback, engineers, or executives and managers, (just to name a few), those who excel in idea creation do more.

Figure 7.2: Sources of Ideas

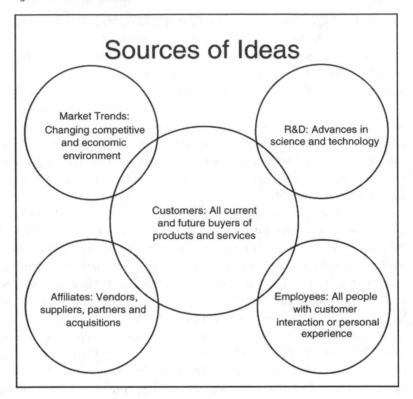

Organizations have multiple internal areas to target for ideas. Every perspective counts. Salespeople provide valuable insight on how their customers feel about products and services. Their personal relationship with customers means that they can provide more in-depth knowledge on their perceptions. On the other hand, engineers may be more aware of technological advances that may make ideas more cost-effective or provide new opportunities for development. Traditional sources such as managers and call center associates, in addition to nontraditional sources including professional partners like suppliers and distributors, each have suggestions and information that could be utilized.

To take internal idea generation even one step further, organizations bring people from across the organization with different competencies and experiences together on a regular basis. Brainstorming sessions— known as "ideation" sessions—allow free-association of ideas and creative inspiration to work together to generate new ideas. Sessions should be focused on a particular type of idea—i.e., long-term possibilities (15–20 years) or short-term improvements.

Internal sources for ideas can be very powerful; however, external sources cannot be ignored. Today's technology provides more advanced tools that make customer observation and market analysis more accessible and less expensive. Focus groups and surveys are still valuable, but new technology-enabled methods can contribute significantly to organizations' understanding of the market and customer trends and trigger ideas. Consider options such as on-line customer chats (where customers can interact with you on-line); Web research (tracking Internet browsers or users to understand and capture preferences and patterns); and on-line testing (where new product ideas and services can be tested on consumers via the Internet). In addition, directly observing how customers actually use products, services and prototypes can provide valuable insight for product extension and improvement ideas.

ASSESS

Obviously not every idea that is introduced can be developed. With scarce human and financial resources, only the best ideas should be pursued and limiting the number of ideas accelerates the product development process. It affords opportunity to apply specialized marketing and developmental expertise to increase speed to market and maintain focus. Assessing all potential product and service concepts in a systematic way is key to successful product development.

Assess ideas based on their core concept. They must be evaluated given the current competitive environment and potential market size, and for cost, functional concept and internal requirements. However, before dismissing a concept that has a great potential but will be costly and difficult to develop, consider options for strategic alliances or acquisitions. Given ever-shorter product life cycles and the speed of technology-based change, a well-timed strategic alliance or acquisition can mean the difference between being the first to market with a financially viable concept and dismissing a great idea as too expensive or cumbersome to develop.

Fully assessing an idea that has potential means creating a complete product proposal, which includes consideration of all likely potential market outcomes and analysis of developmental options. The idea-screening process doesn't end once the decision is made to pursue a concept in greater depth. It takes place continuously but at a greater level of intensity. One of the first things a concept is screened for is strategic fit and that requires consideration of many factors including corporate strategy, competitive advantages and core markets, branding issues and synergies with existing products and services. Questions that should be asked include:

- What market channels do we use now and which do we want to use in the future?
- What is our customer base?
- How will this product affect existing product lines?
- What do we need to do internally to produce this product or service?
- What is the competition like and what will it be like one year or five years from now?

Answering this last question requires taking a long, hard look at what competitors (and potential competitors) are doing. Collecting competitive intelligence, examining the current product environment and then systematically reviewing strengths, weaknesses, opportunities and threats are useful steps to complete this exercise. Staying on top of market conditions ensures that product decisions are not made in a vacuum. Understanding your competition, your customers and your marketplace is key to product success.

Keep your customer in mind throughout. Qualitatively testing a product or service with customers to identify the product's key processes, rigorously assess functionality and to try branding and market positioning strategies can speed actual development. Realistically considering target market size and the cost of entering that market can ensure that you are pursuing a concept with potential instead of just pursuing a good idea.

It's also important to consider:

- Capital investment requirements (what will it cost to produce this product or service initially, as well as ongoing costs?)
- Pricing options (what price ranges can be used? what price breaks or promotions can be considered?)
- Operating margins (will all customers be charged the same? where are we prepared to sacrifice margin for volume?)

The Project Team

It is important to do the right analysis and take the correct approach to development but to have the right resources engaged for a particular product or service under consideration. Using cross-functional teams (as shown in Figure 7.3 below) is the most effective way to assess a product's potential viability. Selecting a group of people from all relevant functional areas (e.g., marketing, engineering, finance, operations) to develop a product or service ensures that the right expertise is available at all times. Having this available expertise, in turn, not only ensures that the team considers the product or service from all necessary viewpoints but also that it wastes no time in developing the idea.

If the product or service idea does not seem to have potential for payback within a given period of time, it may not be worth pursuing, and the project team's time might be better spent developing a different product idea.

Figure 7.3: The Project Team

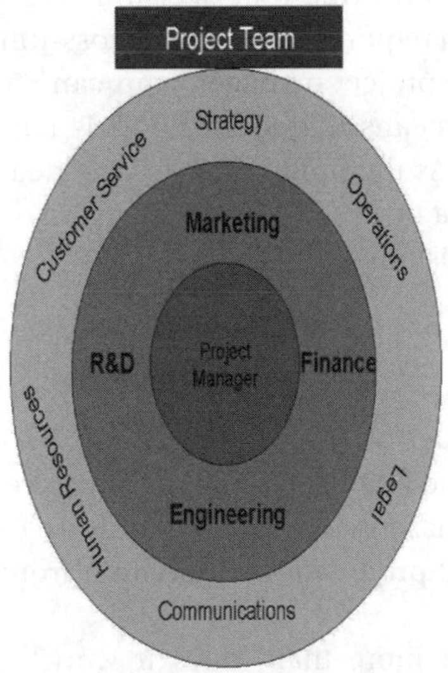

Dedicated cross-functional teams with designated project managers tend to provide the best results. Assigning staff to a team for the duration ensures that the team does not waste time continually familiarizing new people with the concept. It also means that the group members will learn to work together faster, making their progress that much quicker and effective. Ideally, the team should be located in a central place to better promote a quick and easy exchange of ideas although the right technological tools can make virtual consolidation possible.

Many best-practice firms have teams of new product specialists (typically marketers and analysts) that are available to work on projects as they come up. Experience allows these people to quickly integrate into a team and speed a concept to market. While bringing in team members from different areas of expertise as they are needed ensures that no one's time is wasted, it is especially important to get marketing staff involved early. Their input is essential to making sure that the evolving product idea stays attuned to the demands of the marketplace. The lens they provide can save significant time and cost, for they understand which marketing decisions are critical at which juncture in development.

The pace of globalization and technology-driven change are putting more and more pressure on companies developing new products. There is more pressure to not only make the *right* decisions but to make them *quickly*. Ensuring that decisions are made with the best possible information requires the use of a cross-functional team, led by a semi-autonomous project manager, who can consider all necessary viewpoints. It also means that strategic fit is considered up front to avoid wasting time. As the product or service idea is fleshed out, marketing expertise must be used from the start and on a continuous basis to avoid making decisions in a vacuum.

TEST

By the time a product or service is ready to be tested, a significant amount of human and financial resources have already been expended. However, the test phase is the first opportunity to measure the likely success of the actual product and evaluate it from several angles in a live market.

Testing is about more than "does it work?" A test plan should include ways of analyzing both the product and the market. A product may fill a perceived customer need and function perfectly, but if it is not packaged correctly, does not have the specific features a customer is seeking or is not priced competitively, it will fail. Traditional product development processes used testing primarily to check if a prototype functioned. Today's testing often focuses more on product positioning.

Clearly, with all of these considerations, the testing process can be a long one. However, new technologies and marketing models make it possible to test a product or service appropriately without decreasing speed to market. A well-developed testing process actually saves time and resources. Of course, even with the advent of new testing capabilities, actual speed to market will vary somewhat depending on:

- Product or service complexity (the more complex the product, the more parts or the more detailed the programming will affect time to market)

- Regulatory constraints (in some cases, government imposes a certain amount of time in debate or testing)

- Technological or system constraints (in many cases, the staging of product development is dependent on technology development and testing completed in advance of assembly)

- Testing methods (sometimes imposed by government or quality control requirements)

> Many variables may affect how quickly a firm can bring a new product to market. Average speed to market for a new product or service can vary tremendously. In most industries, best practice firms can bring new products to market in three to 24 months.

Regardless of what pace has historically been "normal," today's environment requires quicker, more accurate, more focused testing that provides the answers to make a reasoned decision on a new product or service's future. Even best-in-class organizations have begun changing testing approaches to capture the maximum amount of information and develop the most accurate performance measurements in the shortest period of time. A global leisure services firm tests its new services not only with existing or potential customers but also with customers that have complained about their services in the past. These "critics" are able to tell the firm very honestly what they like about the new concept as well as what they like about competitors' concepts. By screening these critics and being willing to listen, the leisure services firm gets an advantage from its mistakes and the successes of its competitors.

As speed increases, early customer input becomes more important. Using customers to conduct "live" tests of a product or service is not a new idea, but new technologies allow organizations to tap into customers in many new ways. For instance, organizations may use electronic focus groups to survey customers about product features. They can develop computer simulations and bring customers to the development site to work their way through a potential service. Repetitive testing allows considerable customization before a traditional market test takes place. Indeed, a formal market test in varied geographic regions may even be unnecessary for some products and services.

Particularly in the e-commerce world, first to market is often more critical than perfect to market. Consider a limited "live" market test (allowing a limited target market to field test the product or service) with an incomplete product. Such a situation would never have existed just a few years ago, but today's consumer is increasingly tolerant of products they can "tailor." Internet feedback systems can link engineers directly to the customers they are targeting, and customers are often drawn in when they believe a product is designed particularly for their own needs. Customers can thus give you the information you need to complete and perfect your product while actually using it.

Another innovative approach is to conduct short, limited market tests with multiple versions of a product. By varying some features such as price, packaging or message in different versions and comparing results to controls, the organization can better understand what attracts customers to the product. By doing short tests (four to six weeks) in multiple locations simultaneously (or even multiple quick simulations), a new product or service can be evaluated on all levels without delaying market launch.

How does a product or service pass a test? Does the product "work?" Do customers say they will buy it? Does it sell well in a limited market test? It is critical to define key performance indicators (KPIs) at the beginning of any test phase. (These KPIs might include sales targets, endorsements or other factors). Ideally, they should be included in the business plan for the product. KPIs provide the road map for the test; they spell out required threshholds the product or service must attain in tests before a further development can be considered. KPIs commonly include financial standards, but customer satisfaction measures, expected market penetration and so on may also be relevant.

A global communications firm sets specific KPIs for both products and services and portfolios of products. All new products are measured in the same way so that they can be compared. Those products that do not meet the criteria can be quickly "killed" so that the resources can be directed to others with greater potential. By setting KPIs at the beginning of the test process, an organization can develop data to determine the product's chances of success. Set measurable targets and track the product's performance against them in the test phase. If the product does not meet KPI targets in testing, it is unlikely to meet them ever. Products and services that are unsuccessful in tests should be quickly reassessed. What was the reason for the failure? If it was due to a poorly designed feature or an incorrect message, retesting may be called for. If the product fell considerably short of financial targets, by contrast, it should probably be cancelled.

Successful products are really always being tested, because firms continuously monitor their products' ongoing performance. A personal communications firm not only tests its new products against each other but also against its existing products as well. The standards for recently released products may not be quite as rigorous as those of existing products, but they allow the company to track underperforming existing products as well as successful new ones. Some KPI targets will obviously change as the product or service moves into the rollout stage, but others, such as customer satisfaction measures, will remain constant. By benchmarking a product's performance in testing and beyond, against KPIs as well as against other products, customers' continued interest in the service can be determined. As well, customer comments, additional focus groups and further competitor research all allow for continuous improvement.

IMPLEMENT

Getting a product or service ready to launch consumes considerable resources, and speed becomes extremely important when the product is ready to go to market. Implementation needs to be accomplished quickly but not rashly. At one time, most organizations factored in the time it would take to gain full distribution or consumer acceptance for a new product or service. However, with speed-to-market-pressures building, this has become a luxury. Launches need to be planned with bigger expectations and global reach in mind. Especially in today's environment, implementation becomes an exercise in managing concurrent efforts. Staff training, prelaunch sales tactics, distribution, production and promotion all happen at once in the implementation phase.

One way to speed up the implementation process is to acquire, partner with or create an alliance with another firm. Recognizing that increasingly complex products and services demand a broader range of core competencies, many organizations are turning to relationships. Why take the time to attempt to develop a core competency in a new area when someone else can provide it now? Short-term relationships, licensing agreements, acquisition strategies and long-term partnerships are all part of the implementation process for new product development today. A leading apparel firm has capitalized on its brand reputation by entering a diverse number of markets outside its traditional limits. It did not have the required capital or expertise to enter all of the new markets on its own, so it developed a strategy of brand licensing. The firm is able to maintain control of use of the brand and strategic direction of the firm and yet enter new areas while the window of opportunity is still open.

When reviewing the possibility of a relationship, it is important to understand all of the options available. In some cases, a temporary alliance might be the best solution to provide a needed component of a product or service until the capabilities can be developed in-house or for much needed "splash" in the promotion of a product. In other cases, an actual acquisition of another company to bring a competency (and the people that go with it) in-house is the answer. The key to any of these relationships is considering the exact needs for the product or service and the core capabilities, assets or technologies that all parties bring to the table.

The decision to actually begin looking for relationships should be part of the assess step of concept development, but the relationship usually comes to fruition in the implementation of any new product or service. Making a decision to go to market with a partial or test product is also a viable option in today's marketplace for quickening implementation. An implementation strategy that turns customers into development partners can foster a sense of customer ownership, a more robust end product, and most importantly, a brand reputation for being first to market. Especially in some industries, being first to market can be the difference between success and failure. High technology industries are filled with examples of partial product launches. Many start-up companies on the Internet earn their reputations by putting up "shell" services that customers can react to and help develop as they mature. A truly innovative idea can withstand the imperfections of a partial launch. Amazon.com and Dell are strong examples of this.

Bringing a partial product to market must be an intentional strategy. Communications and promotion must be created around that strategy so that customers truly understand their role as development partners and do not perceive it as the launch of a shoddy product. In addition, systems must be in place to make very rapid changes to the product or service as improvements become available.

Moving the sales cycle up into the implementation process has been practiced in some enterprises for a long time. The entertainment industry, for example, has developed and run promotional "teasers" for movies before the script has ever been finalized or the first scene shot. Creating an expectation and a demand for a product before launch reduces the sales cycle after launch thus recouping investment sooner. One recent example of a presales approach that combined innovative use of promotion, technology and low-budget marketing was the *Blair Witch Project*. Use of presales turned this B movie into a blockbuster. Any product or service can be promoted prior to launch. With product life cycles decreasing and the obsolescence increasing, any strategy that reduces initial sales cycle time should be considered.

However, the idea of creating pent-up demand for a product or service before it even exists has not been widely practiced in part because of the risks. Successful presales involve understanding product or service features, meeting development deadlines and meeting or exceeding demand expectations during the actual launch. Promoting a good concept will create demand, but if that demand is not met by the actual product or service, failure may come sooner rather than later.

Any implementation strategy that increases speed to market also increases risk. A relationship will mean a certain degree of loss of complete control, an impartial or imperfect product will not have the its full functions and features, and presales will create expectations that have to be met. However, these risks can lead to greater returns on a successful product by being the first to market, creating customer ownership and building initial demand.

CONCLUSION

The dynamics of today's marketplace demand new products and services:

- Rapid advances in technology and science have enabled things that were not possible before.
- Globalization has created a smaller marketplace for global organizations while at the same time increasing the competition.
- Consolidation and a rash of mergers have blurred the lines between industries.
- New sales channels and marketing tools have allowed small niche players to have a broad reach.
- Consumers are educating themselves about their options. Blind loyalty no longer exists.
- Product life cycles are decreasing while the rate of obsolescence is increasing.

This market demands change and customers can be a key partner in it. Technological change is not only transforming the marketplace, but also changing the development process. Technology has made consumers more reachable for input early in the process. It has provided firms a means of collecting and analyzing information about their target markets, their competitors and the needs and desires of their existing customers. Technology also allows the opportunity to draw in expertise from all over the globe, creating virtual teams and collaborative partnerships.

> "The market needs that a product is meant to satisfy and the technologies required to satisfy them can change radically—even as the product is under development."[2]

This chapter has attempted to highlight some of the best practices in new product development today. It will be up to individual firms to expand those practices, create the new concepts and dare to launch the innovative products and services of tomorrow. Most important, these firms can use and manage their customer relationships to improve and bolster this process.

[2] Marc Iansiti and Alan MacCormack, "Developing Products on Internet Time." *Harvard Business Review.* 108, September 1, 1997.

About the Authors

WILLIAM M. TAKIS

Bill Takis is a Partner in PricewaterhouseCoopers' Amerca's CRM consulting practice and the partner in charge of the Strategic Product Development group within the Washington Consulting Practice.

LORRAINE M. COTE

Lorraine Cote is a Principal Consultant in our Strategic Product Development Practice.

CATHERINE M. STANMEYER

Catherine Stanmeyer is a Principal Consultant in the Strategic Product Development Practice.

Channel Management and CRM

Stanley A. Brown

Oᴿɢᴀɴɪᴢᴀᴛɪᴏɴꜱ ᴀʀᴏᴜɴᴅ ᴛʜᴇ world have a new challenge today. While everyone knows that effective customer care is essential to success, too many organizations ignore the intermediary between the organization and its customer—the channel—and the role it plays in establishing effective customer relationship management.

One of the key questions that an organization must address is its channel and product strategy. Organizations must learn how to properly define and analyze the efficiency of their channels by using proven methods from the channel management theory. This can be done through identifying the conflict of interests that exists between organizations and customers and subsequently defining and implementing appropriate channel strategies to support an effective CRM strategy.

CHANNEL STRATEGY DEFINED

A channel strategy allows organizations to increase their profitability by ensuring that the most effective channel is used to distribute various products and services to customers. This involves better aligning products and services to customer needs and then providing customers with easy access to those products and services through efficient channels of distribution.

As you start down the road to an effective CRM strategy, the answers to some fundamental questions must be sought: What is to be produced, who is going to buy the product and how is it to be sold? This is the channel strategy, and once it is defined, channel management becomes the tactic to make it a reality. It will allow you to target and adjust the channels to the specific needs of the most important customer segments of the organization.

The movement of products from the organization to the customer often takes place through a number of intermediaries within the areas of marketing, sales, distribution and service. These intermediaries constitute the sales and distribution channels of the organization. Typically, the costs of these channels are 20 to 40 percent of the total retail price to the customer.

THE CONFLICT OF INTERESTS BETWEEN THE ORGANIZATION AND THE CUSTOMER

A fundamental conflict of interests exists between the customer and the producer of a product or service and, without fully appreciating this, customer relationship management will not be optimized. The customer seeks the most favorable price and quality while the organization aims to reduce its costs and increase its sales to maximize its profit. The conflict of interests is illustrated in the figure below:

Figure 8.1. Conflict of Interests Between the Organization and the Customer

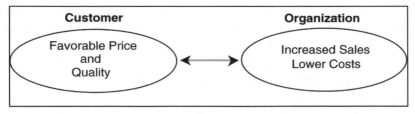

Source: PricewaterhouseCoopers.

Customers focus on elements involved in a transaction, while the producer is more interested in optimizing their investment in the creation and operation of the channel structure and still maximizing profit.

THE INFLUENCE OF THE CHANNELS IN INCREASING THE VALUE OF THE PRODUCT

The characteristics of a product may have a strong influence on the choice of sales and distribution channels. Traditionally, products are regarded to consist of a core, which addresses the fundamental needs of the buyers. For example, an individual's core need for a car could be to be transported from X to Y. With regard to channel management, the concept of core need is extended to include soft areas such as the image of the product. The core need of a car might then be extended from transportation from X to Y to include the value of a prestige brand as well.

Figure 8.2 illustrates the product wheel, which shows the types of benefits of a product or service.

Figure 8.2. The Product Wheel

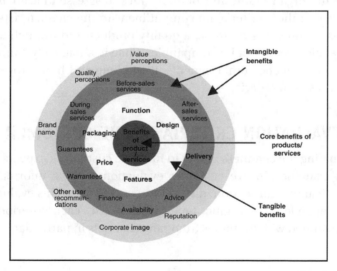

Source: Philip Kotler and Keith Cox, *Marketing Management and Strategy*, 7th edition, Engelwood Cliffs, NJ: Prentice Hall, 1991, and PricewaterhouseCoopers.

The channels normally have great influence on the intangible benefits of the product. These benefits can be categorized by using the following evaluation criteria: information, communication, transaction, distribution and service. The customer evaluates the channels based on these parameters. Therefore, it is necessary to uncover what a given product might demand of the fulfilment of the channels' function. A high degree of after-sales service might demand an intermediary who both supports the image intended by the original organization and demonstrates an expertise in the product.

Take for instance, Bang and Olufsen, which offers exclusive service in their B&O centers. In this case, the value of the intermediary is very high and often demands a close cooperation or maybe even a direct organization ownership. On the other hand, "shelf products" will demand less of the intermediary, and their value will most often lie in their ability to cover the market at low cost. It is important that the chosen intermediary supports the chosen organization strategy to reach the chosen customer segments.

The outer ring of the product wheel contains so-called soft criteria. They include concepts such as image and the perception of the quality level in the organization and brand names. It is essential for many products that these criteria are compatible with the characteristics of the sales channel. For example, a quality product sold through a discount retailer would not be compatible. While it is relatively simple to change and influence other benefits, it is a long and hard process to change these soft criteria.

THE EVALUATION CRITERIA OF THE CUSTOMER

By evaluating the channel's ability to fulfil the customer's expectations we can examine the five customer evaluation criteria: information, communication, transaction, distribution and service. This evaluation is very dependent on product type, which is why each criterion has been illustrated with examples from new channels in particular.

Information

The organization has information about the characteristics, service, price and such of their product, which has to be communicated to the customer. The channels do this by virtue of their large interface with the market. The organization can choose to inform the customer directly or to use its channels. Advertising is often the main method of imparting information about products to the customer and intermediaries.

The Internet is a relatively new medium in the channel structure, and it is very efficient in terms of transmission of information. As a customer it is possible to get exactly the kind of information you want. An example of this efficient information channel might be a car manufacturer's auto manual on the Internet. Such a book can be constantly updated and mistakes corrected quickly and inexpensively.

Communication

A customer needs answers when buying a product or service. Thus it is important that the customer can easily contact the organization in question. In the example of the automobile manual on the Internet, it could be very relevant for the car manufacturer to be in direct contact with the customer. New needs could be identified faster, and defects in a model could be corrected in new models. From the customer's point of view, communicating directly with the manufacturer instead of through an intermediary makes the channel more trustworthy. However, the organization must realize that it takes great effort and many resources to use the Internet as a communication channel.

Transaction

The term "transaction" implies the exchanging of orders, invoicing and payment from the customer to the last link of the channel. It is important that the channel fulfils the customer's need for security in connection with the transaction. The customer must be certain that their payment goes to the right person and that there is no risk of overcharging.

For several years, EDI—(electronic data interchange) has made it easier to accomplish large numbers of transactions between companies. Large companies have greatly reduced their need for human resources by introducing this kind of automatic transaction. However, one of the problems with trading on the Internet has always been the lack of security concerning payments. Customers, particularly those in Europe, have viewed the Internet as a very unsafe channel, even though there are fewer problems with payments made on the Net than with traditional checks.

Distribution

Distribution of a product must take place quickly from the customer's point of view, and products must be delivered at the convenience of the customer. If the product has to be packed and shipped, it should be both protected as well as easy to unpack.

The Internet is also a new kind of distribution. Everything that can be digitalized will eventually be because it is so inexpensive. Banking is one of the areas that takes great advantage of this kind of distribution of services.

Service

Service can be seen as the most important evaluation criteria of the customer. As a customer, it is very important to receive good service in connection with the decision to buy a product or a service as well as after the purchase has been made.

This may include help in installing the product and in the subsequent operating period. The customer must have easy access to assistance, if there are any problems concerning the use of the product. If the product needs repair, it must be done quickly to minimize the inconvenience of the customer.

The quality of the channels' service can be evaluated in many different ways. One is by evaluating the trustworthiness of the channel. It is important that the customer trusts that the channel will fulfil its part of the bargain and do such things as deliver on time and in the way expected. Furthermore, the customer should feel that they have been treated well by a competent, service-orientated, friendly staff. Dell Computer is an example of this kind of service by giving the consumer the opportunity to decide what the computer they are ordering will consist of themselves.

Another way to evaluate the channel is how it responds in the case of product defects. Is it easy to communicate through the channel? Is it felt that everything possible is being done to repair the defect? How easy is it to get in contact and how long does it take before an action is taken? The Internet can supply more kinds of services than many other channels. It is not only possible to receive and repair digital products on-line but also to specify any particular needs concerning the products.

CHANNELS FROM THE ORGANIZATION'S PERSPECTIVE

From the organization's perspective the channels are evaluated using the five criteria: market coverage, control, conflicts, profitability and support. These five areas heavily influence the sales and distribution channels' general performance, and they are very dependent on each other.

If one sales channel is being used exclusively, then there will be higher demands on it to provide training support and perhaps warehousing and billing. This comes with risks, as the sales channel has a closer relationship with the customer and their needs, and thus an organization can suffer loss of control. Therefore, it often becomes a matter of weighing between these parameters since the organization cannot create an optimal situation in all areas at once.

Market Coverage

When analyzing the channels' market coverage it is relevant to distinguish between market coverage of current and of new channels.

Market Coverage by Using Current Channels

To ensure the best possible market coverage, it is essential to have a view of what customer segment the current channel structure covers. This is necessary in order to identify any overlap between the channels' coverage of the identified segments.

Figure 8.3. The Coverage of the Market by Two Channels

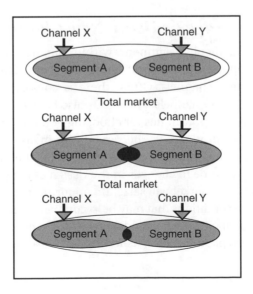

Source: PricewaterhouseCoopers.

In the first situation there is no overlap. Channels X and Y each work with their unique market segment, and there is no subject of conflict. On the other hand, the problem is that the entire market is not covered, which means lost earnings and a possibility of competitors moving into the open areas and then maybe even encroaching on the covered areas as well.

In the second situation, the whole market is covered, but there is significant overlap. This may result in conflicts between the sales channels, and the situation will likely not be the best possible based on the fundamental goal of creating profit. However, the situation may be tolerable, if this surplus supply acts as a shield against new competitors.

In the third situation, the scenario is close to optimal. The market coverage is complete and the overlap small with only minimal potential conflicts. In practice, the situation is seldom this simple. Often some of the channels will be more appropriate than others depending on the characteristics of the product and the strength of the intermediaries.

Finally, competitors can influence the market coverage. For example, in the consumer goods industry, leading brand name suppliers usually want to be represented by the same sales channel as other leading brand names. This ultimately results in an excess coverage between the sales channels.

Market Coverage by Using New Channels

One of the most difficult assignments within channel management is to identify new opportunities to contact customers and make them cooperate with current channels. Often, there is considerable resistance against utilizing new channels. There may also be regulations that limit the organization's opportunities for choosing new channels. For example, certain liquor products can be served only in approved, regulated establishments. However, it is very important for the organization to have a positive attitude to changes in the design of the channels, since other players in the market will seize the opportunity.

Three of the conditions that may help companies to identify opportunities in the market, which would allow for a changed channel structure, are scenario planning, dissatisfied customers and new technology.

Scenario Planning

The technique of scenario planning may be used to identify unfulfilled or changed customer needs. Since customers' needs often move very slowly, a method such as scenario planning shows when the change is significant and thus, when there are opportunities in the market. A great deal of the scenario planning in connection with channel management is about setting some goals that might seem unrealistic at first and letting the creativity around alternative channel structures emerge.

Dissatisfied Customers

Dissatisfied customers are an indication of unfulfilled customer needs. To be able to react to this, it is necessary to uncover what factors affect customer satisfaction in order to measure these factors against current sales channels. An example of using unsatisfied customer needs comes from the computer industry. Michael Dell, founder of Dell Computers, started a new sales channel after having personally encountered inadequate and unsatisfactory service from traditional computer dealers. By starting a telesales service, Dell was able to offer customer-tailored computers and direct technical support. This allowed him to eliminate the intermediary dealer who had created the problem in the first place because of their lack of appropriate product knowledge.

New Technology

In the past couple of years technology has created a number of new opportunities to gain an understanding of the market. Voice response systems, Internet shopping and teletext have now existed for some years and the consumer is familiar with interacting with companies without intervention of a "live" agent. EDI, as another example, has often been characterized as being very cost efficient and capable of individualizing the dialog with the customer, which, in turn, creates greater customer loyalty toward the channel.

One of the problems with using new technology as a sales channel is that customers are often not technologically inclined and do not know how to use the new capabilities. A number of companies have, therefore, chosen to reward customers for using the channel in hopes of creating greater loyalty towards it. For example, SAS, the Scandinavian airline, has offered bonus points for customers who order their tickets via the Internet.

Control

In channel management it is important for an organization to have control of its sales channels and how it communicates with the consumer. The message must be consistent with the soft criteria previously discussed. The organization's degree of control over a sales channel has a great influence on how the channel presents the product and the attached service. The delivery and the environment in which the product is sold is, to a high degree, part of the entire product and image that the customer buys into.

To choose a sales channel with a high degree of control might also depend on whether it is a standard product, which does not require any supplementary service, or whether the product needs to be co-distributed with complementary products. On the other hand, an exclusive distribution offers the opportunity to offer bundled services. For example, most car dealers not only sell cars but also offer insurance, renting, leasing and financing.

Finally, take into consideration the fact that suppliers might want to have a certain feeling of what goes on in the market. By having a completely controlled sales channel, the supplier gains access to market data and the voice of the customer, which are otherwise often dearly bought.

Conflicts

When an organization changes its channel structure or finds new distribution channels, there is a big risk of a conflict of interest with the current intermediaries of the chain if the target group of the new channels overlap the old (see Figure 8.3). Conflicts arise because producers and intermediaries have different interests. This means that the two parties have different goals in relation to marketing and customer loyalty. The organization wants to increase its market share per product, selling in as large batches as possible. Conversely, it is in the interest of the wholesaler to create as many large customers as possible with a broad variety of products that can be delivered together.

The difference in goals deviation is an important reason why conflicts may exist between the supplier and the sales channels. Figure 8.4 illustrates how the differences in interests can be the cause of conflicts between the parties.

Figure 8.4.
Different Objectives Is a Major Cause of Conflict Between the Supplier and its Channels.

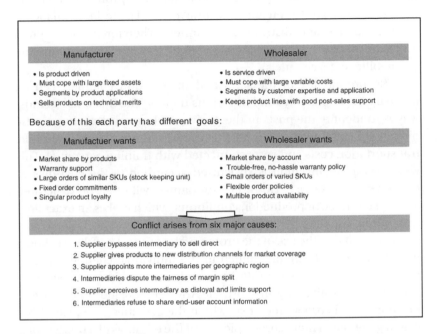

Manufacturer	Wholesaler
• Is product driven	• Is service driven
• Must cope with large fixed assets	• Must cope with large variable costs
• Segments by product applications	• Segments by customer expertise and application
• Sells products on technical merits	• Keeps product lines with good post-sales support

Because of this each party has different goals:

Manufactuer wants	Wholesaler wants
• Market share by products	• Market share by account
• Warranty support	• Trouble-free, no-hassle warranty policy
• Large orders of similar SKUs (stock keeping unit)	• Small orders of varied SKUs
• Fixed order commitments	• Flexible order policies
• Singular product loyalty	• Multible product availability

Conflict arises from six major causes:

1. Supplier bypasses intermediary to sell direct
2. Supplier gives products to new distribution channels for market coverage
3. Supplier appoints more intermediaries per geographic region
4. Intermediaries dispute the fairness of margin split
5. Supplier perceives intermediary as disloyal and limits support
6. Intermediaries refuse to share end-user account information

Source: PricewaterhouseCoopers.

In some business sectors the relationship between organization and intermediary is only at the transaction level, while in others it is like a partnership. If the product requires great technical insight and a lot of service (for example, photocopiers) the organization and intermediary would have to work together closely to ensure consistent customer service, training of personnel and so on. On the other hand, it is often possible to sell ordinary commodities without a close, binding relationship between the partners.

The management of current sales channels, as described above, can be destroyed if completely new channels are introduced. However, this does not mean that it is not possible to sell to different channels without conflicts arising. Fundamentally, the organization has two possibilities of avoiding conflicts in its channels: differentiation of either product or customers.

Profitability

Basically, the organization needs the channel to be profitable. It is normal that up to 20 to 40 percent of the final price of a product is made up of costs to sale and distribution channels. Therefore, it is of great importance that the organization is able to measure and evaluate the profitability of its channels.

The profitability of the sales and distribution channels can be made up in various ways and in various depths. The first and foremost way is to identify the posts in the profit and loss account that can be directly assigned to the channels. These would include, for example, transportation costs and costs connected with training personnel. This works if the organization is structured according to the channels or customers they service. However, companies will often be structured along geographic or production conditions, which makes an exact division of costs difficult.

Furthermore, the use of the profit and loss model has the weakness that the fixed costs are distributed in the individual channels. Therefore, activity-based costing (ABC) methods are used in many places to calculate the profitability. In short, the ABC method allocates the organization's fixed costs to the areas where the activities take place. That way, it generates a more correct picture of the earnings of a product and how much each channel draws on these costs. However, the ABC model is not perfect either, since the division of costs does not take into account how many products and customer-specific costs there are in each channel. When costs have been distributed, the turnover per sales channel can be decided, and this way the profitability of the channel can be determined.

Support

Often the support will consist of activities such as marketing, promotions, training programs, repair warranties, material in connection with demos/exhibitions or flexibility in connection with stock, delivery and selection. In general, a good support program should address the following areas: finance, customer service, order/delivery and information/marketing.

This can seem like a one-way flow, where the sales channel has the sole benefit. The advantage to the supplier is that they gain influence on how the product is presented to the customer but at the same time the support helps to bind the sales channel closer to the supplier. The support ensures the channels have incentive to continue the trade with the supplier and, thereby, create a loyalty effect. From Figure 8.5 you can see how loyalty coheres with the degree of support.

Figure 8.5. Connection Between the Degree of Support and the Loyalty toward the Channel

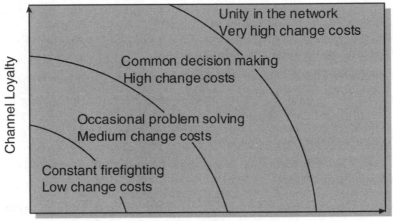

Source: PricewaterhouseCoopers.

As it appears in Figure 8.5, it is possible for a organization to increase the loyalty of the intermediary of the channel by increasing the support. The farther away from the top left corner, the greater mutual dependency there is between organization and channel. Such a relationship can be named a partnership, where each gains by a close cooperation.

CONCLUSION

When evaluating the channel strategy of the organization, it is important to ensure that the channels match the demands from the primary customer segments of the organization. The teamwork between the two sets of evaluation criteria is central when evaluating whether the channels perform satisfactorily and the customer relationship management strategy is effective. It is, therefore, incumbent upon the organization to measure the channels' performance from the perspective of both the customer and the organization.

In the same way it is not sufficient to determine whether a sales and distribution channel is *profitable* in itself, if the other organization criteria have not been taken into consideration: market coverage, control, conflicts, profitability and support. Furthermore, a profitable sales and distribution channel can be outright harmful for a supplier, if the profitability has been achieved at the expense of the value-creating function of the channel for the customer.

To be effective in designing a channel and product strategy, the organization must:

- identify and understand customer needs
- effectively deliver products and services to meet those needs
- enhance revenue by attracting new members and improving the retention rate of existing ones
- improve the cost efficiency of services

In addressing these challenges the following should be taken into consideration:

- There is a strong correlation between customer satisfaction and customer retention. For example, one study found that 95 percent of customers who rate service as excellent will repurchase from an organization and are unlikely to switch. Compare this with only 60 percent of customers who rate service as good.

- IBM found that a 1 percentage point increase in overall customer satisfaction translated to $257 million in additional revenue over the next five years.

- The key to enhancing revenue opportunities is linking particular products and services to particular customer segments through the appropriate channels.

About the Author

STANLEY A. BROWN

Stanley Brown is a Partner in PricewaterhouseCoopers' America's CRM consulting practice and leader of its Center of Excellence in Customer Care. His primary focus is CRM in the Financial Services and Government Services consulting practice.

Embracing the e-Channel

PricewaterhouseCoopers

ELECTRONIC BUSINESS: THE NEW HORIZON IS HERE

Is the business world on the verge of a new paradigm? In mid-1998, PricewaterhouseCoopers asked executives and senior managers of leading companies—all members of The Conference Board's Information Management Centre—to describe their e-business progress to date and their outlook for the future. This research study on electronic business confirms what many of us already know through experience: electronic business is changing the way corporate leaders see their business world and the way they operate within it. These changes, moreover, are likely to accelerate in the near future.

Three decades ago, a new electronic world of communication called the Internet appeared on the horizon. Today, this new electronic world is no longer a thin line in the distance; it is here surrounding us and is challenging the very notion of distant horizons in time or space. With the same rapid pace, the growth of e-business is bringing the world into faster, closer reach for many corporate leaders, changing both their strategic vision and their operations.

What does e-business mean to leaders today? Although electronic business is relatively new, it is already having a profound impact on business strategy and operations. E-business is not limited to mere messaging; it includes ways of helping companies meet their goals, both in the marketplace and in the back office. More significantly, all signs point to a near-term surge in new e-business applications in both the strategic and operational realms.

e-Business Impact on Strategy

Clearly, respondents believe that e-business can help them serve their customer better, a key strategic goal. This is an extremely important finding, since many companies today are reorganizing to become centered around the customer. As brick-and-mortar storefronts yield to 24-hour relationships, these new dynamics can help companies accomplish a key goal—to provide premier service "anywhere, anytime" the customer wants.

More importantly, some companies are exercising an active leadership role in finding such applications. They recognize that e-business has strategic importance for all companies: over one-third have a dedicated team and/or senior executive involvement to support the transformation ahead. In measuring the success of their e-business strategies, executives say they will look to customer loyalty as a key indicator. In other words, e-business has gone far beyond a mere means of communication; it is a way of building lasting relationships and increased revenues in the process.

e-Business Impact on Operations

Meanwhile, on a parallel track, the technology of e-business itself is enabling companies to accomplish new operational goals. Managing technology and quality of information remain key operational concerns for managers, and they see process streamlining and cost control/efficiency as clear ways to gain competitive advantage. Despite the challenges, one very positive sign is found in some emerging operational uses of e-business, such as customer call centers, intranets that link business partners, and data warehouses that improve customer relationships. Other key findings include plans for using enterprise-wide data warehouses and the increasing use of data marts.

A New Link

Yet the best of e-business is still to come. Only a handful of executives see themselves as "leading" the e-business movement. Moreover, many potentially valuable uses of e-business are still in the planning stage. This is because executives have other priorities and because they face practical challenges in making full use of e-business. These findings show that the use of e-business is bound to grow in the future. As followers see leaders succeed, they will attempt to become leaders themselves. As we look at the signs contained in our survey, we are truly seeing the future, and it is e-business.

THE TOP FIVE FINDINGS: SUMMARY

1. Most senior executives (over two-thirds) identified their top challenges as meeting customer demands and managing technology—in particular technology change and integration. These two areas clearly outranked the other 10 areas offered as choices.

2. Executives aim to create competitive advantage in various ways, but primarily through premium service, process streamlining and cost control/efficiency. These same executives showed awareness of e-business, but only one out of five rank it high as a competitive factor today.

3. Senior executives have staked out three different stances toward e-business. About one-third are e-business leaders or innovators, another one-third have decided to enter the field but are not sure when, and the final third are undecided.

4. Whatever they think of e-business, corporate leaders today are surrounded by it. For every 10 firms represented in our survey, nine routinely use e-mail, seven make full use of a company Internet site, and six have an intranet. Most of the others make selective use of these tools. In addition, a majority of respondents reported that they are using or planning to use a number of other e-business tools, including customer call centers, electronic data interchange, and business unit "data marts" (sub-segments of the data warehouse). Other innovations are in the planning stage.

5. Most executives are measuring e-business success through not only improved quality of information but also increased loyalty of customers. Both of these were cited by more than seven out of 10 executives as key performance metrics.

About the Study

In spring 1998, PricewaterhouseCoopers and the Conference Board embarked upon an industry-wide survey on electronic business. Eighty-three business and IT professionals from 76 companies representing virtually every industry sector responded, and a group of industry and e-business experts were assembled to analyze the data and address its implications. Seventy-five percent of participating companies were international, 18 percent were national (US), and 7 percent were local/regional. Their organizational experience with e-business varied from those still in the planning stages to those who had completed a significant project.

Forty-seven percent of the respondents reported total worldwide revenues of over $5 billion, and 32 percent reported total worldwide revenues of less than $1 billion. More than half the respondents were in two sectors—industrial/manufacturing (34.1 percent) and financial services (23.3 percent). The remainder were fairly well divided between consumer projects, utilities, oil & gas, transportation, entertainment/media/communications, the public sector, and others.

Eighty-one percent of respondents who were either executives or senior managers answered on behalf of their entire firm; the rest focused on their own business unit.

Survey questions were administered by The Conference Board's Information Management Center as part of an initiative aimed at studying e-business as a path to strategic market advantage. Respondents were asked questions concerning their e-business experience and their plans over the next three years. The areas covered were:

- Key challenges being faced by their organization
- Factors affecting competitive advantage in their industy
- How e-business activities are initiated, managed and owned
- Goals, challenges and issues surrounding e-business initiatives
- Decisions about e-business leadership
- Lessons learned from e-business initiatives
- Areas in which they had or planned to invest in e-business-enabling technologies in the next three years

THE TOP FIVE FINDINGS: DISCUSSION AND ANALYSIS

1. What Are the Key Challenges that Confront Senior Management Today?

Findings

Both "meeting customer demands" and "technology change and integration" are considered critical challenges by 67.3 or 67.5 percent of the executives surveyed. Cost reduction, once the major challenge facing most companies, is no longer ranked as high, even though it continues to receive management attention.

Figure 9.1. The Key Challenges

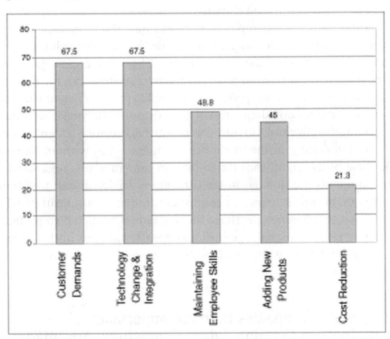

Analysis

In a world of wrenching change, companies are more concerned than ever about finding new ways to meet customer demands. They recognize that this involves improving employee skills and providing new products and services while continuing to stay ahead of the competition. Many are going further, re-examining the fundamentals that drive business success and looking to exploit new technologies and business models to meet this challenge. Many companies that successfully made reducing costs and improving processes a priority in the past realize that their future success will depend on continuing these practices and more.

Recommendations

Electronic business is one prescription for meeting customer demands in today's fast-paced, increasingly global marketplace. Based on the coalescence of numerous strategies, processes and technologies, e-business changes the rules of competition, leveling the playing field among large and small companies and reducing the importance of issues such as physical distance.

E-business leads companies to re-examine their assumptions governing supplier relationships, time-to-market and the value propositions they present their customers. The economics governing e-business are different and defy conventional thinking; for example, transaction costs can drop significantly, value can be created with little or no additional capital investment and customers may take on some of the administrative tasks involved in product acquisition, often for free.

But operating in the world of e-business is not without its costs. Because of the significant differences in how markets, organizations and products are defined in the e-business environment, traditional forms of business management usually require modification when moving into e-business. Perhaps the most important challenges facing companies contemplating e-business are the changes in the areas of tax, legal, regulatory, financial, human resources and internal control and compliance practices.

2. How Do Companies Rate the Importance of e-Business in Creating Future Competitive Advantage?

Findings

Today, 78.8 percent of executives are seeking to gain competitive advantage through premium service. At the same time, 61.7 percent of these executives are examining how to further streamline processes and improve cost control/operating efficiency. While 61.3 percent of these executives are very aware of e-business, only 20.0 percent consider it critical at the moment.

Analysis

Most senior executives recognize information-enabled enterprises to be the business model of the future, a model that will eventually help them provide their customers with far better service. They are not, however, ready to jump in, forgoing the more traditional approaches to incremental improvement that have worked before. For all its potential, e-business still entails uncertain outcomes. For successful businesses without a compelling reason to change, e-business may involve a transformation that is too dramatic to justify, or even contemplate, in the short-run.

Executives who have chosen to move ahead on e-business are for the most part focusing on incremental improvements to infrastructure, driven by opportunism rather than policy. The greatest danger in the focus on operational issues is that it may constrain a company's longer-term options in exchange for smaller, but increasingly more elusive, short-term gains.

Recommendations

In 1997, 135,000 companies were involved in business-to-business electronic commerce, a number that is expected to explode to over 435,000 companies by the end of 2000; 24 percent of business sales are expected to come through electronic technologies, and 26 percent of business purchases will be made via new electronic technologies by 2002. Clearly, organizations that ignore the importance of e-business as a source of competitive advantage do so at their own peril.

Companies that have successfully integrated e-business into their operations can capture the full range of advantages it provides, including stronger relationships with customers, distributors, retailers, suppliers and business partners. They will develop an ability to differentiate themselves strategically from their competition by being market-driven and highly proactive. They will better assess the risks and costs of allowing competitors to move ahead in the battle to develop and utilize information more fully. The successful company will be aggressive, moving forcefully, but purposefully, to reap the potential of e-business.

Figure 9.2. Path to Competitive Advantage

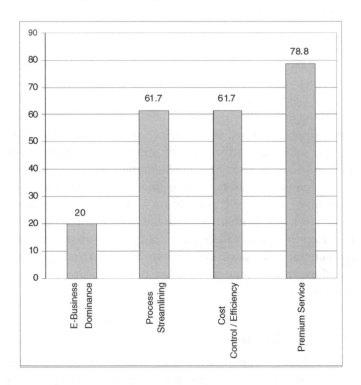

3. How Aggressively are Companies Planning to Move Toward e-Business?

Findings

Of those responding, 13.6 percent consider themselves e-business leaders, and 20.0 percent see themselves as innovators who will seize e-business opportunities when they see them. Most respondents are either waiting to decide when (34.6 percent) or whether (the remainder) to enter the larger e-business arena.

Analysis

In today's marketplace, it is not only speed that matters but also an organization's ability to anticipate and respond to developments. New corporate alliances are forming that strengthen market position; new business models are appearing that represent fundamental changes in thinking about what a business is and how it should operate. Virtual corporations, business communities and on-line auctions are all business forms that have added new complexity to the business of business.

In the face of these changes, just over a third of respondents already have begun to focus on moving aggressively into e-business. While it is not necessary or practical for every company to be a leader or an innovator, clearly most companies recognize that it would be unwise to fall too far behind. That is why a third of respondents indicate that their companies have begun positioning themselves to be fast followers.

Recommendations

Where there is vision—where there is a willingness to accept change—there is a basis for growth. Therefore, the keys to future success include management's commitment and its ability to select the right people to lead the e-business undertaking. Management must choose leaders who can work together to formulate sound strategic scenarios and identify the scope and size of the investment and personnel needed to guide the move to e-business.

Organizations evolve through four stages in the course of building sound e-business models: presence, integration, transformation and convergence. At each stage, they build on and refine capabilities, skills and insights critical to their future performance.

Presence. The first stage in business-to-consumer e-business commonly involves the development of an electronic presence, usually a Web site, which presents information about the company, its products and its key differentiators. The corresponding stage in the business-to-business world is typically the use of electronic channels such as EDI to suppliers and key partners. The goal is to improve timeliness, cost effectiveness and reach. Risks are small, except for companies that decide to go no further.

Integration. The second stage brings closer interaction as customers and suppliers work together on-line and as vendors customize content for their users. Exchange of critical information brings greater understanding and value for all players, adding to the required commitment, but offering significant competitive advantages. Tax, legal, risk management and internal control and compliance issues loom larger as real business transactions take place. Prompt and effective customer service becomes critical.

Transformation. In the third stage, organizational transformation begins as executives distinguish between their core and non-core competencies. E-business allows them to more easily unbundle operations, retaining only those critical to market position. And with transformation comes additional challenges involving organization, staff training and retention. Other considerations include outsourcing non-core operations, changes in processes and systems and paying attention to legal and audit considerations.

Convergence. Finally, in stage four, companies can achieve true integration with other organizations both inside and outside their own industries. Over time, this will produce cross-industry supply chains that will come together to create networked organizations and markets. These new forms can best be described as dynamic customer-centered networks that may exist for only a single contract, a single customer or a single instant. Customers gain convenience and choice, and firms benefit from being part of extended, cross-industry value networks.

4. Do Companies View e-Business Merely as a Way to Perform Existing Functions Better or do They Have the Vision to See How it Can Help Them Operate in a Totally New Way?

Findings

At most companies, the communications-enhancing aspects of e-business are already commonplace: 92.4 percent of respondents have adopted e-mail and messaging, 72.4 percent have an Internet Web site, and 58.4 percent have intranets. Within the next three years, companies plan to move much further into e-business, embracing interactive technologies and information-rich processes to add new, deeper dimensions to their relationships with customers.

Analysis

Clearly, the overwhelming majority of respondents are capitalizing on the e-business tools that provide effective communications, cost reduction and operational efficiency. For the most part, they have not achieved the benefits to be derived from exploiting approaches that drive top-line revenue and those that add a new dimension to their businesses.

Still in the planning stage for many companies are company-wide data warehouses (planned by 41 percent) and enterprise resource planning (ERP) links to other firms (32 percent plan to have these links). These are the e-business technologies that offer such important benefits as enhanced relationships with customers, suppliers and business partners to build efficiencies—and economy—into operations at every level.

Recommendations

No company wants to be left in the shadows of the past. Those committed to leadership must recognize the full potential of the e-business model before their competitors gain an unsurpassable lead. E-business presents companies with the opportunity to achieve strategic superiority, create global sales opportunities, strengthen customer relationships, streamline the supply chain, enhance operational efficiency, reduce transactional and overhead costs and optimize human resource utilization. Achieving these objectives, however, requires an understanding of the scope of the process, a commitment to succeed and the appropriate investment of resources.

For companies to totally change the way they do business will require a holistic approach, one that will enable them to add the capabilities needed to enhance their relationships with customers, suppliers and business partners.

Figure 9.3. E-Business Capabilities

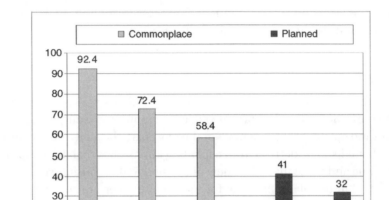

5. How do Executives Measure the Success of their e-Business Initiatives?

Findings

For greater than 75 percent of those surveyed, a key measure of the success of e-business initiatives is whether they build customer loyalty; 72.5 percent of respondents measure success by their ability to increase the access, accuracy and usefulness of information.

Analysis

Although companies measure e-business success through its impact on customer relationships, improvements in their decision-making ability, and achieving a competitive edge, respondents are still at the stage where e-business capabilities are used primarily to enhance internal communications. Today, there is not enough recognition of the connection between e-business capabilities—such as partnering outside one's industry (11.5 percent)—and results, such as lower customer service costs. And 50.7 percent of respondents rank that as very important.

Recommendations

Companies must begin to align their goals with their e-business philosophy and investments and they must carefully analyze what actions it will take to achieve success.

Executives understand that the e-business model will help them maintain and even enhance customer relationships, but they have not as yet placed sufficient emphasis on the transaction mechanics—such as customer order entry, self-service, on-line procurement and supplier information exchange—that are necessary to achieving this advantage. Customer order entry was ranked important by 33.8 percent of respondents; self-service by 40 percent; on-line procurement by 31.3 percent; and supplier information exchange by 41.3 percent.

Companies must develop a holistic process for addressing all the components of e-business if they are to achieve their goals. They must begin by analyzing the real and potential opportunities e-business offers, including the ability to open markets, develop new products and services and provide unique combinations of efficiency and value. Then they must make a commitment to invest the necessary resources to move forcefully into this challenging and rewarding future world successfully.

Figures 9.4. Measuring Success

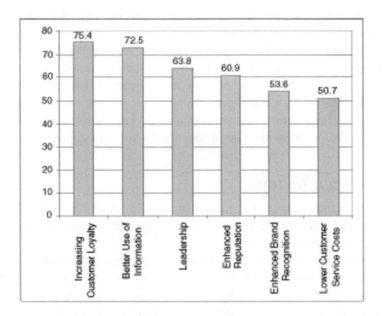

Figures 9.5. E-Business Drivers

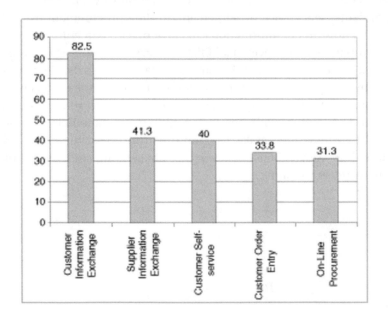

CONCLUSION: THE CHALLENGES THAT LIE AHEAD

The marketplace is constantly evolving. We are in the midst of a sea change sparked by the convergence of globalization, deregulation, customer assertiveness and technology. Our response to these developments is called electronic business, a new model that may have as profound an impact on business as did the coming of the Industrial Revolution. In order to maximize the power of this new development, it is critical that your organization approach it in the right way. First, you must time your entry into e-business to minimize risk while maintaining preparedness. Second, you must understand the breadth and depth of the changes that your organization must undergo to achieve success.

You must address e-business as an integral part of your organizational philosophy. Taking a holistic approach is critical because your e-business initiatives must become part of the vision, goals, strategies, structure and operations of your organization. It affects everything from the foundation of your business—that is, what it is you do—to how you do it—your governance, physical presence, the kinds of people who work for you and the skills they must have.

The challenges you face moving forward involve:

1. Understanding what e-business is. It is not the same as e-commerce, the form of e-business most talked about at the moment. Whereas e-commerce involves the marketing, selling and buying of products and services on the Internet, e-business extends to encompass what you are as an organization—your philosophy, your markets and your value to customers.

2. Understanding all the effects e-business can have from creating new sources of shareholder value, improving customer loyalty, reducing costs, opening new markets, creating new products and services, achieving market leadership, streamlining business processes to managing risk and compliance.

3. Understanding the interdependency of every component of your organization when creating, implementing and integrating e-business initiatives into your current strategies and structures.

4. Understanding that complete buy-in from management at the highest level is the only way to succeed when you embark on a transformation to e-business. The initiatives you put in place must be business-driven and involve senior-level business champions. Do not forget, however, that you need skilled people at every level.

5. Understanding that e-business is an evolving area that will take
    future investment and constant attention to developments. In
    other words, you must transform your organization into a change-
    embracing entity, one with a culture that accepts that every tomor-
    row is different and all developments are worth examining for the
    benefits they may bring.

6. Understanding that tomorrow's business model is fundamentally
    different from today's. That model, however, will be based on rela-
    tionships that have been built, maintained and enhanced over
    time. It is clear even today that what we are witnessing are the first
    stages of the development of globally networked business enter-
    prises—what are now being routinely described as virtual e-busi-
    ness communities. These communities are the next stage in the
    evolution of the corporate business model and to deal with
    them—and perhaps become a major player—you must work now
    to lay the groundwork for future electronic relationships with your
    key constituencies.

As the global information economy evolves, these e-business communities will learn and adapt. They will create open, collaborative environments that transcend the traditional barriers to business
relationships. Information databases will give community members
up-to-date insights on markets, including customer needs, supplier
capabilities, economic conditions, delivery options and services. A
variety of electronic market mechanisms will come into play—auctions, consortiums, free agents—to help establish financing rules, pricing, discounts, taxes, contract terms and warrantees. And interactions
among market participants will be flexible and secure, with the possibility that the sequence of events leading to each sale, each supplier
transaction, and each customer interface will be unique. This dynamic
information and supply chain, made possible by a shared electronic
infrastructure, is the essence of the fully realized e-business model.

The opportunities and the rewards are virtually limitless. The challenge is finding the best way to seize those opportunities and to begin
collecting those rewards through near-term actions.

About the Author

The above chapter is extracted in part from PricewaterhouseCoopers' 1999
publication entitled *Electronic Business Outlook.*

e-Channel Management:

ELECTRONIC-CUSTOMER RELATIONSHIP MANAGEMENT

Andy Pritchard
Peter Cantor

"67% of Web transactions are never completed, largely because top e-commerce sites have made few provisions for real-time, on-line customer service and support."

Source: *USA Today*, June 1 1999

CREATING BALANCE

Since the time they first appeared, call centers have been plagued by a problem that has been difficult for operational managers to reconcile:—how to ensure that the balance is maintained between operational cost-efficiency and the provision of customer service that meets or exceeds customer expectations. Call centers were originally created because organizations needed to cut costs and make interaction with customers more efficient. Early call centers were often sweat shop-like environments with a focus merely upon number of calls handled and talk-time (known as "hard" metrics).

This focus was further exacerbated by the growth in the 1980s of tele-sales and telemarketing, where measurement of agents was often purely on sales and hence throughput continued to be a primary operational measurement within the center. Even today many call centers focus primarily upon the measurement of efficiency in the call center rather than a combination of both measures of efficiency and of customer satisfaction (softer metrics).

However, there is now universal recognition of the importance of customer interactions on customer satisfaction and of customer satisfaction upon revenue through increased retention and subsequent business. In addition, increased retention leads to a corporation being able to make more effective use of costs on the sale of additional products to existing customers, rather than on winning back defectors. Consequently, it is not surprising that the strategic intent of many call centers has moved from one of throughput to one of enhancing the customer experience, leading to increased retention.

FROM SELF-SERVICE TO ELECTRONIC-CUSTOMER RELATIONSHIP MANAGEMENT (eCRM)

But the world is changing dramatically with the Internet becoming increasingly seen as the panacea for all things that touch the customer—the customer-facing processes. It is true that the Internet has significant potential for increasing revenue, decreasing costs and for retaining customers through improved customer service. However, the majority of organizations embracing the use of the Internet in this context have focused to date wholly upon the first two at the expense of the third. Self-service, a low-cost, on-your-own approach has been developed, whereby clients are given direct access to perform transactions via the Web often without regard to the appropriateness of those transactions and without consideration of the process changes required. This enables organizations to deflect calls away from the call center, but at what cost?

In the rush to embrace the new world, in most cases little consideration has been given to the implications of self-service as it relates to resolution of problems. Customer contact with human agents is typically cumbersome and inefficient, where it is even available, and self-service applications are poorly designed. Although cutting the costs to the organization, most such applications do not add value for the customer in terms of ease of use, the provision of new and enhanced service or indeed in terms of making best use of the customer's valuable time.

Furthermore, responses to e-mails are often delayed and inaccurate in terms of content. Despite increased customer expectations

regarding their speedy response, many organizations still regard reply-
ing to e-mails from customers as a low-priority activity and responding
to them is a backroom activity (not dealt with by front-line customer
service representatives but by a team of people that do not have any
direct contact with the customer). Stories abound of organizations
printing off e-mails and passing them to an administration unit that
deals with them—when they have the time! Their responses are typically from scratch without the use of template letters or standard para-
graphs that are the norm in other written customer communication.
This leads to inaccuracy, a lack of urgency and a lack of consistency in
dealing with customers.

In most cases the Web self-service applications have little or no
integration with the organization's other customer-facing applications
and data repositories. Such an approach means that an enterprise-
wide view of the customer is not achieved, either at the operational
level (i.e., to support customer care processes) or at the strategic level
(for customer data analysis and segmentation). These are the challenges that must be addressed.

CHALLENGES IN DELIVERING TRUE ELECTRONIC-CUSTOMER RELATIONSHIP MANAGEMENT

There are many challenges in moving to a true electronic customer
relationship management (eCRM) environment, including:

- **Consistency:** Developing an Integrated Interaction Channel
  Strategy
- **Balance:** Getting it Right between Self-Service and Agent-Assisted
  Interactions
- **Technology:** Adopting the Right Technology at the Right Time
- **Change Management:** Recognizing that this Is Radical Change
- **Customer Expectations:** Gauging Customer Expectations of Web-
  Based Service
- **Legacy Customer Care Environment:** Avoiding Building on a
  Foundation of Sand

Each of these is explored in more detail in the following sections,
together with examples of leading-practice organizations, which have
risen to these challenges.

Consistency: Developing an Integrated Interaction Channel Strategy

The development of an integrated interaction channel strategy that addresses all current and Web-based technologies and that is designed to enhance the overall customer experience rather than merely cut costs is a key part of moving into eCRM. eCRM will be multiple integrated channels. The high cost of customer acquisition, the ability to pass and access information quickly and the one-to-one relationship which can be facilitated by pan-organizational data access, has led to a shift in the importance of customer care. Companies are required to compete not only in the traditional areas of price and product distribution but also on pre- and post-sales support.

To see eCRM as purely a strategy to cut costs could have catastrophic effects. Internet and Web technologies provide opportunities to support personal service based on an individual customer's needs and provide interactions with the company that are able to match or exceed a customer's expectations. A loosely planned strategy will result in unsatisfactory customer experiences that if experienced widely enough will undoubtedly result in lost revenue, which may eventually kill the business.

The strategy developed therefore must:

- be integrated across all relevant interaction channels
- be integrated through the use of consistent customer data
- answer the question "how do my customers wish to contact my organization?"
- consider which interaction channels will be most appropriate for which types of customer and for which types of interaction/ transaction

Existing channels must be considered along with new ones. In sales, a company may have existing retail outlets, a direct sales channel or telesales operations. For customer service, there may be a call center that can be contacted by phone, fax or e-mail. However, a strategy for the future may include kiosks and on-line access to account and customer information via the Internet. These channels must be integrated into existing operations seamlessly and must be provided with access to consistent, constantly updated customer data.

The channel strategy must be integrated both across channels and across areas of the business. A successful strategy will therefore need to span all parts of the value chain from marketing, product development and sales to distribution customer service. In the areas of sales and customer service, the strategy adopted will depend on the value of the customer to the company and the cost of providing the channel.

CASE STUDY

The impact of the strategy on the business dynamics can be illustrated in the computer industry.

Compaq needed to react to its competitors' success at selling on the Web and do so quickly. A strategy was developed to undertake a Common Global Internet Program. Compaq decided to rapidly build three or four initial Web-based applications within a six-month time frame, develop core expertise and infrastructure and prioritize and continue a long-term development program. The first step was to develop some guiding principles. These were to provide a customized, personalized view for customers into Compaq and provide consistent Internet-based functionality to support worldwide solutions.

At Compaq, the Internet now provides customers, major accounts and global accounts access to information, ordering capability and support services. It enables:

- on-line information requests (responding to questions and request for literature immediately)
- catalogs viewing (the ability to access color catalogs and spec sheets while on-line
- price quotation
- provision of payment/shipping information
- provision of order status and fulfillment information
- completion of surveys/questionnaires
- customer e-mail feedback
- resellers and channel partners access to information, on-line ordering and support services

The benefits to the customer are clear: sales support for customers and resellers; information available 24 hours a day, seven days a week (24x7); real-time order taking and order status; and a cost-effective customer feedback channel. It has now been rolled out to support Compaq's operations in 15 countries and has resulted in $40 million per month in orders.

Despite the obvious efforts required in this business solution, reducing the number of customer service repesentatives (CSRs) needed and significantly improving accuracy have been possible, resulting in savings of $1 million per year in the call center.

In addition to the above capabilities, a configure-to-order (CTO) solution has been developed at retail outlets. These CTO applications allow retail customers at a store to configure and order products from Compaq through the Internet. This enables sales of higher-end systems in stores, allowing Compaq to make direct sales to customers while maintaining their relationships with retail outlets. Customers can do this through more than 5,000 retail stores, which has resulted in $5 million per month in sales.

In order to get an eCRM strategy right, it is necessary to understand the company's customer profile. In considering such a strategy, it is important to know the percentage of customers with no Internet access at home or at work, as well as customer access to other interaction channels. Further, the propensity of the customer base (or different segments of it) to use the Web for customer service rather than other channels needs to be established by the organization. In summary, it is necessary to establish:

- current interactions by customer segment by interaction channel
- expected interactions by customer segment by interaction channel

This profiling needs to take into account trends for Internet take-up, and once established, it needs to be continually reviewed.

Individual customer trends, habits and preferences as well as those of customer segments can be monitored using behavioral analysis. For example, use of different channels (by type of interaction) and satisfaction can be monitored across the same dimensions. Such analysis is key to ensuring that an interaction strategy is not only implemented in a coherent and integrated way but also with the flexibility to enable the use of interaction channels by customers to drive the strategy moving forward. Data-warehousing and data-mining techniques are key to the implementation of such an analysis framework.

In many businesses, in order to provide a customer-centric service, an Internet-enabled call center will be at the core of the business process model, so it can support the full customer life cycle from pre-sales and order provisioning to post-sales support.

In summary, interaction channels must be readily available to customers who wish to use them and be integrated through consistent service and the use of consistent customer data across all interaction channels.

Balance: Getting it Right between Self-Service and Agent-Assisted Interactions

It is incorrect, however, to view the future of customer care as being simply a choice between either Web-based self-service or traditional phone-based interaction. This fails to recognize that as we move forward, we will begin to see more and more integration between the channels with which organizations interact with their customers. Technology is moving customer interaction to a new level, with both an increase in new channels (Web, e-mail, interactive chat, kiosks, etc.), together with the combining of channels to enhance the quality of the interaction. Most notably in the latter category, we are seeing the rise of "collaboration" and "interactive chat" technologies, which are enabling the agent and the customer to interact over the Web in real-time, and in the case of the former, while simultaneously undertaking a voice phone call.

The possibilities for enhancing the customer experience here are enormous—imagine the following scenario around a telecommunications company:

CASE STUDY

A business customer has a question about a charge on their bill and checks their account status on the Web site of their telecommunications supplier. Based upon the ID number and password to their secure area, the screens provided show the specific information for that customer. In addition, they personalize themselves to that customer, including displaying information based upon the customer's usual behavior (i.e., the information the customer usually queries) and the reason for visiting the site. Targeted marketing information is also provided.

Despite the information available, the customer cannot reconcile the differences in their own calculation and the figure that is both on the bill and available on-line. They push a "call me back" button on the Web page and then enter some details, including reason for call (bill query), and the number where they can be called. The customer also enters a time when they can be called back. In this case, they select "immediately."

The Web call is routed within the call center through the ACD (automatic call distributor) to the most appropriate agent, in this case one who specializes in bill queries for the segment of business customers to whom the calling customer belongs. The computer telephony integration (CTI) within the call center pops a screen to this agent, which contains details of the caller, together with reason for the call, and details of what the customer was looking at the time of call.

The outbound call[1] (to the telephone number entered) is automatically made, and the customer and agent begin their conversation. The agent is able to confirm that they are both talking about

---

[1] In reality, the outbound call could be made prior to routing to the agent and popping the screen. In this way if the line was busy, or if an answering machine, fax or similar instrument was encountered, details of the required call could be stored and tried again later. Thus, the agent's time would be optimized and they would not waste time waiting for calls to be answered.

the bill by "pushing" an image of the bill to the customer using "collaboration" technologies. This is confirmed over the phone, and the customer is able to pinpoint the queried charge immediately. The agent is then able to explain how the charge is calculated and to "push" a page with details of this calculation to the customer for printing. The agent is then able to introduce the customer to a package that could potentially save the customer money, together with other packages that provide enhanced facilities and push details of these to the customer, including comparative pricing information and features of the package.

The agent automatically directs the customer to another page on the Web site where they are able to sign up for one of the packages. The agent and customer end their conversation and the customer is asked to fill in a survey regarding their satisfaction and signs up for an enhanced package. The customer, pleased with the service provided, sends an e-mail to 10 colleagues, together with posting a note on the organization's bulletin board.

The key element of this scenario is the use of the Web to enhance the experience, not merely to cut costs. It is true that the customer did much of the initial work on-line prior to calling the call center and that the wrap-up in terms of the additional order was carried out without agent intervention, both of which resulted in cost savings. However, the use of multiple interaction channels to provide information and clarity to the customer had an immediate impact upon the quality and effectiveness of the response to a perceived customer problem.

Indeed, the use of combined interaction channels for this purpose may well have led to the call being completed more quickly, since the agent was able to clarify the situation immediately through the detailed information contained within the page pushed to the customer. Agent talk-time was decreased in this scenario, bringing about time savings almost as a by-product!

The following chart demonstrates the key ways in which the integrated use of the interaction channels in the scenario above impacted the customer in terms of an enhanced experience and had immediate impacts upon the organization in terms of revenue enhancement and cost savings.

Figure 10.1: Increased Revenue and Decreased Costs

	Enhanced Experience	Revenue Enhancement	Cost Savings
Initial query investigated by customer on the Web			X
Unassisted capture of details of query			X
Auto-identification of customer, routing to relevant agent and callback customer	X		X
Ability to push Web page of bill to customer	X		
Ability to undertake Web/voice combined interaction	X		
Rapid identification by both parties of queried charge	X		X
Ability to push page with details of how charge is calculated	X		
Overall rapid resolution of problem	X		X
Auto-upsell of new package		X	X
Ability to sign up for package on-line	X	X	X

In addition, there is likely to have been an impact of the enhanced experience on longer-term revenue enhancement, particularly in the above example where the customer was happy with the experience and indeed advertised this fact to others. Imagine if the customer had found it difficult to contact the call center about the bill query or had to spend time repeating their name or other details. What if there had been uncertainty over which bill they were looking at or which charge? Imagine the reaction of the customer after all of that if they had been presented with an up-sell offer.

It is therefore essential to ensure that the balance between unassisted/self-serve (including e-mail), agent-assisted and wholly voice calls (where the customer can dictate instructions) is carefully planned to provide self-serve maximum value to the customer and not just to reduce costs. But can the organization influence this balance or will it be wholly customer-driven?

Of course, at the end of the day customers will choose the interaction channel that is used, but it is often possible to influence their choice. For example, EGG, a UK financial service provider gives a higher rate of interest if you agree to conduct all of your business (including customer service) via the Internet, and the adoption rate has exceeded expectations. Under any circumstances, the customer may decide that they want to speak to a customer service representative (CSR), and allowing them to easily do that through devices such as call-me-back buttons is likely to be a requirement of an eCRM implementation.

Therefore, as part of the development of an integrated interaction channel strategy, an organization can:

- understand the desired balancing required between assisted, unassisted and wholly voice interactions for different customers (or segments of customers).

- understand the likely balance based upon the desire of customers for voice interaction. This will differ by customer segment, by industry, by geography and over time. Transition planning must take this movement over time into account.

- under some circumstances, influence this balance. However, this influencing must be based upon a rounded decision regarding the appropriateness of an interaction channel for the types of interactions. A decision to remove another interaction channel to force the use of Internet and Web-based channels must not be taken lightly without due consideration of the potential impact.[2]

The success of newer interaction channels will be based upon their ease of use and the customer experience gained from their use. It is extremely important to note that a combined channel (e.g., collaboration combining Web and voice) must be viewed as a separate channel in its own right, as well as a potential alternative route from each of the component channels to escalate for a higher level of action.

Technology: Adopting the Right Technology at the Right Time

As demonstrated in the scenario above, Web technologies that have the potential to enhance the overall customer experience are beginning to become available. With the expected dramatic rise of interactive digital TV and its consequent penetration in the home, such technologies will increasingly become both available and be used. An eCRM solution will require deploying new technologies to achieve transparency and visibility across the value chain of the business and between the business and its customers. There are different technological options to consider in calculating what technology is appropriate to the customers and requirements of the business. Figure 10.2 on the following page outlines some of the key ones that are becoming available today.

---

[2] It worked very successfully for Cisco systems in a business-to-business environment where, due to the nature of Cisco's business, the customer base overwhelmingly consisted of technically savvy Internet users.

Figure 10.2: Appropriate Technologies

Technology	Abilities
Web Collaboration	• Web-initiated enquiries can be integrated with voice calls and queued for handling by the appropriate agent • Initiation by the customer of both inbound and outbound calls can be achieved • CSR can "push" Web pages, applications and updates to the customer providing such information as quotes, copies of the bill etc. • Collaboration can be used as an escalation route from an unassisted Web call
Interactive Chat	• Direct customer interaction with a CSR via the Internet • Access to customer's history through the transfer of last click or click stream (which Web pages are accessed in which sequence) on the initiation of an inbound chat session • Has the cost advantage over a voice call that the agent can undertake multiple simultaneous chat sessions with different customers
Universal Queue	• Seamless integration of all interaction channels to ensure that voice and data transactions are delivered to the most appropriate CSR with customer history being viewed by all CSRs

	• E-mails, interactive chat, standard voice calls, video etc. integrated into single channel
Problem Resolution (Knowledge Management and Self-Learning Search Technologies)	• Provision of the information needed for customer problem resolution • Customers access to existing knowledge base • Knowledge communities between the company/customers/suppliers where know ledge is transferred between users within an access point and framework provided by the company • Record voice calls, translate them into text, distill out common questions and answers to feed into knowledge environments
e-Mail Response Management	• Tracking, management and control of the e-mail received by an organization and ensuring that e-mails are routed to the person best suited and able to respond • Provision of automated standard or customized responses to queries and questions
Customer Care Robots	• Intelligent software agents monitoring customer activity and providing offers based on appropriate triggers
Voice Recognition and Processing	• Recognition of individual's voice patterns for security purposes • Voice to text capabilities • Text to voice capabilities

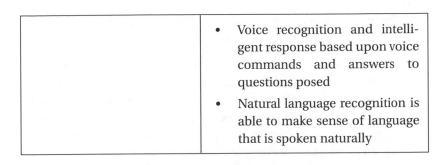

| | • Voice recognition and intelligent response based upon voice commands and answers to questions posed |
| | • Natural language recognition is able to make sense of language that is spoken naturally |

In addition to these emerging Internet and Web-based technologies there are a number of others that in many cases are already an integral part of the modern call center but are key to the provision of quality eCRM. These will need to be integrated with the above technologies to provide a heterogeneous solution for eCRM:

- CRM package applications, covering functionality from marketing and campaign management through remote sales to customer care and agent support within the call center. These applications are themselves becoming increasingly more Web-enabled with a number of newer vendors providing products that have been designed from the ground up.

- Data warehouses and data-mining tools allow reporting on a 360-degree view of the customer and supporting the segmentation of customers and customer groups.

- Interactive voice response units (IVR, IVRU), which enable the routing of calls based upon the number keyed upon the phone: ("If you have a product query, then please key 1…")

- Computer telephony integration (CTI) provides such facilities as intelligent routing, based upon both agent skills set and availability and upon customer requirements and profile.

- Dialers do the bulk of outbound calling of customers, primarily for marketing and sales campaigns. These significantly reduce the time spent by agents dialing phone numbers and waiting for the customer to answer. They provide facilities that connect an agent only when they have ensured that a live customer is on the other end of the phone.

There are a number of key points that will impact the successful use of technologies in the provision of eCRM:

- *The readiness of different customers to take up technology.* The readiness of customers (particularly the mass-market segments) to take up the Internet as a common way of interacting with corporations will be key here. Geographical variations upon the speed of this take-up can already be observed, with the US being way ahead of Europe, for example.

- *The performance versus customer expectations of that technology.* There will be a significant time-based impact here, with, for example, customers refusing to accept things (particularly in terms of response times) that they did six months ago.

- *The integration of new technologies with existing ones.* This applies in particular to call center technologies as detailed above. The development of a technical solution for a traditional call center with CTI is already a complex systems integration with multiple technologies and suppliers involved. Additional Web and Internet-based technologies will be challenging for many organizations.

- *The design and development of a technology foundation that enables timely deployment of the right technology.* It is key that this foundation is established early in the process and is not just added as a bolt-on farther down the line. The foundation established should be architected to enable the rapid deployment of additional technologies as required, and it should provide a foundation based upon emerging Internet standards (in particular XML)[3].

- *The use of customization provided by Web applications.* Customers are beginning to expect a degree of customization in their use of the Web. Organizations can make increasingly more use of such facilities in terms of both providing better service and in more effective and better-targeted marketing. The successful use of such personalization technology, which provides the customer with the information they require and does not "clutter" their screen with other information that is irrelevant to that customer will be key.

- *The maturity of technology and uncertainty of who will succeed in this technology space.* Although vendors are moving fast to provide industrial-strength Web- and Internet-based products to support the call center, many of the products in the table above (Figure 10.2) are only now beginning to mature.

---

[3] XML stands for Extensible Mark-Up Language

Organizations are likely to have to plan for providing services that require a combination of technologies available. Adoption of the right technology at the right time, and for the right customer segments and transactions, is an intricate process.

CASE STUDY

At Gofly.com, a UK on-line travel service (www.gofly.com), customers can start the process of booking a flight but they can request a callback at any point in the process. The customer can also choose when they would like the callback to occur. A fare discount of £2.00 is received on all return trips booked over the Internet.

At the 1800flowers.com home page (www.1800flowers.com) you can link to customer service. A customer has a choice whether to e-mail, call toll free, connect to on-line customer service (eQ&A Chat), chat on-line or look at the frequently asked questions (FAQ) area of the site.

Those who do not position themselves to take advantage of these newer technologies as they become industrial-strength will lose out. Organizations must move fast, but they must recognize that the deployment of some technologies may not represent a "lock-in" to that technology (it may be a temporary solution until a known, more functional technology is fully developed), and that it may make sense (for a whole host of reasons) to replace initial products or deploy additional technologies later. Such an approach is counter to the way of working that is regarded as best practice by most IS organizations today.

It is therefore recommended that an eCRM strategy is adopted that establishes the correct foundation for the future, that (as far as is practical) enables a "plug-and-play" approach to technology components, and that makes use of technical "proof-of-concept" prototypes before full-scale deployment.

Change Management: Recognizing that this Is Radical Change

Developing the strategy, defining the architecture and choosing the appropriate technology components is not the whole solution. The implementation of that technology must provide an IT infrastructure capable of supporting an integrated channel strategy underpinned by customer-centric thinking and action, which will be achieved only through effective management of the transition. There is a requirement to recognize that the transition from call center to an eCRM operation is a fundamental change to the way the business functions. This affects many key areas of a call center operation, including:

- Organization Design
- People and Culture Changes
- Business Processes
- Management Processes
- Training and Recruitment Requirements
- Performance Measurements

Organization Design

Organization change will be an inevitable consequence of implementing a Web-enhanced customer service strategy. As customer usage of multiple access channels grows, it will become increasingly important to manage customer information independently of channel and location. A key part of the process is to design and implement an organizational model to support the CSRs who deliver service to the customer. If the nature of the services has changed, then the organization will need to reflect this. Companies are increasingly recognizing the need to restructure the whole customer service organization to support a customer-centric view of the world.

The customer contact center structure will need to be able to embrace the emerging customer care roles as the Internet redefines the way companies interact with their customers. The provision of business tools with which to drive sales and profitability at an individual customer level necessitates the transformation of customer care functional groups into service teams fully enabled to manage customers across traditional processes.

It is also important to recognize that there will be number of new tasks and responsibilities within customer service that must be organized and managed. Such activities include understanding and predicting what customers choose to do over the Internet, managing e-mail responses and interactive communications and resourcing a contact center to manage multiple points of customer access. As a result, both the CSR and the management structures need to change to ensure responsibilities are mapped to business activities in an appropriate manner (the right people are assigned to the right tasks).

A program to redesign the organization will therefore be an integral part of a transformation to an eCRM customer care environment.

People and Culture Changes

A strategic policy toward customer care implies an investment in profitable long-term customer relationships, measuring customer service against the customers' standards and responding to their changing customer service requirements. For some businesses this will require a change in their attitudes about the roles of their CSRs and to attitudes within the customer service arena.

The Internet is changing the way people do business. It is essential that an organization's people are prepared to adapt as rapidly as the environment in which they are working. Their skills and attitudes must reflect these changes. As illustrated above, a customer may start an enquiry via the Web site and then decide to talk directly to a CSR. Staff need the right skills to be able to thrive in this kind of environment:

- Flexibility—to meet a customer's needs as they change through an interaction
- Fast thinking—to receive details about a customer midway through a transaction and assist them with the rest of it
- Customer focused—to ensure the solution presented to the customer is the most appropriate to their individual needs
- Sales oriented—to identify opportunities to upgrade services received by customers and cross-sell other products
- Multi skilled—to deal with customers over the telephone and write professional and courteous responses to e-mail enquiries
- Multi tasking—to service a number of customers on interactive chat calls at one time

Traditional telephone-based skills will not be enough in an e-CRM environment. Additional technical skills that are required to properly service customers include an ability to understand the business dynamics and the profitability of different customer categories.

This knowledge base and skill set is very different from the profile of CSRs working in a sweat shop–like environment. If a company wants to provide service that delights its customers over the Internet, it must be prepared to invest in its workforce and nurture a culture that focuses on customer service excellence, support its people in delivery and build on its experiences to plan customer service for the future.

Business Processes

The use of the Internet to support the customer care operations has redrawn the business process model that corporations must now adopt to succeed. Leading business processes in the new environment have moved from being product oriented, through departmental and then cross-functional, to customer-driven. Each subsequent stage of evolution has built upon the foundations of the previous, but the latest stage truly requires a mind set change to succeed.

Processes must therefore be engineered to meet the needs of the customer and must be developed both to support customer-driven "events," and to provide the organization with a single 360-degree view of the customer. This is a tall order, since it requires balancing a design of sufficient quality with a reduction in cost and transaction time, while simultaneously providing processes that are flexible, increase revenue and improve customer loyalty and both enhance and make use of enterprise-wide customer data.

In addition to identifying the business processes, it is necessary to ensure that the business processes cater for each customer-facing scenario. Well-defined business processes (or "interaction flows") should support each type of customer interaction. A CSR may be taking a customer phone call, communicating via interactive chat or helping a customer over the Web or through a kiosk.

CASE STUDY

AOL provides on-line support to its subscribers who can initiate an interactive chat session if they have technical questions, request problem resolution or billing information. The service is free. Response times can be quicker than making a phone call and continuity of support from an individual CSR can be maintained while the enquiry is resolved. AOL customer service operation benefits as one CSR can handle multiple real-time queries at one time.

This service can be compared to the service model of service providers providing free Internet access like Freeserve and Connect-Free. They provide a free e-mail customer service but to speak to CSR, it is necessary to phone a premium rate telephone number.

Both service models are perceived as valuable by their customers and the growth of free-service providers has been achieved without a terminal decline of subscription-based providers.

The key elements in developing business processes for the new world are therefore:

- an outside-in approach, with the customer at the heart of the process (looking at processes through the eyes of the customer)
- streamlining processes across existing functional boundaries to provide the best service to the customer
- designing processes that enable problems and enquiries to be resolved at the first point of contact
- providing the customer with the ability to help themselves

Management Processes

Management processes are the tools used by the contact center management to ensure the sales and customer service areas are properly supported. In order to ensure that all operational needs are met, it is necessary to:

- provide in-depth support to the CSR teams in the provision of best-in-class sales and customer service
- develop expertise within customer service by identifying individual and team training needs
- collect and interpret management information
- control and monitor the workload of the sales and customer service teams
- encourage staff

Training and Recruitment Requirements

As can be seen from the sections above, the move to an e-CRM environment affects all aspects of the contact center, from technology and business processes to culture and management style. All the changes identified to any aspect of operations will require training for both managers and CSRs. CSRs will require both technical and behavioral training to meet customer expectations and managers will require new skills to manage the new environment contact center.

As well as providing current CSRs with training, recruitment policies need to be reviewed and tailored to ensure that new joiners have the necessary skill set to work in the Web-enhanced environment. While telephone screening will remain important, assessment will be required by other methods. This will include a combination of psychometric testing, role-playing, team workshops and computer skill testing.

The assessment should let the company ascertain not only whether candidates have the right skills but also if they have the potential to develop and, importantly, have the staying power to work in a dynamic and rapidly changing environment. The new eCRM environment may reduce the number of voice-to-voice interactions required with a CSR, but each contact must still reflect a company's chosen image. In order to do that, the staff must be equipped and trained whether working with the customer by phone, fax, e-mail or the Internet.

Performance Measurements

Once the contact center is ready to operate, it will need to measure and manage its performance. These measures should be identified at the design stage to reflect business imperatives and so the systems can be designed to deliver the required information. However, performance measurement can relate to a number of different areas:

- customer service efficiency
- cost savings
- customer retention
- customer profitability
- customer satisfaction

A company must decide upon the measures that it will monitor. This will depend on its customer service goals and must balance business and operational performance indicators. Here, we will focus on two elements of performance: customer satisfaction and operational performance.

Customer satisfaction has traditionally been measured by customer satisfaction surveys and through complaint handling. However, it is key to ensure that satisfaction is truly measured in the most effective way. This is generally regarded today as being as a proactive request for feedback as soon as possible after the interaction. This is due to the following key facts:

- Unless it is soon after the interaction, feedback is diluted by other life experiences, and the customer's true feelings regarding the experience are lost.
- Surveys draw only responses from extremes of experience—either people who had very good or very bad experiences. This tends to skew the figures.

The Web enables the eCRM operation to gain (almost) immediate feedback in a relatively anonymous way, and in doing so it uses as little of the customer's time as possible. This feedback can be solicited as part of the interaction itself.

But principles of self-service provide a potentially major pitfall to the company. If a customer telephones with a problem or complaint, then the company has the opportunity to resolve it and repair (or even improve) their relationship with the customer. In today's customer service environment a customer may be aggrieved but not complain, just taking their business to a competitor. With the provision of self-service via the Internet, a customer's frustrations may never be aired. "In cyber space, no one can hear you scream"—not even the call center agent.

This emphasizes the importance of well-designed interaction processes and robust contact channels that meet customers' needs. Performance measurement must now be two-dimensional—how satisfied are they with the channel that is being used, and how satisfied are they with the organization's products and services? In terms of operational performance, the measures from different channels must be reported individually as well as in a consolidated format to represent overall customer care performance, for example:

- number of interactions received (hourly, daily, weekly, monthly)
- type of interactions received (e-mail, calls, chat sessions)
- number of interactions answered (hourly, daily, weekly, monthly)
- number of interactions outstanding by channel at the end of each day
- average response time (overall, by phone, by e-mail, via chat—typically measured in terms of percentage of calls/interactions received within a given number of seconds or minutes or hours to receive a response)
- average duration of interaction (overall, by phone, by e-mail, via chat)
- CSR time available, in work mode and unavailable
- "clickstream" measurement and capture (which Web pages and in what sequence)

Some measures will be specific to the type of interaction, for example:

- e-mails—average time required to acknowledge them
- chat—total number of requests
- chat—number of seconds to respond
- chat—number of simultaneous chat sessions handled by Web CSR
- number of transactions switching from Web only to live CSR or visa versa

Systems need to be able to support the performance measurement gathering described, by collating data and enabling customer needs to be captured either directly over the Internet or via CSRs within the contact center.

It can be seen from the above descriptions that the transformation from call center to eCRM is not a simple task. It requires a clear strategy, business case and guiding principles. It is also important not to try transform everything at once. The change should be a staged transition within a framework for change. Without the correct executive buy-in, budget and commitment it will fail and potentially decrease customer satisfaction.

Customer Expectations: Gauging Customer Expectations of Web-Based Service

Being able to provide Web-enhanced customer care is in many respects a starting point. Customers are using the Internet as part of their daily lives more and more and will continue to do so as long as it makes it easier for them to do business with the company. The Internet will continue to provide opportunities for businesses by enabling them to manage costs, improve the value of their customers by retaining their loyalty and still provide excellent service to customers.

The Internet is still not the appropriate channel for many customers who are not comfortable with it, just as many consumers are still reluctant to use interactive voice response to access services and information over the phone. In planning further Web customer care, companies must develop ways of retaining the customer as the focal point for all Web-based initiatives. This will ensure that Web initiatives are targeted at the right customers and for the right reasons as evidenced by the case example below.

CASE STUDY

EGG, a UK financial services provider, has introduced a credit card with a competitive interest rate and a cash-back scheme (which could be in the form of a cash credit to the account or redeemable coupons). This may not sound too innovative, but there are some interesting features. The company has set up a shopping zone with Internet links to different retailers. Transactions through this shopping zone receive double the credit normally received. EGG charges £2.00 for printed statements or telephone service calls for information that is available on the Web site.

The Web will continue to change the landscape for businesses and customers alike. With proper planning, large corporates will be able to compete with niche players by offering truly personalized service. Smaller companies without legacy systems will be able to continue to reduce time to market for new products and target the profitable customers of their competitors.

Customer segmentation may unknowingly conflict with customer expectations and the customer may never know to complain. Customers will want to align themselves with fellow consumers with similar interests, not based upon the company's view of how customers should be grouped. Thus the incentives of options offered based on this segment may be different. Customers may be redrawn into communities (people with like interests) not segments.

Legacy Customer Care Environment: Avoiding Building on a Foundation of Sand

The Internet may appear to be a cheaper communication channel and in many cases it will be, but if customer interaction is limited to just that area there is a danger of trying to paper over the cracks and hiding current inadequacies in the call center's existing channels in the hope that self-service will provide an immediate improvement on bottom-line cost. If a company has problems with its current call center operations, then it is not ready for an Internet strategy until it solves those problems. In all cases, the move to eCRM must be part of a major customer interaction program that aims to bring the whole of the call center and customer interaction operations to a leading-practice position. This can be and has been done, as the following case study demonstrates.

CASE STUDY

A major European credit card company was faced with: customers with multiple cards; new competitors in the form of US specialists, supermarkets and utilities; and mounting price competition and declining loyalty. In response, it embarked upon a program of smarter customer acquisition and retention and service improvement, together with strategic cost reduction and an improved product.

At the core of this program was the transformation of its existing separate call centers into a single virtual call center. However, this was not done in isolation, as the company took steps to consider how customers wanted to contact them. It therefore defined how customers could access customer service in the future and identified how it could reduce internal hand-offs and consequently improve resource effectiveness through achievement of "right place, first time" customer service.

The program required redesign of the customer service processes and organization model including resizing, a new management structure and a fundamental change in the technological platform. This was a major change program undertaken over two years that is itself part of a longer-term strategy geared for revenue growth on a recalibrated cost base.

Attempts to merely bolt on a Web-based interaction channel to the current call center operations is unlikely to succeed if your customers perceive it as exactly that. Further, unless optimization of the operation across the board in respect to customer interaction is achieved, then the full benefits possible from eCRM *will not* be achieved, and indeed a detrimental effect to the customer experience is possible and perhaps likely.

SUMMARY

We have clearly come a long way, with the most effective organizations in the customer interaction business being those that have a business strategy is industrialized intimacy[4]—using technology both to drive efficiency and to provide support to enhance the customer experience. Leading-practice organizations in the call center space are those that successfully maintain the balance between these two business drivers.

The key issue here is that the human interaction has been removed from the equation. This leads to two potentially damaging effects:

- It may become more difficult for organizations to identify and recover a difficult situation at an early stage since it is far easier for a trained CSR to ascertain the level of a customer's frustration during a telephone conversation than it is for the organization to spot that when the customer is navigating through the process on their own via a self-service Web application.

- The Web has to a great extent leveled the playing field. A customer more easily identifies competitors, and upstarts can easily develop a market presence on the Internet. In this situation, customers are likely to compare wholly on price rather than differentiating on perception, customer care, loyalty and other factors.

So, what has happened in this new model to the balance between efficiency and customer care effectiveness? Clearly there is a danger of moving backwards in terms of the customer experience of interacting with an organization. The customer, being driven to a lower-cost channel may feel removed from the organization and therefore less loyal, no longer having a voice in the level of service provided.

However, there have been a number of recent technology trends, which if capitalized on can help rather than hinder the enhancement of this customer experience. Firstly, the integration of self-service and call center technologies, and secondly, the provision of Web applications that customize themselves for an individual customer or targeted group. It is the integration of such technologies, together with refined processes and information in a way that enhances the overall customer experience rather than depersonalizes it, which is already beginning to separate the leaders from the laggers in this space.

---

[4] Kolesar, van Ryzin and Cutler, "Creating Customer Value Through Industrialized Intimacy," *Strategy & Business*, 3rd Quarter 1998.

About the Authors

ANDY PRITCHARD

Andy Pritchard is a Senior Director in PricewaterhouseCoopers' CRM Management Consulting practice in the UK. He specializes in delivering complex CRM solutions to large pan-European and global clients. He has been instrumental in the development of PricewaterhouseCooper's thought leadership, particularly in the area of eCRM.

PETER CANTOR

Peter Cantor is a Principal Consultant in PricewaterhouseCoopers' CRM practice in the U.K. He is a member of the CRM team within the Information, Communications and Entertainment group.

The Customer-Centric Organization in the Automotive Industry— Focus for the 21st Century

J. Ferron

To be effective in executing a CRM strategy, organizations must put the customer front and center—sometimes referred to being customer-centric. That is easy to state, and visions of what that entails abound. But being customer-centric requires that an organization enlist our three CRM substrategies—customer strategy, channel product strategy and infrastructure strategy—and link them inextricably together. Organizations that have been effective in CRM have defined customer-centric models that give greater recognition to customer needs, the channels available to them and the products and services available through them. The automotive industry seems to be tackling this head on and increasingly at e-speed.

Powered by access to information unparalleled in history, consumers today are redefining the way business will be done. Fading rapidly is the old model of force-feeding them goods and services. Replacing it is the notion of "making it easy for consumers to do business with you," says Patricia Seybold, author of *Customers.com*.[1] Or as Bill Gates, CEO of Microsoft commented in his book, *Business at the*

---

[1] Patricia B. Seybold, with Ronni T. Marshak, *Customers.com: How to Create a Profitable Business Strategy for the Internet and Beyond*, New York: Times Business, 1998.

Speed of Thought[2] "A manufacturer or retailer that responds to changes in sales in hours instead of weeks is no longer at heart a product company, but a service company that has a product offering."

Many companies have already awakened to this new paradigm and are moving to create the consumer-centric organizations that will be necessary to service this new customer. But what is a consumer-centric organization?

The consumer-centric organization:

- conducts business through the consumer's eyes and shares unfiltered insight within the enterprise
- is able to do business anytime, anyhow from anywhere
- is always easy to do business with
- creates a compelling consumer experience and innovates services as well as products
- adds value in the eyes of the consumer
- integrates the product and information

According to a recent poll published in *USA Today*, 44 percent of US-based CEOs list customer loyalty as the number one management challenge.[3]

WHY CONSUMER-CENTRIC?

Retaining customers is a key issue for all automotive channels (including vehicle, parts, finance, leasing and rental) in business today because companies have learned that loyal consumers translate to relationship revenue over the life cycle of the product or service. As more and more of these consumers demand a higher level of service, the enterprises that are able to provide it will dominate their market segment, strengthen their brands and defend their position within the industry.

In a recent *USA Today*[4] article writer Greg Farrell assembled some interesting information on the lifetime value of a customer. Excerpts from the article detail the following:

---

[2] Bill Gates with Collins Hemingway, *Business @ the Speed of Thought: Using a Digital Nervous System*, New York: Basic Books, 1999.

[3] The Conference Board, Heidrick & Struggles.

[4] *USA Today*, July 7, 1999.

"It's the new real advance in marketing," says Peter Sealey, an adjunct professor of marketing at the University of California at Berkeley. Sealey, former head of marketing at Coca-Cola, uses the Coke and GM examples in presentations to would-be marketers. "There can't be a marketer who's not brain dead who's not doing this now."

Several developments have pushed marketers toward the life-time value approach:

- Consumers have less time. Marketers know consumers don't want to spend time on brand decisions; most will stick with the tried-and-true.

- It costs a lot more to capture a new customer than to care for one you have.

- The Internet is giving marketers a better idea of who their regular customers are. More important, marketers can figure out exactly how much it costs to acquire customers on the Web, so they are compelled to figure out how much each of those customers is worth.

That principle remains in place today. "We value loyalty at General Motors," says Martin Walsh, general director of marketing for Cadillac. "And we recognize the value of moving customers from one division to another."

What is new is the ability to use the Internet as a tool to deepen ties with heretofore-anonymous buyers. "We're focused on the life-time value of the customer," says Gateway Computer CEO Ted Waitt. "There's a lot more in that relationship than just the box." Gateway is using the Internet to build loyalty. It offers a year's Inter-net service with the purchase of a new computer.

The loyal customer is worth more than the sum of her pur-chases. A faithful General Motors customer can be worth $276,000 over her lifetime, including the 11 or more vehicles bought, plus a word-of-mouth endorsement making friends and relatives more likely to consider GM products.

Certainly from the perspective of these well-known brand manage-ment organizations, the consumer-centric impact on future business gains have been recognized.

It can be done. The capital markets have rewarded a number of companies (e.g., Coca-Cola, Procter & Gamble, Compaq, Dell) for a more customer-focused—CRM approach to business, and the median price-to-earnings ratio for the top consumer companies is over 30. Capital markets demand profitable growth and high asset utilization. The most effective way to facilitate this demand is for organizations to have a superior ability to meet customer needs in the present and future.

Today in the automotive industry, the consumer knows what their personal sense of value is, whether it is pricing, design or product performance. Consumers can get information, can find inventory, negotiate the deal and insure and finance the purchase all with more information than sales staff at traditional dealerships. Although the consumer cannot yet consummate the purchase electronically, they will soon come to expect to complete the transaction, follow order status, get a just-in-time notification and be able to finance the car and apply for insurance on-line. "Within five years, this industry will have to learn how to sense and respond to market forces and deliver customized vehicles rapidly," Harold Kutner, VP of GM's World Wide Purchasing organization told the leaders of Canada's autoparts industry recently. "The auto industry's decades-old habit of pushing product will have to go. I stand here before you today and tell you this system is going to die, and it's going to die fast."

Reporting on the conference, the *Toronto Star* wrote that for automakers, "the neatest trick of the 21st century will be giving customers more product diversity while reducing manufacturing complexity. Offering more for less—and faster.

- Design products for customers' needs and desires on a faster time schedule
- Reduce the number of platforms while building as many different models as possible from remaining core underpinnings
- Eliminate wasted effort and wasted materials
- Simplify where possible from vehicle engineering to manufacturing processes.

To address these challenges, the automotive industry has begun to experiment with a number of alternatives in several marketplaces. Volvo began testing factory sales on the Internet last year in Belgium. Daewoo said it wants to begin direct Internet sales to customers in California by the end of 1999. Ford is trying to shorten its order-to-delivery cycle to

15 days with a new effort with Trilogy (Ford.com) and GM is experimenting with ways to cut inventory and speed deliveries through specific programs like a Cadillac program called Custom Xpress Delivery and general revisions to its entire "order to delivery" processes.

Manufacturers have also begun to look back into their supply chain. They are redistributing assets with spin-offs like Delphi and the Ford-announced intent to free its component make, Vistcon. Shareholder pressures and the need to wring more efficiencies out of the supplier network are spurring experimentation. GM and VW are experimenting with modular assembly plants that researchers at the University of Michigan's Office for the Study of Automotive Transportation say have the potential to eliminate 75,000 jobs if implemented in US assembly plants. Most importantly, however, all the automotive companies are beginning to drive their organizations to the consumer-centric model. Jacques Nasser, CEO of Ford Motor Company perhaps put it best: What is a consumer company? It's an enterprise that is continuously gathering unfiltered consumer insights worldwide to:

- connect with current and potential customers and anticipate their present and future needs
- translate consumer needs into a competitive advantage, using fast cycle time and generation of breakthrough products and services
- focus on building sustained relationships
- effectively manage a portfolio of brands
- continuously grow shareholder value[5]

Borrowing from the consumer-centric business model that has driven Dell Computers' phenomenal success, Michael Dell has begun to tackle other industries. A recent article in *Automotive News* described his entry into the automotive retailing field.

"With his investment in CarsDirect.com, computer entrepreneur Michael Dell is pushing the automotive business closer to the day when shoppers, without having to visit a showroom, will simply point-and-click their way to a new-car purchase. Dell says it can build a computer to a customer order in less than five hours. That just can't be done in the car business. But in some areas, such as supply-chain management and electronic commerce, Dell is pointing the way.[6]

---

[5] PwC, *Interview with Jacques Nasser*.

[6] "Dell Points the Way" *Automotive News*, May 24, 1999.

THE AUTOMOTIVE INDUSTRY IN PERSPECTIVE

The Automotive Industry comprises three highly integrated processes:

- New Product Development—perform research and development, define product and deliver concepts and engineering product and associated components
- Demand Fulfillment—develop a production plan, process orders, plan material requirements, manufacture and assemble product
- Customer Acquisition and Retention—product pricing and configuration, brand image and equity, customer communication and needs assessment, sale and delivery of product, services, financing and insurance.

Linking these processes together is key to success. That is, the integration process represents the automotive industry's move towards consumer-centricity, faster innovation and mass customization of products and services.

Figure 11.1: Consumer Centricity in the Automotive Industry

According to Jeffrey F. Rayport, associate professor of business administration at the Harvard Business School, "mass customization creates a feedback loop with customers that enables a company to react quickly to changing demand and even sense the fate of the business several years down the road." As companies move in the direction of consumer-centricity they will benefit from the links they have established with their customer base. These benefits include market penetration, product loyalty and more efficient production.

New product development covers what is done by suppliers as well as the traditional OEMs. It includes research and development, design for manufacture, market research and strategy, as well as developing products, prototyping and now collaborative product design. The mission of new product development is to establish an entity capable of providing world-class education, research and technology applications to all areas of the value chain. In addition, the new product development process recognizes the hot areas within the automotive community where change is occurring and the drivers of that particular change. This includes specialty vehicles jointly developed, joint engine programs and even the "dot.com" relationship services seen around the products. Product development has been expanded to encompass service aspects of the industry.

Demand fulfillment includes make-to-order, order-to-delivery, and modular assembly and logistics. The challenge of this process is to integrate the total supply networks through the use of enterprise-wide linkages that will provide seamless information flow throughout the value chain. As a result, companies will benefit from a high performance, low cost, highly integrated end-to-end system that is synchronized with true demand and is connected to demand creation.

Customer acquisition and relationship management includes sensing customer needs, product pricing/configuration, brand equity/image, customer dialogue (two-way communications), positive acquisition experience and after-sales relationship around the products and its use. This process focuses on customer insight, demand creation, innovation and analysis. Customer acquisition and retention relationship is driven by the informed customer who has individual and often elevated expectations for product attributes whether they are quality, performance, fuel efficiency, "greenness" or friendly local service. The individual customer focus helps companies utilize solution-based and lifestyle selling and provides multichannel coverage and synchronization. More importantly the focus on individual needs encourages innovation as companies work toward targets "one-to-one."

Figure 11.2 is key to expressing one possible evolution of consumer-centricity. It implies new behaviors that are more consumer focused than manufacturing focused. We call this new behavior category Vehicle Brand Ownership (VBO) and believe it will replace some of the traditional OEM actions if, for example, should an OEM chose to divest or lower their asset base of operations in assembly, stamping and distribution, and focus on building the shared enterprise activities around brands and innovation.

Figure 11.2: A New Paradigm of Consumer Centricity

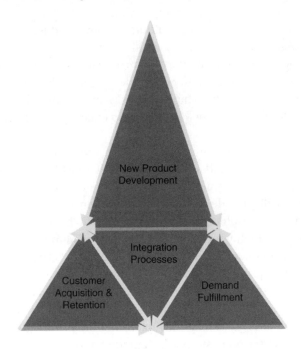

The elements of the diagram express the components and their intersects. Changing the focus off the key parties will result in a reallocation of assets, both machinery and intellectual property.

AUTOMOTIVE INDUSTRY TRENDS

While automotive business trends, such as globalization, mergers and acquisitions and retail consolidations have dominated headlines with respect to shareholder value and margin pressures, there is an equally important consumer-centric impact that these trends have on the enterprises' core processes:

Process	Trend	Consumer-Centric Impact
New Product Development	• Vehicles are starting to contain a much higher degree of electronic components, telematics and PC chips. • Global collaborative product teams and global, flexible platforms. • Cycle times are falling due to increased modularity, fewer platforms, and increased supplier responsibility and collaboration.	• Higher potential for service offerings tailored to consumer needs encompassing environment, entertainment/communications safety, productivity and comfort. • Best-in-breed quality and globalized features with local market variations. • Ability to deliver vehicles that better meet customer demands due to shorter product development lead times.
Demand Fulfillment	• OEMs are beginning to move from push-to-pull based manufacturing systems. • Suppliers are assuming a higher degree of responsibility including	• Highly customized vehicles with shorter delivery cycles. • Lower costs, more information sharing and shared

	liabilities in the delivery/design of components.	"success" payments for the best performance.
Customer Acquisition and Retention	• More shared information is available because of the Internet and the addition of new retail channels and alliances—those organizations that have more impact or power than the traditional brokers/middlemen. • New retailing formats and access points, chains superstores, satellite service, etc. • OEMs focus more on dialoguing with the consumer.	• Customer-driven and customer-shaped distribution services will led to rapid experimentation in service innovation and new channel allies (e.g., Yahoo, AOL). • The ownership experience is being unbundled to accommodate differences in consumer process of access and utilization (purchase and service relationship). • More information to share but also privacy issues.

Each of these trends moves the industry closer to a consumer-centric nature and in the process drives change into the associated suppliers and service providers. This change will redefine the entire supply chain and provide those companies that are first to address these market needs with the opportunity to gain market share. The next section of this paper details the trends and impacts of consumer-centricity on the traditional original equipment manufacturers.

ORIGINAL EQUIPMENT MANUFACTURERS

Benefits/Impacts: The advent of consumer-centricity will draw the OEMs closer to their end consumers while taking millions of dollars out of the inventory flows. The model will force more collaboration between the OEM and automative suppliers.

Within the automotive industry new strategies are constantly being devised aimed at heightening customer satisfaction and loyalty. But are these strategies really working? The following charts depict customer satisfaction between 1994 and 1999 and suggest that despite improved product quality and many efforts to improve the level of service to the customer, relative levels of satisfaction did not mirror that improvement.

Figure 11.3: Customer Satisfaction in the Automotive Industry

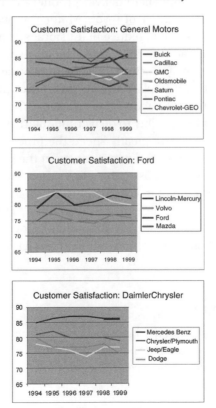

Source: University of Michigan

Part of this judgment about the OEMs stems from the fact that many consumers do not get the specific new vehicle that they wanted, settling for a close match. Bruce Belzowski, senior research associate at the University of Michigan, suggests that 75 to 85 percent of new cars are purchased directly from the dealer's lot, and every day that consumer sits in the car is a reminder of the mismatch in the process. Yet, the industry, through rate subsidies, inventory support programs and consumer incentives, still spends inordinate amounts to foster such dissatisfaction. Indeed, distribution, selling and marketing, dealerships and transportation account for 26 percent of the transaction price of the average new vehicle.

Hoping to dramatically reduce cost and at the same time improve customer satisfaction, Toyota announced (and then modified) a commitment to build a custom-order Camry within five days at its' plant in Ontario, Canada. To do this, Toyota has implemented an extensive network of just-in-time suppliers to deliver product to their site up to 24 times per day. Real Tanguay, VP of Toyota Motor Manufacturing Canada Inc. indicated that this would reduce plant storage requirements by 37 percent and reduce carrying inventories by 28 percent. Each of the OEMs has experimented in custom delivery but few have been successful in the endeavor. The implications to the entire value chain of the Toyota initiative can be enormous. A key factor of this speed to market will rest on the suppliers' ability to deliver modularized components to Toyota on a timely basis. To greatly speed the process, many of these cycles will have to be simplified and/or occur at the same time.

The key suppliers to the assembly plants then will have to become the overall integrators of the components and parts needed for the major "chunks" of the vehicle to be assembled. They will become responsible for the synchronizing execution using pull signals that react to consumer requirements. Inventory at each stage of the process is thereby reduced.

Scenario Visioning

There are a number of likely changes to be expected in the industry as shown in Figure 11.4. Each of the four scenarios within the Figure has merit and would change the face of the automotive industry.

Figure 11.4: Scenario Visioning for OEMs

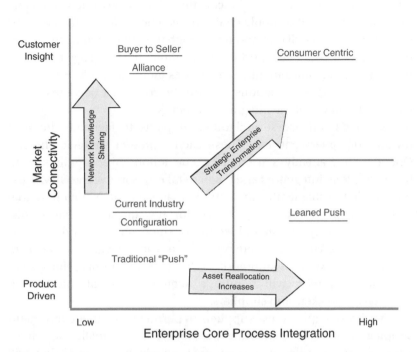

AUTOMOTIVE SUPPLIERS

> Benefits/Impacts: Consumer-centricity benefits the automotive supplier in their collective ability to reduce inventory, collaborate on innovation of products, retain margin and reduce prices by connecting to their own suppliers' processes effectively. The impacts are dramatic to the automotive suppliers in that their systems are geared to push signals rather than pull.

Automotive suppliers will play a vital role in the move towards consumer-centricity. The traditional tier structure in the automotive industry has already begun to transform itself to support this shift. Joseph C. Day, president and CEO of Freudenberg-NOK, feels that "with a major shift occurring in the automotive supplier tier structure, warranty cost issues, increased expectations and merger mania, the automotive industry must think out of the box, target total costs, embrace lean systems and focus on value for the consumer." This new role will enable the early stages of the supply chain to become customer focused and flexible enough to pull the product through the value chain. The emerging industry e-commerce portals will facilitate the exchange and sharing of demand management as well as design processes. Therefore the automotive suppliers' relationship with the consumer becomes a fundamental element of the integration process.

Suppliers can use several different paths to facilitate the shift toward consumer centricity. These each represent strategic choices. One that has already started for some automotive suppliers is to become system integrators and begin to take on some of the OEM's historical role in subassembly and supply management. Not all potential system integrators appear prepared for this quasi-automaker role, however, for many are still wedded to a business philosophy of "lowest-price parts and cut everywhere possible" to win the wars and stay lean in the cyclical world of automotive schedules. In contrast, the system integrator approach will require a seamless flow of information between automakers and suppliers.

It will also require these suppliers to partner with other component suppliers and become modular partners. For the smaller suppliers, knowing the new rules of engagement with which they must align will be more critical than ever.

Another possible approach for suppliers is to maintain their current product offerings but improve their information "link" to their OEMs. Gary Burgess, Product Development Information Officer, GM North America, says, "At GM, we want to help our suppliers and make it easier for them to communicate with us. We believe in partnering with our suppliers on various projects, and the concept of e-engineering will help us do that in a more efficient, cost-effective way". Burgess also claims that "in the manufacturing world we live in, the goal—of course—is to achieve breakthrough product development cycle time and get your product to market faster. This, in turn, increases sales, improves margins and delights our customers because they get the best product we can offer. Without electronic collaboration, none of this would be possible."

VBO-led enterprises (suppliers/OEMs/retailers) will strategically link demand and customer information and core processes from retail to design for the next competitive advantage. Push-to-pull transformation will accelerate when a part/module/vehicle is produced based on customer demand and replenishment needs, rather than on forecast and retail incentives "push to move iron." Transformation begins by connecting and then synchronizing information flows within the business entity. These efforts are by nature collaborative and will cause the formation of communities of leading players within the supply chain who will lead the way to consumer-centricity.

Scenario Visioning

Scenario 1—Suppliers will assume more assets of production and have greater responsibility in the supply chain as an enterprise moves towards modular assembly. They may consolidate or integrate themselves at the assembly level to reduce the cycle time and cost while improving quality.

Scenario 2—Suppliers will enhance connectivity with OEM partners of their choosing and continue to offer the same or affinity products but focus on improving their cost structures and product quality as well as information systems.

Scenario 3 (Most Likely)—The supplier community will reorder, with some becoming systems integrators providing full assemblies and/or integrating other suppliers' products. The supply networks will be more collaborative, dynamic and fluid, covering production, design and innovation.

Regardless of which scenario plays out in the industry, the supply chain will be transformed from a push to a pull distribution strategy by providing the informational power needed by the suppliers to service the customer.

The goal for suppliers is to replace the complex, redundant and costly multiple connections that exist in the automotive supply chain today with a highly reliable, secure business network to ultimately reduce production costs and improve profitability.

DEALERS/AUTOMOTIVE RETAILERS

Benefits/Impacts: Dealers acting in traditional ways are in the most precarious position of all of the key players in the consumer-centric evolution. The dealer community is squeezed on one side by the OEM and on the other by the consumer who has the new information technologies.

Retail distribution is a battlefield where competitive advantage will be determined in the automotive industry. This is because the automotive industry presents specific characteristics that have a major impact on retailing. These include:

- Competitive markets
- Channel conflicts (such as intra-brand dealer competition)
- Market maturity (lack of growth in volume or value)
- Price erosion (increased "discounts" to consumers)
- Fast-changing consumer legislation
- Product convergence (and therefore increased need for service innovation)
- Overcapacity and excess assets in production and distribution
- Brand clutter and lack of clear differentiation of attributes of customer value
- Increased consumer focus

This has created an environment where the value proposition offered a customer is now much more important than the product itself. The vehicle purchase process is a combination of propositions that can be combined to create value to the customer.

Figure 11.5: A Customer Value Proposition

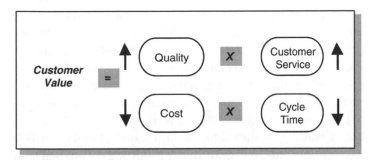

Source: PwC

What does this mean for automotive retailing?

- Customer preference for a specific channel is the result of complex choice and trade-offs between price, services, convenience and risks.

- Services (including after-sales services) are used to lower or hide direct product-price competition and are a significant source of profits for some channels.

- Mature markets develop many alternative channels that use various formats.

- The retailing model in existence is based upon push methods of inventory distribution.

- The competitive advantage for a manufacturer begins to derive as much from channel management as from other elements of the marketing mix.

- Shared insight by consumers is now possible.

- Segmentation of after-sales services is used to address specific customer segments with a differentiated offer (though the product itself is the same).

Many retailers are reacting to the changes by increasing service levels, offering one-price/low pressure selling, weekend and evening service hours, money-back guarantees and a clean and pleasant environment for customers. An example has been the rush to implement one-price selling while neglecting the complexity of such an implementation such as the migration of management responsibilities from traditional "closer" to that of a "merchandising" manager. Many retailers have simply delivered a market message of one-price, or value pricing without creating a credible fulfillment process.

But, according to the National Automobile Dealers Association (NADA),[7] in 1998, the average dealership still had only a total net profit before tax of 1.7 percent—up slightly from 1.4 percent in the previous year, and the majority of that came from service and used vehicle and parts sales. In fact, over the past seven years, the new-vehicle department of the typical dealership has been little better than a break-even operation. (Larger dealers earned an average of $207 per vehicle, compared to a loss of $66 per vehicle at smaller dealerships.) Thus, dealerships have had to rely on the service and parts end of the business to deliver profits. However, as manufacturers have reduced warranty work by as much as 40 percent from previous years, because they are building better automobiles, this market is now not secure for the franchised dealership.

Studies also continue to show significant consumer dislike with buying a vehicle from a dealer. According to the NADA 1998 Industry Analysis, heading the list of complaints are:

- Broken promises
- Complicated price negotiations
- Intimidating environment

And now the dealer environment is faced with yet more challenges:

- **New Entrants**—AutoNation, CarMax and Priceline.com have been changing the retailing model either by purchasing dealerships or, in the case of Priceline, simply using dealers as distribution channels.

- **Dealer Consolidations**—Manufacturers have launched several consolidated company-owned retail operations throughout the

---

[7] *NADA 1998 Industry Analysis.*

country. The purpose is to deemphasize intra-brand competition while offering more coordinated selling and service. Depending on local state legislation, a company would hold either majority or minority ownership in the outlets. In response to these moves, the NADA and several state dealership associations have launched intense lobbying to prevent such factory-owned retailing efforts.

- **Third-Party Brokers**—Consumers, empowered by emerging e-commerce technology as well as their experience with other retailing processes, are reassessing the overall value of the traditional customer relationship. They are increasingly finding alternative retail structures or end-running the current system through brokers or affinity groups. On-line buying services are quickly becoming a method for purchasing a new vehicle while almost avoiding the dealership altogether.

- **Factory Direct Sales**—Korean automaker Daewoo was the first to announce factory-direct Internet sales in North America. Since the company is new to that market, it will not have to contend with the franchise issues that established dealers are wrangling with. The company promises it will conduct the entire process on-line, including buying, financing and delivery. The pilot program was launched in California at the end of 1999. It should also be noted that Daewoo initially tried to control the retailing process through manufacturer-owned retail outlets, but due to limited initial success and prohibitions in many states, the company is in the process of rushing to sign traditional franchise retailers to boost their sluggish product launch in the US.

Scenario Visioning

Scenario 1—Dealers will be replaced, leaving new vehicle selling to the OEMs, and become merely a delivery point with a focus on services, warranty, used cars and add-on services. (Very unlikely).

Scenario 2—Dealers will become part of the e-commerce communities as they become more Internet savvy and learn to live with the new medium by addressing Internet consumer's individual expectations.

Scenario 3 (Most Likely)—Dealerships will continue to consolidate, with some extending the VBO reach into new regions and new channels, which will be collaboratively built. Large chains will focus on building retail brands and evolving their own CRM efforts that compliment the CRM efforts of multiple brands.

The automotive dealers are in the least favorable position of all of the key players in the automotive industry. Dealers are caught between the OEM's desire to connect directly to consumers and the emergence of new entrants and therefore either new competitors (or allies) that are more than willing to accept a lesser role.

The next section will focus on the consumer—the driving force of these change elements.

CONSUMERS

> Benefits/Impacts: The consumer is the biggest winner in the consumer-centric automotive industry. Increased access to information has given consumers considerable power, and in the future that access will have even more impact through negotiated pricing and services.

To be a consumer in the Western world today is to be powerful and harried at the same time. And ironically, the latter condition fosters the former. In its "Time in America" survey, Day-Timers found that the majority of working Americans feel time pressure every day. This is reflected in their decisions about car buying and servicing, where they increasingly are less and less inclined to shop for and service their vehicles in the traditional manner. Through the power of the World Wide Web they are defecting to nondealers for increased savings and convenience. They are interested in minimal service requirements and a painless buying experience.

Figure 11.6: The Shift to Non-Traditional Channels

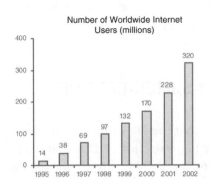

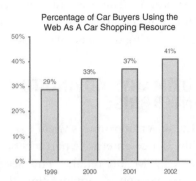

Industry statistics indicate that 1 to 4 percent of new cars were bought through Internet services in 1997, and that according to estimates, 33 percent of new car buyers will use the Internet to car shop in 2000, up from 16 percent in 1997. Industry forecasts suggest the number could reach 41 percent by 2002. More than one-quarter of all used vehicle buyers already check the Internet while shopping, according to the J.D. Power and Associates Used Autoshopper.com Study.

The direct marketing model pioneered by Dell Computer that allows for mass customization and requires short product lead times to satisfy consumer demands is gaining in popularity across the business spectrum. Some automakers are experimenting with mass customization already. DaimlerChrysler's Smart Car in Europe allows consumers to chose any combination of colored plastic panels for their vehicles. The vehicles can be customized at the retail outlet in less than two hours. Ford's Focus, new in the US in 1999, is also experimenting with vehicle customization. Buyers can order one of several inexpensive bundles of equipment to customize their cars.

As the OEMs get more adept at analyzing and acting on the vast amounts of customer information they have, they will get better and better at meeting consumer needs.

Scenario Visioning

Scenario 1—There is only one scenario—the consumers win. More data, more competition, more focus on needs—no question, the consumer is king or queen of this new model.

SUMMARY: MOVING TO CONSUMER-CENTRIC ENTERPRISE

The power consumers wield assures that the status quo is unacceptable. Hence enterprise partners have to make choices. However a supplier, OEM or retailer chooses to make the transition to the consumer-centric organization, the risks and challenges are plentiful. The transition to consumer-centricity will impact each of the elements of the increasingly dynamic network working to produce, relate and innovate faster than competitors. The high asset base and low margins of the automotive industry mean that some will fail and consolidation will accelerate. For an organization to be truly CRM focused, the starting point is information: Who are my customers and what are their needs and aspirations? This information will fuel collaboration for new products, services and promotional ideas. But it is not as simple as that to be successful. There are many points of contact that the manufacturer has with its suppliers and the total value chain:

- suppliers/ integrators
- parts/component manufacturing
- assembly
- distribution
- the retail channels (dealerships and repair facilities, etc.)

and that the consumer has several points of contact with various interaction points within this network or its enterprise allies.

Each point of contact has valuable information to help the organization make it easy to do business with. Each point of contact has information that can affect new product development, customer satisfaction, marketing and more. The key will be securing the consumers' permission to use these interactions to better innovate in their interest. This will be a collaborative effort, shared by the allies.

This information must be collected, shared and used for continuous improvement. Channels must be embellished with new capabilities and ease of use. Products and service offerings must be refined and flexibility must be created—that is true customer-centricity and the essence of CRM.

"It's a gradual process; the forces start to grow and, as they do, the characteristics of the business begin to change. Only the beginning and the end are clear; the transition in between is gradual and puzzling."[8]

About the Author

J. FERRON

> J. Ferron is a Partner in PricewaterhouseCoopers' America's CRM consulting practice. His primary focus has been CRM and eCRM in the Automotive sector.

---

[8] Andrew S. Grove, *Only the Paranoid Survive: How to Exploit the Crisis Points that Challenge Every Company and Career*, New York: Doubleday, 1996.

Part Four

Step Three:
The Infrastructure
Strategy: Overview

OVERVIEW

To a large extent, the ability to track customer information and measure return on investment of individual customers will depend on your infrastructure strategy—the process, technology and organizational foundation that must be laid to enable the CRM strategy. Sales and service personnel need to be able to better collect information and to track and understand a customer's current and future needs. The information can then be shared across all parts of the company, enabling the entire organization to work toward the same objective. If the infrastructure strategy is well focused on CRM, it will support this process and define the organizational changes required to effectively and efficiently manage relationships with customers.

Chapter 12, "The Tools for CRM: The Three Ws of Technology," seeks to address the integration of process, technology and organization in more detail. When companies combine and link the Web, work flow management and data warehousing—three critical technological forces—they open opportunities for electronic customer relationship management—eCRM—a process by which they can learn about customer desires and fulfill their needs, all through automation. Consider the following: If you look at why customers leave a company, it's usually because they could not get the information they needed when they wanted it or they are being asked for the same information repeatedly—"Does anyone know who I am? Does anyone care?" Customers are using telephone, e-mail, fax and electronic data interchange to get information. And how you touch the customer, the speed and the care taken once connected, is critical. If a customer makes a hotel reservation through a call center, the hotel front desk where the customer later registers should be connected to the first touch point; the person doesn't want to be asked for his or her address again. The call center, in this case, should be as its name implies the center of the relationship, one that reflects the entire organization and its desire to add value to the customer relationship.

Chapter 13, "Using the Tools: Database Marketing, Data Warehousing and Data Mining," provides us with a case study on Hachette Filipacchi Media (HFM), an international publisher with 123 magazines in 31 countries. Its challenge was simple—leverage the potential of its millions of customers into a strategic tool to maximize revenue and improve profitability. Of course that is not a simple task, and the lessons learned will prove valuable for those embarking on the development of an integrated infrastructure strategy. Getting close to the customer translates directly into the need for a central customer database, one that contains every bit of information regarding the relationship with the customer, during the entire life cycle of the relationship. Companies must realize, too, that such information might be useful for product development and quality as well as customer support.

We close with Chapter 14, "CRM in the Telecommunication Industry: A Case Study of Swisscom," and the challenges that it faced in the development and implementation of a loyalty program, its first step in becoming a CRM company. The case study explains the challenges, Swisscom's CRM understanding, the design and implementation of its now successful Joker Loyalty Program and the tools and strategy to support it. The case study highlights the strategic challenges, the design principles and the success factors during implementation.

As the CRM strategy unfolds, Part Two provided a context to target customers and key customer needs (our customer strategy). Part Three provided the framework for the product and channel strategy (clear focus on which products to offer which customers through which channels). Part Four, provides guidance on the process, technology and organizational components that must be considered (the infrastructure strategy) to ensure the CRM strategy can be enabled and that is what is found in the chapters that follow.

The Tools For CRM:

THE THREE Ws OF TECHNOLOGY

Lawrence Handen

OVER THE PAST five years, three technologies have emerged as a foundation for process improvement and automation: the Web (Internet), work flow management and data warehousing. Many companies have gained significant improvements through each of these. The data warehouse streamlined and improved the decision support process, work flow automated and expedited tasks within a process, and the Web provided a way of connecting processes and people regardless of location. It also provided a window into a company for customers and suppliers. But because these technologies still represent disparate processes, even companies with well-designed systems find they have many steps and activities that can fall through the cracks. The multiple processes entailed in taking a customer order from beginning (order entry) to end (provisioning), are still fraught with pitfalls.

For instance, one of the problems is that by itself, a company's Web site doesn't achieve anything. From the customer's point of view it represents one-way communication; it certainly does not guarantee sales, being in a sense, a notepad where the customer can enter his or her wants. Some organizations have Web sites that customers can use to enter orders for service. However, in many instances, this is little more effective than having a customer service representative take an order by hand and pass it on—again by hand—to the next stage in the sequence.

If a Web site is linked to a data warehouse, which can gather and analyze customer responses, then the organization begins to have true support for its marketing decisions. Further, work flow technologies make it possible to link the Web site to a seamless chain of processes leading to prompt and efficient fulfillment of customer orders. By linking all three technologies, companies can achieve far greater automation. In fact, it should be possible to take an order with little or no human intervention from beginning to end. And if a Web site has features that draw customers in and make them want to return to the site, it can facilitate a highly effective, ongoing way of learning about the customer and building a relationship, as illustrated in the electronic customer relationship management (eCRM) example later in this article.

Recently, organizations have been finding they can better exploit the individual investments already made in Web, work flow management and data warehousing technologies by making these three technologies work in conjunction—the three Ws.

THE PARTS

Each of the three technologies performs a role that is analogous to a human function. The Web acts as the eyes, ears and mouth of the process by absorbing and presenting information to the user and by collecting responses. The data warehouse serves as the brain and central nervous system. Its job is first to absorb the information being passed to it by the Web and then to formulate a response based on current, external and historical information. It can "think" and provide a organization with advice. The work flow management engine serves as the arms and legs that support the data warehouse and execute its decisions. To explain the powerful benefits of linking these technologies, it is useful to look at the potential and the limitations of each separately.

The Web

The Web has created a near-perfect market, eliminating many of the time and distance costs of working with multiple vendors and supporting various channels to access customers. The Web has enabled organizations to reach out to people who affect their operations, including suppliers, alliance partners and others in the company's business units.

Customers and suppliers can access information themselves instead of using intermediaries such as customer service or sales representatives. For example, customers can check pricing plans or other value-added services available from a telco, or they can collect information about coverage areas for wireless service and compare these. This obviously has the potential of decreasing the cost structure for organizations.

Although organizations have found the Web to be an effective tool for interconnecting users and processes, they have been less successful in using it to manage work activities within or between processes, for instance, between order entry and provisioning. To solve the issue related to scheduling and routing tasks within a process, organizations have relied on work flow technology.

Work Flow Management

Work flow management systems automate the procedures by which documents, information and tasks are passed among participants. These systems employ defined work rules or sequences of activities. If an employee needs to order a piece of equipment, the work flow engine can, without human prompting, check to ensure that spending is authorized for such a purchase. Work flow provides a strong framework for customer-centric business processes, such as order management and customer service. Work flow allows users to route customer communications, along with an associated "virtual folder" that combines documents, voice messages, e-mails, faxes, videos or Web pages containing information about the customer. The information can be transmitted to the appropriate customer service points at the right time to produce the one-call resolution that customers have come to expect.

Like the Web, work flow also has a critical shortcoming. The technology has been most effective when used to automate routine tasks, for instance, in getting approval for an equipment purchase. The work flow engine reacts to stimuli, taking in data and sending it out. It does not learn or draw inferences. Consequently, it is not good at supporting tasks that require complex decision making: Did I order all of the right equipment, did I get the best possible price, is the equipment in stock, and will it be delivered as quickly as possible? To answer this need, organizations have built data warehouses capable of supporting such complex decisions and providing information critical to process improvement.

Data Warehousing

In effect, a data warehouse, by viewing inputs several times, develops an institutional memory. Organizations have built data warehouses to unleash the business value locked away in their operational systems. Like a conventional reporting system, a data warehouse contains information about a organization's customers, its products and its marketplace. The difference is that a data warehouse extracts information from existing internal and external sources, then standardizes and consolidates that information, and finally stores it for easy access and retrieval. For instance, in the context of customer relationship management, a data warehouse can take demographic information from outside the company's systems and analyze it against its own billing records in order to discern the buying preferences of its base of customers.

Today, organizations use data warehouses as an overlay to their existing IT infrastructures. A data warehouse relieves operational systems from providing intensive real-time reporting capabilities, and it can also provide a platform on which other systems (such as order entry, campaign management, purchasing and billing) can be integrated.

WORKING TOGETHER

All three of these Ws (the Web, work flow management and data warehousing) can be made to work in conjunction, supporting the whole enterprise and maximizing an organization's investment. It is usually possible to achieve this integration without dismantling existing systems. Rather, through bridges and patches created using commercially available software applications, these systems can be converted into a powerful end-to-end structure supporting all of the processes entailed in a organization's value chain. Organizations without legacy systems can deploy integrated three-W systems and structures through commercial applications.

It is important to begin such a project by establishing a process baseline. That identifies all of the critical revenue-generating processes, including customer-facing processes such as order entry, trouble ticketing (indicating that the customer has a problem), and some provisioning activities, as well as processes entailed in supplier dealings. Additionally, each process has an envisioned outcome (the outcome for customer relationship activities, for instance, is profitable sales). Each process is evaluated to determine that its outcome is correct and that it is achieved efficiently.

The next step is to envision the environment that will support the right outcomes, first adjusting processes, and then systems. The work can begin to build an integrated system from the ground up (in the case of an organization without legacy architecture) or to apply the kinds of system modifications needed to link separate legacy architectures. Enhancements can be made incrementally in each of the three systems and structures. This is a complex undertaking, and it can take from nine months to two years to fully deploy a three-W integration. However, an organization can expect to see results within five months of beginning such integration. For its supply chain process, one organization experienced a 200 percent reduction in cycle time, using 30 percent fewer people to process these transactions, and it achieved a 99 percent accuracy rate—all in less than six months from installation.

Most organizations will aim for 25 percent of their transactions to be carried through e-commerce channels. Experience indicates that this will yield a 5 to 10 percent incremental rise in gross revenues in the first year, with even greater increases for early adopters.

A THREE Ws CASE: eCRM IN THE TELCO INDUSTRY

One of the examples that best illustrates the value of integrating the Web, work flow management and data warehousing technologies is electronic customer relationship management (eCRM). As carriers develop Web sites as alternatives to traditional sales, service and distribution channels, they struggle to make the interaction effective without the benefit of human intervention. One of the best ways to enrich the customer experience is to use technology as a means of first anticipating and then fulfilling a customer's need. The concept is fairly simple, but the mechanics associated with the implementation can be difficult.

Ideally, the eCRM can allow personalizing of the customer experience. That can help the carrier achieve particular business goals, which may differ at specific stages of the customer relationship. For example, for a new customer it is useful to adjust the Web content to present what the customer is searching for. The eCRM can provide the customer with relevant information without knowing the customer's identity. Rather, by asking certain questions, the system can develop a profile of the user, one that assigns this potential customer to a particular demographic. This is called overt matching. Furthermore, by observing and recording which Web site elements a customer clicks on, the company can conduct "covert matching." If, for instance, the Web site includes a price calculator, and a customer accesses this calculator often, then the carrier learns that this user is probably a value shopper. If, on the other hand, a user clicks on various feature descriptions, then the carrier can see that this customer is a feature shopper.

Subsequent visits to the site by these same customers might either underscore these first findings or add greater dimensions to the carrier's understanding of the customer. For known customers, application tools and databases to filter and segment customers (known as collaborative filtering) or rules-based technology can be used to predict behavior when demographic and buying behavior information is known. Consider this example: Marketing wants to launch a campaign to sell more wireless service and will target users known to be highly mobile. Filters would help the marketers rule out customers from relatively poor demographics. This process saves both time and money that might otherwise be squandered by marketing to those who would neither want nor be able to afford the product or service.

One of the greatest challenges that organizations face is how to get customers to log on to their Web sites. Clearly, the intrinsic value of the service is important, but there is a great deal more that organizations can do to ensure that customers log on in the first place and that they come back repeatedly. Organizations can include a wide variety of content, such as describing events and discussing issues in the company's area of coverage. They can develop their sites as portals to other interesting sites. The Yellow Pages offer a dramatic opportunity: Imagine the value to customers of logging on to a organization's Yellow Pages and being able to link from these directly to the listed merchants, from whom they could buy goods and services.

What is the value of this sort of content for the organization? With repeated visits by customers to its site, the organization gains more and more information that can be used to pinpoint customer desires. And the more often a customer visits the organization's site, the more likely he or she is to be exposed to—and possibly hooked by—the organization's additional offerings.

Integration Points

Of necessity, an eCRM focuses on integration points with other operational systems that can provide the information necessary to drive the predictive model that anticipates a customer's needs. These integration points include the following:

- **The Web interface**—A Web sales channel will allow the capture of valuable customer information at a low cost of service. Captured information may be the result of user profiles, site navigation preferences and the like to which predictive logic would then be applied. The captured information might include frequent visits to a rate comparison tool or link; frequent visits to a particular product, indicating a product preference; or a profile of a large family, representing potential demand for additional services.

- **The order/provisioning system**—This system records customer service orders and interactions occurring through all sales channels. Service orders can be recorded in the eCRM environment, and the customer's profile and the corresponding predictive model scores can be updated immediately. A score is a number derived from a set of criteria relating to a particular marketing question. If a company were trying to sell disposable diapers, someone with a baby would have a high score; a user with several children might have a higher score. Integration with network provisioning allows eCRM to target customers with products and offers that can be provisioned in that customer's area.

- **The trouble ticketing system**—Trouble ticket is the method used to indicate that a customer has a problem. This information can be fed directly into the eCRM system to improve predictive modeling and identify customer needs. For example, an overdue trouble ticket could signify a poor customer relationship. The eCRM could generate both a Web banner for the user acknowledging the problem and a subsequent call from a customer service representative (CSR) to rectify the issue. Similarly, a customer with frequent troubles could signify a high-cost customer for the carrier.

- **The call center**—Web-based eCRM infrastructure can be leveraged to internal call center channels so that offer and response data are tracked in the call center in the same manner that these data are tracked for the Web channel. Links to call centers immediately capture the latest customer information profiles in the eCRM environment and allow customers' scores to be updated immediately. The eCRM environment can also be linked into an intelligent scripting engine that can tailor the script used to communicate with or up-sell the customer. That enables real-time generation of call-center CSR scripts.

Once a profile is established a user begins interacting with the carrier's Web site. Whether the user is browsing, ordering, checking a bill, tracking status or just answering a question the eCRM is tracking this customer's activities and storing the selections in the data warehouse. Based on the profile, the work flow engine will trigger a background search to see whether there are any preprocessed messages or advertisements scheduled to be delivered to the user. A good example is a reminder to a customer to initialize his or her voice mailbox if it has remained dormant for two weeks after activation.

The work flow engine will then present this message to the Web layer in the form of a reminder to the user. At the same time, the eCRM system uses closed-form calculation, which is a device intended to look for a specific, expected result derived from the data warehouse to set up real-time message and menu options for the user. A good example of this real-time response occurs when a valuable customer orders a second phone line and logs on to check for installation status. As the work flow engine interrogates the provisioning system, it returns a response that indicates that the service order is past due. Based on the value of the customer, the past due status and the number of status checks performed by the user, the data warehouse and decision support system may indicate that they risk losing the customer. Given this deduction, the workflow engine automatically triggers the issuing of a "loyalty bond," a certificate a customer can either apply against the bill or allow to grow in value, and the user is notified via the Web.

CONCLUSION

To succeed in today's highly commoditized and competitive global marketplace, organizations are striving to improve and automate the business processes that deliver value to their customers, suppliers and employees. The greater the automation and efficiency that can be achieved in such processes as on-line billing, business-to-business bonding, on-line order entry and electronic customer relationship management (eCRM), the more effectively they can achieve profitable sales growth. The architecture needed to support such automation is difficult to implement, but it is finally possible, thanks to the power of an integrated Web, work flow management and data-warehousing platforms.

About the Author

LAWRENCE HANDEN

Lawrence Handen is a Partner in PricewaterhouseCoopers' America's CRM consulting practice. His primary focus is CRM in our Telecommunication, Information, Communication and Entertainment Consulting Practice.

Using the Tools:

DATABASE MARKETING, DATA WAREHOUSING AND DATA MINING

Eric Falque

FILIPACCHI MEDIA BACKGROUND

Hachette Filipacchi Media (HFM) is a subsidiary of Lagardère Group, a leading world publishing group of with 123 magazines in 31 countries. With more than 50 titles in France, 26 in the United States, and 18 in Spain, Hachette Filipacchi Media covers nearly all segments of the market: women's magazines (*Elle, Elle Deco, Woman's Day*), leisure (*Première, Quo, Car and Driver*), current events (*George, Paris Match, Le Journal du Dimanche*) and also TV, sports and kids' magazines. The company's publications are read in millions of households throughout the world (47 million readers in the United States alone).

The Challenge

With such a large customer base, the management of customer information is a major challenge. For most companies, keeping an accurate and up-to-date name and address file of such magnitude would be overwhelming. The addresses alone would come from active and inactive subscriptions, contests, mail-order business, letters or call centers. HFM had an even greater challenge to leverage this information to achieve customer relationship management and to achieve customer loyalty and repeat sales and be able to cross-sell new business to its existing customer base.

As a leader in its market, HFM had a large customer base, but only limited information (name, address) within it. To be proactive, and have the ability to use the information it had, the tools to mine the data had to be more sophisticated. Otherwise, the costs of attracting and keeping its customer base would continue to escalate.

Action Taken/Lessons Learned

With the help of PwC, HFM is now in the process of developing a data warehouse that will help achieve CRM by increasing the value of its considerable assets in order to generate important financial profits and to develop a major competitive advantage.

The path to CRM required the organization to simultaneously think through a number of steps to ensure that each was cost justified and would also lead to an effective implementation with a high chance of success. The process steps were:

- Understanding the current environment
- Identifying true costs and benefits
- Assessing the organizational and process implications to make it a reality

HFM is now in the process of implementing its CRM data warehouse project. But as you will note, that is only a small part in the refocusing of the organization to a customer-centric model from a product-centric one. A data warehouse is a tool, but put in the hands of an artist or master craftsman, it can and will offer rich CRM rewards—closeness to the customer, improved customer care and improved organizational profitability.

UNDERSTANDING THE CURRENT ENVIRONMENT

Subscribers Are Strategic

As with any other magazine publisher, subscriptions represent an important part of Hachette Filipacchi Media (HFM) revenues, accounting for more than 30 percent of total HFM sales in overall value and more than 50 percent for some key magazines. Subscribers are strategic as they represent a revenue base as well as a readership base that advertisers look for when considering in which magazines to place their client's messages. Subscriptions are a stable portion of the business as distinct from retail sales, which can fluctuate greatly.

Customers are strategic assets, and the more you know about them and their habits, the more capable the organization will be to develop targeted products and services that will be successful in attracting customers. The more you know about your customer, the greater the likelihood for cross-selling opportunities and the better able you are to retain them, which is equally important. Moreover, subscribers constitute a reliable source of information for the firm, which allows improving the customer relationship (useful data on loyal readers).

Retention is Necessary for Survival

Generally speaking, it is necessary to identify and to segment customers depending on their value to the firm. With that information in hand, an organization is more capable of targeting to the more profitable. This is particularly challenging for the publishing industry, which can effectively communicate with its subscriber base only by achieving a better understanding of this customer base. In so doing HFM has the potential for improved customer retention (the renewal of subscription rate is around only 65 percent) and to attract new subscribers in the most profitable category, instead of spending huge amounts of money trying to attract new readers indiscriminantly. Indeed, renewal of subscription is from four to six times more profitable than recruitment.

Retention Offers Must be Targeted

Magazines always have to recruit new readers to survive and to grow. There are many ways to do this is—all more or less expensive—from coupons or simple sales promotions to awareness marketing (through sponsorship of sporting or fashion events or direct mailing (sending out offers to a portion of the customer base). Only a few HFM magazines, however, will recruit through direct mailing, as it is the most expensive strategy.

At the end of the day, recruiting costs are high whatever the strategy, (often more than US $25 per magazine) and have to be minimized. Thus, as a first step, it is much more profitable for HFM to encourage readers' loyalty than to recruit new ones. But to develop that loyalty, the offer needs to be targeted to a customer's changing needs. It needs to be able to predict this change and offer a product best suited to it. Firms have to learn to develop a deeper understanding of their consumers in order to be proactive. This is the aim of Customer Relationship Management.

At the same time, in order to grow, HFM must recruit new clients, but recruiting costs have to be more oriented and targeted to be really efficient. Having an effective database that can identify the characteristics of its loyal customers will allow it to target to customers that resemble same group—look-alikes. Thus, HFM has to focus on gaining a deeper knowledge of its customers and therefore must invest now in a more detailed customer relationship database to be able to recruit in the future.

Dependence on Outside Sources Causes Some Vulnerability

Few companies have their own data warehouse with enough information to manage customer relationships properly. Thus, they have to share or to buy addresses of suitable potential customers based on lifestyle or other demographics. This is an expensive alternative and one that may not be sufficiently targeted. While the organization may not be capable of having a larger target, the quality of names and addresses may be suspect and thus the acceptance or "pick-up" rate may be quite low (less than 1 percent). The firm becomes rapidly dependent on its data supplier for its strategic advantages.

This is the true for HFM. It had to work with outside sources to collect customer information. The organization currently buys data from outside sources (collectors, brokers etc.) to complete their existing data warehouse. They also partner with other companies to collect and share customer information (manufacturers data) and distributors' loyalty cards, for instance). In addition, the organization works with specialized companies to organize focus groups or to follow samples of consumers during a given period of time.

Thus, at the moment HFM is not the only owner of its customer/client information and is dependent on others to create its strategic advantage. This is not an acceptable position because that same partner is likely to sell the same information to HFM's competitors.

Targeted Information Gathering Ensures a Deeper Knowledge of Customer Behavior

HFM will enhance its address database in order to build a larger data warehouse with strong information on each client. This might include information such as: social category, housing conditions, purchasing power, frequency of purchase and so on. With a strong CRM data warehouse, HFM will now be in a position to gain greater leverage in the marketplace by becoming closer to the utopian "one to one" marketing relationship, which offers both cheaper and more efficient solutions to target heavy buyers. In doing so, the organization will be able to personalize its marketing approach—direct mail, Internet, cross selling—through better knowledge of the customer profile. Advertisers know precisely who they target. By owning the information source and profiting from this knowledge. HFM will also enhance its position in the market. The new CRM data warehouse offers the company an opportunity to develop partnerships and to make profits in the data business through agreements with targeted partners to obtain a better control of address sales and to benefit indirectly from these addresses sold. At least two options are available to them:

- Addresses sales/partnerships with direct marketing companies or brokers
- Exchange of addresses with targeted companies

IDENTIFYING TRUE COST AND BENEFITS

Benefits

Costs and benefit analysis has always been touted as being essential but all too often neglected and given minimal attention. Not only must the organization know its short- and long-term costs, it must establish milestones and goals to assess whether estimated benefits are realized. With a customer data warehouse (CDW), it is not uncommon for development costs to escalate and because of that the purpose and benefits of this database must be rethought. A proper analysis will ensure that the initiative does not go off track or be sub-optimized.

Figure 13.1: Benefits of CRM Database

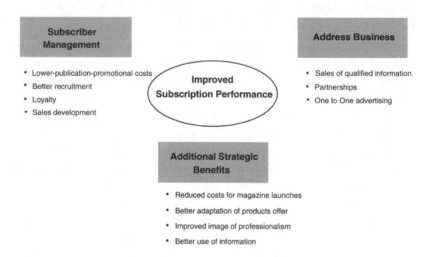

As shown above, there are three main benefits to be gained through a more effective subscriber/CRM database: Subscriber management, additional strategic benefits and the address business. Let's look at each of them in isolation:

Subscriber Management

There are at least four main benefits related to subscriber management:

- Partial substitution of external addresses (New addresses will no longer have to be purchased from external list suppliers.)
- External sales of qualified addresses (List developed through data mining can be sold to other non-competitive organizations.)
- Improvement of the renewal of subscription rate (Lists and offers are more relevant and the chance of acquiring new customers increases.)
- Increase in margin for renewal of subscription (The cost of advertising and promotion can be reduced by taking a more targeted rather than a shotgun approach.)

A CRM data warehouse seems to be especially appropriate for organizations that require subscription management. Effective management can lead to a drop in publication promotional costs and possibly to better loyalty and commercial developments to recruit new clients. It becomes easy to extract, for example, single women in their 30s who read HFM magazines, instead of doing it magazine by magazine. This subscriber management improves the image of professionalism of HFM and the feeling of proximity of the consumers. Subscribers became associated as a community of readers with like interests, and articles are tailored to their needs. Moreover, by having this new competency, HFM can lay emphasis on the fact that strategic risks with data suppliers (such as collectors and brokers) are reduced.

Additional Strategic Benefits

For these organizations that are able to implement a customer data warehouse (CDW), there are many benefits to be realized. As highlighted in Figure 13.2, these benefits fall into six primary categories:

1. **Strategic Marketing**—A CDW will allow you to better segment your customer base. Then, knowing who your customers are, their preferences and likelihood to switch, different pricing options can be proposed. In the long run this will make your direct marketing program more cost effective.

2. **New Product Development**—Knowing your customers, their needs and the profile of other preferences (magazines purchased, in this case, will provide valuable input into the extension of the product line with new articles as well as products to be developed to attach to the existing competitive offering).

3. **Channel Management**—A CDW will ascertain channel preferences—through which channel (mail, newsstands, Web) do they want products or services delivered? Moving customers to lower-cost channels will require incentives, which may vary based on current habits and likelihood of switching.

4. **Sales Productivity**—By knowing channel preferences and existing purchase patterns, resources can be better allocated and balanced. By resources, we mean both human and investment in technology. Why invest in more sales people, or branches/retail outlets, if, in fact, the movement is to the Internet?

5. **Customer Equity/Relationship Marketing**—Some customers are more loyal than others, and some can be enticed easily by low-cost introductory offers. By gaining that information and storing it on the CDW, better, more targeted offers can be developed and implemented.

6. **Customer Care**—The ability to customize offers and create true one-to-one marketing cannot be achieved without a CDW. Customer satisfaction and care and ultimately customer loyalty can be greatly enhanced.

More than simple benefits, we can talk about considerable strategic stakes for the firm that implements clients' data warehousing.

Figure 13.2: Customer Data Warehouse

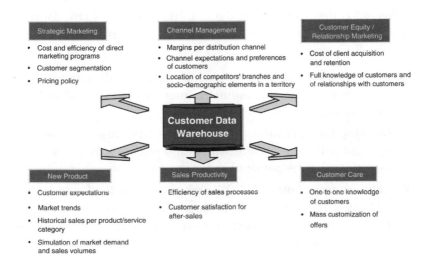

Address Business

The data warehouse allows you to sell qualified addresses directly or through brokers after having used them. Since this data can be sold for several million dollars, this is one way to help pay for data warehouse costs.

Although many organizations have not taken this to these natural extensions, the selling of addresses is also an opportunity to develop relationships and joint marketing opportunities as well as to make profits in the data business: Agreements with targeted partners to obtain a better control of address sales and to benefit indirectly from these addresses sold. Additional revenues can be obtained from:

- Addresses sales/partnerships with direct marketing companies or brokers
- Exchange of addresses with targeted companies (by means of sharing and trading of customer lists)

Costs

No benefit comes without costs and, in the case of a CDW, some of these costs can be quite substantial. Generally, these costs fall into four primary categories.

1. **Initial Investment Costs**—This will include both hardware and software as well as the resources (internal and external) to build the database.

2. **Running (or Operational) Costs**—The CDW must be constantly updated with current information and practices. Without it, the investment will be outdated and ineffective.

3. **Enhancement Costs**—A CDW contains more than names and addresses. It must contain demographics, purchase habits and preferences. There is a cost to obtain and populate the database with this information.

4. **Workforce Costs**—Staffing costs are involved in maintaining the CDW, including the users in the marketing, IT and sales departments.

These costs must be estimated early on in the process to ensure that costs do not exceed long-term benefits.

Figure 13.3: Data Warehouse Costs

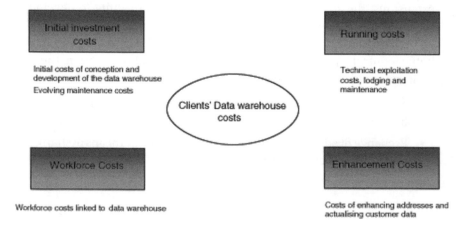

1) Initial Investment Costs

The initial investment for a data-warehouse implementation project can be quite large. Costs can include general and detailed concept design costs of the computing tool and technical development as well as project management and technical assistance. Obviously, costs depend on the existing technology and support environment.

In the HFM case, those costs are principally concentrated in Year 1 but, as the databases of other magazines in the HFM Group are added, these could lead to incremental costs in the years to come; evolving maintenance costs (the costs to make changes and updates to the CDW) could exist from Year 2. By their nature, these costs can hardly be predicted.

2) Running Costs

The costs associated with operating the CDW (including the facility and management of the CDW), can be either sub-contracted or treated internally. In both cases, costs will probably increase over time, as the database grows and new uses are found. It is also possible to mix the two options of in-house versus outsourced operation of the CDW. It is sometimes recommended that one can sub-contract for the launch and then bring it in-house once it is operational (this solution is less expensive).

3) Enhancement Costs

The existing HFM data must be enhanced to be efficient: HFM has only names and addresses in its database for the moment, plus isolated information bits. Buying habits, personal preferences, buying power and move must be attached to each customer profile. Moreover, this customer profile must be updated very often: 15 to 30 percent of addresses change every other year.

Enhancing addresses and updating customer data can be either subcontracted or done internally. If subcontracted, the cost of enhancing addresses depends on the number of addresses that will require update. In HFM's case, they chose the second option, which made HFM the real owner of those data-rich addresses:

- the client asset is strategic for HFM, which needs to be the only owner of customers' data

- this solution is better to regulate data costs, without being dependant on sub-contractors

- it is always possible to share those costs within the parent company (Lagardère Group)

Moreover, this "proprietary solution" gives the opportunity to exploit external as well as internal information, which leads to a better knowledge of the client. They know more about the customer than any one of their list suppliers.

4) Workforce Costs

Obviously, such a big project as data-warehouse implementation generates specific workforce costs. This project requires technical qualifications, at least at the beginning: a full-time IT department must work on this project. The firm will generally have to recruit qualified project leaders and then train employees in this new data system. And with these new data, the marketing organization will have to be adapted with, for example, the creation of a centralized marketing team or external providers of services. Employees with a marketing profile should be recruited.

ASSESSING THE ORGANIZATIONAL AND PROCESS IMPLICATIONS TO MAKE IT A REALITY

New marketing and technical expertise are required to take advantage of a data warehouse. To be able to do this, the organization must first evaluate its internal competencies to determine if subcontractors are necessary to support the initiative and at what time. In HFM's case, it was necessary to subcontract technical tasks, at least at the beginning, to be quickly more efficient and independent.

Start-up and Project Management

It is also typically necessary to centralize the project management function within the organization itself. These are many sub-activities that will be necessary in designing, building, enhancing and using the CDW.

Each will have its own project timeline and dependencies on other sub-activities. Coordination is essential to avoid slippage. In most cases, the conceptualization and database development should be subcontracted. The lack of internal competencies makes the assessment by an external specialist indispensable. A transfer of competencies is still possible if someone from HFM, as an example, is part of this project and if knowledge transfer occurs.

Technical Exploitation

Technical exploitation (lodging, maintenance) in most cases is also subcontracted and then bought in-house. This solution guarantees that the process is not delayed by facility availability or technology lead times and that there will be rapid production in the planning phase. Teams will be trained in parallel in order to improve internal skills. After six months, HFM will be able to set up an international database with trained and operational internal teams. Moreover, this internal administration gives the group the total control of this huge client asset, which is highly confidential.

In the case of HFM the data-mining expertise was initially subcontracted under centralized control of HFM. For the most part it is more efficient to have an external source deliver these technical skills as internal resourcing decisions will not be required and thus be affected by delays in resource commitment.

Marketing Management

Marketing management should be shared between the organization and its operating divisions. In the case of HFM this would be the different magazines. The aim of this step is both to reinforce the role of marketing in HFM as being required across all titles and realize a common approach to the CDW.

SUMMARY

New information systems such as a CRM data warehouse collect marketing information from various sources and enable an organization to be more effective in customer retention and marketing. That data warehouse must contain not only basic demographic data but also customer preferences and habits. Within some organizations this information will include:

- Customers' expectations and preferences
- Previous relationship with customers
- Frequency and volume of customer purchases
- Correlation between types of purchases and customer characteristics
- Knowledge of the lifetime value of each customer
- Evolution of customer satisfaction

With these strong data on its buyers, HFM will be able to set up a one-to-one advertising strategy and develop an efficient proactive marketing approach:

- To focus on key consumers and maximize their retention.
- To develop cheaper and more efficient marketing strategy than massive advertising. HFM can be sure of its data and spend more money on high-potential customers and less money as a whole (nothing is wasted).
- Develop and personalize direct marketing programs.

This one-to-one strategy represents an enormous market potential.

About the Author

ERIC FALQUE

Eric Falque is a Partner in PricewaterhouseCoopers' EMEA CRM Consulting practice. As EMEA leader in Relationship Marketing, Eric's primary focus has been in the Consumer and Industrial Products as well as Information, Communication and Entertainment areas.

CRM in the Telecommunication Industry:

CASE STUDY OF SWISSCOM

Michael Hobmeier
Urs Briner

COMPANY PROFILE

The telecommunication provider Swisscom is the former Swiss monopoly offering fixed line, mobile and Internet services to all customer segments in its home market and in eight other countries. Deregulation in January 1998 had a dramatic impact on Swisscom's position in the marketplace. Its strong financial performance since liberalization as well as its successful going public in October 1998 demonstrated Swisscom's capabilities to react quickly and to become a CRM-focused company:

- Twenty months after the liberalization, Swisscom is still the dominant market leader in all service areas.
- Within the last 12 months, the volumes in fixed-line and mobile communication increased by 12 and over 60 percent respectively.
- Earnings and profits increased dramatically compared to the previous year.

These developments occurred despite a large number of competitors entering the market in all product and service areas and prices dropping dramatically within a few months of privitization.

Swisscom's strong performance has been reflected in its stock price since going public. This case study describes the development of Swisscom in becoming a customer-oriented company for the residential market and will highlight how it established a comprehensive loyalty program in order to become more customer-focused and customer-driven.

In 1996 Swisscom faced internal and external challenges that made the company aware of its lack of customer orientation. Internally the voice, mobile and data (Internet services) product lines were very powerful, but no organizational unit was responsible for marketing activities across the product lines. Bundling of products became difficult (e.g., the bundle of an ISDN with an Internet access). Customer retention was treated at the product level. Segmentation of customers became very difficult due to the lack of customer information across the various product groups:

- Most of the data available was stored based on a single access of a customer.

- Proactive cross- and up-selling and the recognition of most profitable customers was not possible.

- Recognition of high-value customers had not been possible thus far.

Externally the market deregulation in January 1998 was the main challenge. New competitors were entering the market, customers were becoming more demanding, especially in terms of pricing and services, and the market offerings were becoming more diverse. As a result, customer loyalty was practically nonexistent, and accordingly it was believed that customers intended to switch to other telecommunication providers for specific services. This jeopardized revenue and margin development. In addition, disloyal customers decreased referrals, required to win them back investments and costs for service and support. Experience with other telecommunication companies revealed that the winning back of one customer can cost between $US300 and $1,500 per line.

The following consequences have been derived based on Swisscom's position in 1996:

- *The more we focus on the customer, the higher their loyalty*—Product orientation has to be replaced by *customer orientation* in the marketing and sales activities.

- *The longer a customer stays with a company, the higher the profit —* Active caring for and retention of Swisscom's customers will increase profitability and shareholder value in the long run.

STRATEGIC CUSTOMER RELATIONSHIP MANAGEMENT AT SWISSCOM

Swisscom's CRM vision has been derived from its internal and external challenges and was based on one question: How can we retain our most important customers in the most efficient and effective way? In order to achieve its CRM vision, Swisscom developed three strategic CRM elements:

- A market segmentation in order to recognize high-value customers.

- A positioning concept in order to keep number one for all important target with its product and service offer.

- A concrete CRM implementation road map in order to realize the customer orientation and to establish long-lasting relationships with its most important clients.

The following graph summarizes Swisscom's strategic CRM understanding:

Figure 14.1: Strategic Customer Relationship Management for Swisscom

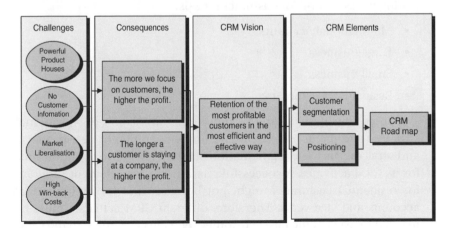

The next section will explain the three strategic CRM elements for Swisscom: customer segmentation, positioning and the customer relationship management road map. These elements built the foundation for the implementation of CRM programs such as the Joker Loyalty Program, which will be described later.

Customer Segmentation

Loyalty can be seen as the feeling of owing something to somebody. Customers will become loyal when they get more than expected. The customers' needs determine their expectations and will become important for segmentation. If Swisscom is able to exceed the specific needs and expectations, then these customers will remain loyal. The following criteria must be fulfilled to get effective segmentation:

- The size of the segment is big enough
- The structure of the segment is homogenous in itself and distinct from other segments
- The segment is stable in its need-structure over a long period of time.

Swisscom has segmented its customers on two levels: A basic segmentation valid for the entire company and a specific segmentation for a single loyalty program.

Basic Segmentation

The basic segmentation has been used with a corporate focus and distinguishes four major customer groups:

- Multinational Accounts
- Large Business
- Small Business
- Residential Customers

These four basic segments determine Swisscom's organizational structure and the development and implementation of new products and services. The basic segmentation of Swisscom is also of importance for its CRM activities. A successful relationship management program for residential customers might not be successful for multinational accounts and vice versa. Therefore, different CRM activities must be realized for each of the basic customer segments according to the CRM road map.

Specific Segmentation

Additional questions relevant to each segment must be answered in order to realize a single CRM program. Some of these questions are listed below:

- Should everybody be admitted to the CRM program or should it be restricted to certain target groups?
- Do customers have to register themselves or is the CRM program automatically relevant for all customers in the target group?
- Should the CRM program be segmented itself in terms of benefits or service quality (e.g., should premium customers benefit more than average customers)?

Swisscom put a lot of emphasis on customer information gathering when setting up its loyalty program. The answers to the above questions determine the segmentation and structure of each specific CRM program or activity:

- Focusing on residential customers at the beginning but broadening the customer base later for small companies
- Everybody can join the program; there are no restrictions on access.
- Registration for the program is mandatory in order to get information about the customer, the household and the lines and services they currently have with Swisscom.
- There will be only one program structure for all customers at the beginning in order to keep it simple. Segment specific offers might come up later based on the information gained.
- Within the Joker program, the more profitable customers in terms of revenue generation must benefit more than others.

This segmentation enabled Swisscom to gain household information about profitable customers in order to keep them loyal and about non-profitable customers in order to make them more profitable.

Strategic Positioning

Every customer-oriented activity positions a company in the minds of its target groups, and three levels of positioning in the telecommunication industry:

Level 1:   The basic prerequisite for positioning is a good technology.

Level 2:   Positioning with prices/tariffs and exit costs (the costs of leaving) are possible as well, especially in the short run.

Level 3:   The main positioning possibilities in the long run lie in the areas of customer care, service quality and total bundling of products and services.

These possibilities are summarized below. Swisscom had to position itself strategically in each of the three levels before designing and implementing a single loyalty program.

Figure 14.2: Positioning Possibilities in the Telecommunication Industry

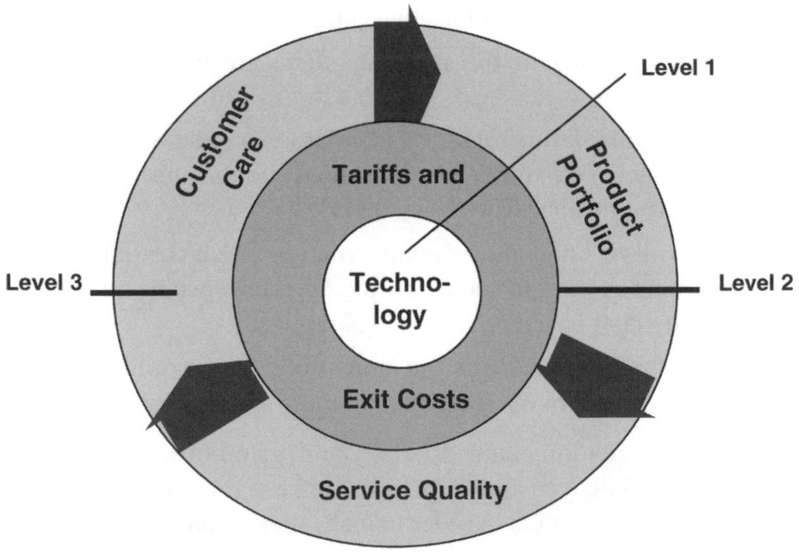

Source: PwC White Paper on Customer Retention for Swisscom

Level 1: Technology—Providing the right technology such as communication clarity or network coverage: Swisscom currently has the advantage of being the best provider in terms of network coverage in mobile communication. However, in future, this advantage will not be sustainable.

Level 2: Tariffs and exit costs—The tariff structure will become less transparent in future due to the additional competitors entering the marketplace. Swisscom currently has higher rates than its competitors, but the company can retain customers over the short term with an increase of the exit costs, making it expensive for customers to leave (e.g., pre-selection, charges for changing provider contract duration). These activities are not very user-friendly and therefore not of strategic value for Swisscom in the long run. Nevertheless, according to several studies in the telecommunication industry, customers will accept moderate price differences as long as they include better service.

Level 3: Product and service quality and customer care—An attractive range of products and services available (the product portfolio), high service quality and a state-of-the-art customer care will help in positioning Swisscom beyond price and tariff structure. Swisscom is currently known as an innovative service provider offering products and services before others. Implementation of a more effective service organization, development and implementation of the Swisscom call center and the development of vertical industry solutions will help for the strategic positioning of Swisscom on this level.

The Swisscom loyalty program focused on Level 2 and 3 in terms of positioning:

- In terms of price and tariff structure, the loyalty program became one important element of Swisscom's pricing strategy. The financial benefits for members were estimated to be between 3 and 6 percent of total purchases (revenue generated from airtime etc). The more products and services used, the higher the financial benefits. The program made it more difficult to compare prices between Swisscom and competitors.

- Level 3 is the main positioning area of the program. A state-of-the-art call center supports the program member and ensures high quality service. In addition, the member profits from new products and services such as a calling card that allows members to make calls without cash from every public phone. Additional benefits are planned for the future in order to position Swisscom as an excellent telecommunication provider on Level 3.

Relationship Management Road Map

Swisscom has been able to derive the customer relationship management road map based on customer segmentation and positioning possibilities. This road map highlights the activities or programs that must be implemented in the area of customer relationship management. The customer relationship management road map is the combination of segmentation and positioning and enabled Swisscom to realize its vision in retaining its customers in the most efficient and effective way. The following figure gives an overview of some CRM activities Swisscom intended to implement. (Note that there is one additional customer group identified, "channel partner," the intermediary between Swisscom and its true customers).

Figure 14.3: Swisscom's Loyalty Road Map

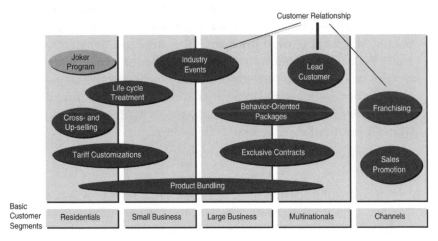

Source: PwC White Paper on Customer Retention for Swisscom

Not all of the programs have been implemented so far. The next section focuses on the Joker Loyalty Program launched in February 1999. It is an important first step towards customer relationship management in the residential-customer segment.

THE JOKER LOYALTY PROGRAM

Joker is a loyalty program similar to those bonus air miles offered by certain airlines. Residential customers can get points for using most of Swisscom services (fixed-line or mobile telephones, Internet services, telco devices etc.) and can redeem these points for Swisscom services, air miles, or adventure weekends. The Joker program enables Swisscom to obtain information on customers, households and preferences across all products and services. It took 12 months (February 1998 to February 1999) to develop and implement the program. This section explains the key elements of the program's design and infrastructure. In addition, it will highlight initial market reactions and give an outlook for the future.

Goals

The Joker Loyalty Program had the following goals:

- Attract 20 to 50 percent of the residential-customer base within the first 12 months after the launch.

- Reduce the customer defection churn rate by 50 percent in order to secure market share and to decrease win-back costs.

- Increase the revenue from Joker members by 5 to 15 percent with cross- and up-selling.

- Obtain customer information across the product lines in order to recognize profitable customer segments.

- Establish a customer-contact platform, a common interface to log complaints and issues across all distribution channels and product lines in order to start a dialog with the customers.

Program Design

The program design is based on the concept of the loyalty pyramid with its six levels. The loyalty pyramid allowed the management of Swisscom to find answers for all strategic design questions in its customer relationship management program. Swisscom management followed the loyalty pyramid from the top down and defined the basic elements of the Joker program based on the agreed goals. Figure 11.4 gives an overview of the elements in the loyalty pyramid:

Figure 14.4: The Loyalty Pyramid

The strategic decisions in each level of the loyalty pyramid will be highlighted in the next sections:

Customer Behavior

Participants in the customer loyalty program should become loyal to Swisscom across all product lines. Cross- and up-selling should be taken into consideration in the loyalty programme offer. In addition, a personal loyalty card will enable participants to call without cash from any public telephone, charging the call to the next monthly bill and gaining loyalty points in addition to that.

Targeting

Everyone can join the program for free. There are no restrictions and no entry charges. This way Swisscom was able to obtain the necessary customer information from a broad customer base. At the beginning, there is one program for everybody in the residential-customer segment, but based on the analysis of more than 20 target groups, Swisscom derived four segments that had to be treated differently with the offer:

- Premium Customers—Behavior Goal: Keep them loyal at all costs.
- Profitable Customers—Behavior Goal: Keep them loyal and intensify cross-selling.
- Average-Spending Customers—Behavior Goal: Bundles and cross-selling.
- Unprofitable Customers—Behavior Goal: No benefits without higher spending.

Positioning

One strategic advantage of Swisscom is its product and service portfolio, which encompasses fixed-line communication, mobile communication and Internet services. Swisscom's position as full service provider is therefore very important. In addition, price is not the key positioning factor for the Joker program. It is not a short-term price strategy of Swisscom but a long-term benefit for its customers. The main characteristics of the Joker were innovation, surprise, and full service provision as well as excellent product and service quality.

The competitive situation required price reductions, but Swisscom was not willing to position itself as price leader. The Joker program is one element in the company's pricing strategy of Swisscom but it did not want to initiate a price war. The Joker focused much more on service quality and the benefits of a long-lasting customer relationship. The association of the points rather than money with positive, non-telecommunication benefits (such traveling, wellness and such) lead to a decrease in the pure price competition.

Program Offer

The program offer had to be simple, highly visible and easy to understand to attract a majority of customers. It should be impossible for competitors to copy the program in a short period of time. Several principles had to be combined in the Joker offer:

- **Bonuses**—Each member of the Joker program gets a personal Joker account. Members can register all communication products in their household (e.g., mobile phones, Internet and fixed lines) and collect bonus points based on their communication behavior (communication for 1 Swiss franc will score one point). Asking for information about the whole household enables Swisscom to get important information about the family's communication behavior involving several products. Two additional points-collection possibilities have to be granted: The family that uses several products must get additional points in order to increase cross-selling behavior and to attract profitable customers. Additional points will be awarded the more a member communicates. Points can be redeemed either for Swisscom products or services, for air flights or for other special offers including holidays and entertainment such as theater and musicals.

- **Rebate**—Every member of the Joker program gets special rebates on certain new products and services at Swisscom's retail outlets. This will attract more people to the points of sale and increase the penetration of Swisscom products in the marketplace.

- **Recognition**—Every member of the Joker program gets an exclusive treatment based on his or her personal Joker card. With the loyalty card, coinless calls can be made from every public phone.

The combination of these three types of offer results in a flexible Joker program structure:

Figure 14.5: Joker Loyalty Program

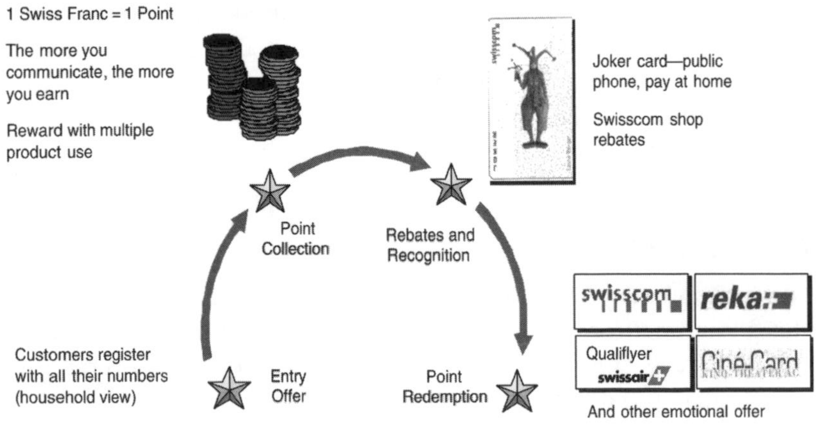

1 Swiss Franc = 1 Point

The more you communicate, the more you earn

Reward with multiple product use

Joker card—public phone, pay at home

Swisscom shop rebates

Point Collection

Rebates and Recognition

swisscom   reka:¬

Customers register with all their numbers (household view)

Entry Offer

Point Redemption

Qualiflyer   Ciné Card
swissair

And other emotional offer

Cost and Benefit Structure

A loyalty program is not just a short-term marketing campaign but a long-term investment. The costs associated with the development, implementation and operation of such a program are enormous. Therefore, it was important to carry out a detailed analysis of costs and benefits and to get top-management involved. A budget shift from traditional marketing and sales activities to the Joker CRM program became necessary.

On the cost side, the main element was the cost for the redeemed points. The direct benefit for customers is responsible for 75 percent of the total costs.

Figure 14.6: Cost Structure for Joker Loyalty Program

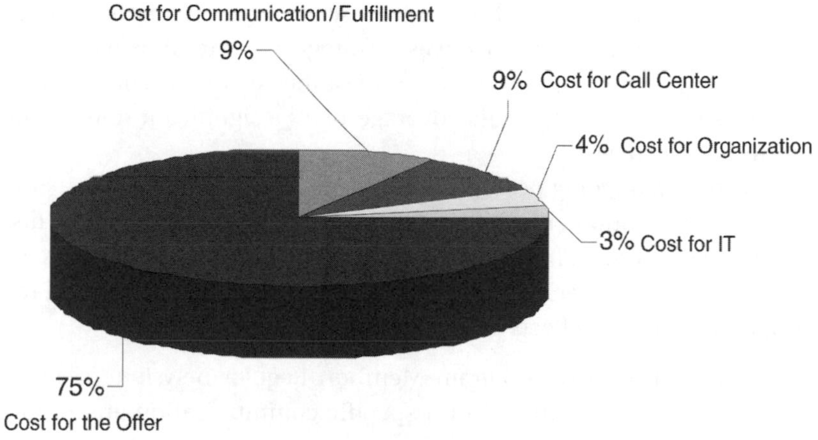

Cost for Communication / Fulfillment
9%

9% Cost for Call Center

4% Cost for Organization

3% Cost for IT

75%
Cost for the Offer

On the benefit side of the Joker program, three main categories had been identified:

- **Benefits from cross- and up-selling:** The attractiveness of having several products and services from Swisscom is higher for Joker members. The members get additional points when they have more than one product or service assigned in the program. In addition, they benefit from new products and services.
- **Benefits from the reduction of the win-back costs:** Due to the higher loyalty, the expected costs for winning back lost customers can be reduced.

- **Benefits from securing basic customer turnover:** Due to the Joker program, customers will not defect so rapidly and often.

Each of the benefit categories had to be quantified and compared with benchmarks from other loyalty programs. The assumptions for the cost and benefit categories enabled Swisscom to derive a financial business plan as well as a net present value calculation for the Joker retention program. The financial business plan has been developed for three different scenarios in terms of program penetration in the marketplace (20, 35 or 50 percent penetration). All scenarios had a payback period below three years.

Communication

The basic requirements for communicating the Joker program could be derived from all levels above in the loyalty pyramid and had to fulfil strategic and tactical objectives: Strategically, the objective is the positioning of the program in the mind of the customer: The program brand as well as strong media coverage plays a significant role for the strategic objectives.

Tactically, ongoing perception of the latest offer is important. Several communication channels must be integrated to launch and distribute the messages: Internet, special events, television, radio, teasers, newspapers and others. An ongoing dialog between Swisscom and the program members reflects effective communication:

- Swisscom to Joker Program Member: Regular newsletters, point statements and target-group-specific communication are important elements.
- Joker Program Member to Swisscom: The main communication contact of the Joker member is the call center where agents redeem points and inform customers about the latest developments in the program.

The customer and household information Swisscom gained when members joined the program allowed the company to target its communication and direct marketing to specific groups.

The loyalty pyramid with its six levels was Swisscom management board's decision on implementation. The Joker infrastructure (processes organization, and information technology) was set up based on the agreed program design.

Joker Infrastructure

The Joker infrastructure secures the successful launch in the marketplace. Defined and trained processes, an effective structure and an effective IT environment are the main elements concerning the infrastructure in such a program.

Processes

The project team estimated that the Joker Loyalty Program would require more than 500 Swisscom employees during its launch period, and they had to be trained before that time. Loyalty programs such as the Joker have two different types of processes: The first is marketing processes such as defining new points collection or redemption offers, producing a member newsletter or similar processes. The second is operational processes such as information about point status, processing applications or similar processes.

Most of the operational processes have been concentrated in the Swisscom call center. For example, points redemption is possible only through the call center. This concentration of operational processes in the call center reduced the amount of interfaces and training. There are two additional advantages to strong involvement of the call-center agents: On the one hand, the infrastructure enables the agents to carry out outbound telesales activities (outbound selling of offers) for Joker in low-intensity phases. On the other hand, the amount of people in the call center enables internal service and support availability to all Joker members.

Organization

Budget responsibility for the whole program has been allocated to a new organizational unit that acts across the product houses with a customer focus. This makes it possible to analyze programs profitability and to secure proper handling of responsibility. Other loyalty program such as Swissair's frequent-flyer program divide up responsibilities and activities through spin-offs.

The Joker organization consists of a Joker management, a financial controller, a call center organization, a program design team (acting together with a responsible product manager from the product houses), a responsible team for campaigns and communication as well as an IT and data-mining team. The organization can be summarized as follows:

Figure 14.7: Joker Organization

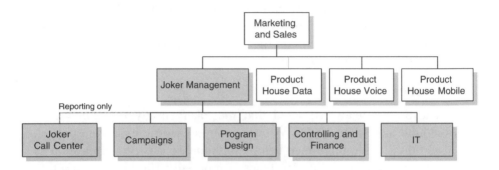

Information Technology

Three main systems became important for the operation of the Joker loyalty program: The Customer Loyalty Software (CLS), the Swisscom Data Warehouse (DWH) and the Campaign Management System.

- The Customer Loyalty Software (CLS) administrates the program member addresses as well as points collection and redemption. This system is customer-oriented and summarizes all accesses of the customer's equipment. For example, a family with two fixed-lines and two mobiles has one Joker account. This enables Swisscom to analyze the overall communication behavior of that family across all products and services. The call-center agents and the staff in the Joker organization are the main users of CLS. In future, the staff at Swisscom's points of sale will have access to CLS, too. In addition, partner systems (such as mileage programs) and the fulfilment center (for mailings and points statements) will be integrated as well.

- The Swisscom Data Warehouse (DWH) is the second important system and provides the necessary transactional information such as billing information to the Customer Loyalty System. In future, the data and information gathered in CLS will be available in the DWH too. This enables Swisscom to carry out more detailed analysis (e.g., with data mining) in areas such as customer behavior, new Joker offerings, reactions to the introduction of new products and services or the existence of target groups. The main users of the DWH are the marketing staff, product house managers and the Joker management.

- The Campaign Management System (CMS) will become the third important element in the IT environment for target-marketing campaigns and win-back activities. Customer reaction to certain campaigns will be gathered in the campaign management software. This will enable Swisscom to target its customers more effectively while reducing marketing and communication costs. The main users of the campaign management system will be marketing and communication as well as the call-center agents.

The three elements CLS, DWH and CMS, build the basis for the administration and management of the Joker. These elements have a close relationship with each other.

Implementation of the Joker

The Joker program design as well as its infrastructure had been implemented within a short period of time. The next section will highlight the respective project-management approach, market reactions and an outlook for the future.

Project Management

The Joker program was implemented based on a structured project approach and good project management. At some stages, it was difficult to coordinate several activities across different organizational units. Standardized platforms for meetings as well as regular progress reports were crucial for success and progress management. The project was implemented in three stages: business plan, implementation and test and teaser.

Figure 14.8: Project Phases and Key Activities

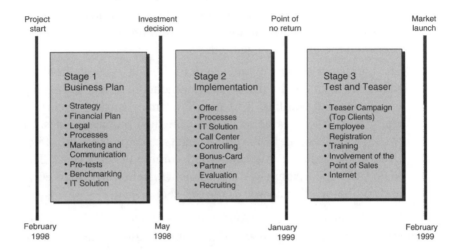

The Joker program was launched successfully. From a project-management point of view, the key challenges were:

- Getting personal commitment from the management board

- Establishing an aggressive timetable to keep all involved project members focused

- Establishing regular communication within the project team as well as formal decision points/milestones

- Managing interdependencies in a project with more than 80 people involved

- Establishing good relations with the product houses to keep them committed

Market Reactions

Given that all the preparatory activities were performed secretly, it was possible to create a surprise and a sustainable advantage in the marketplace. Swisscom's direct competitors became aware of the program only after its launch, and they were thus unable to react in advance, which gave Swisscom positive feedback from customers and the press who perceived Swisscom as innovative.

The first market reactions were positive. More than 25 percent of the most profitable customers joined the program before its launch based on a teaser promotion, and more than 500,000 members joined the Joker program within the first six months. The press published several articles, and TV and radio was positive in most cases.

Outlook for the Future

The Joker program is one example of an aggressive initiative to make a company more customer-focused. The Joker is not a stand-alone activity but works in close relation to other CRM initiatives within the customer relationship management road map for Swisscom. The key challenges for the Joker program in future will be:

- Target the customer behavior to develop new products and services.
- Increase the effectiveness of the information use.
- Keep the attractiveness of the offer for specific target groups (e.g., premium customers).
- Improve support processes (especially in the call center).
- Combine the campaign management with the Joker more effectively.
- Set up win-back programs.
- Include future possibilities with the new technologies such as smart cards.

SUMMARY

Swisscom has made a successful turnaround within a very short time. Its stock price has shown an increase in shareholder value coincident with the launch of customer loyalty programs. So far, Swisscom became CRM—focused due to the following aspects:

- CRM is a strategic topic and has gained management attention.
- Swisscom has established a CRM strategy linking its positioning and customer segmentation with concrete implementation programs.
- Swisscom has recognized that the use of customer information is the source for improvements in marketing and sales activities.

- Swisscom has launched long-term programs in order to serve customers better.

Customer relationship management activities will never come to an end. Therefore, it is important to keep customer orientation in mind to enhance existing programs and to implement additional initiatives, too.

Swisscom has clearly established a linkage between improved performance (profitability and shareholder value) and CRM. But they have also found that success in CRM cannot be established without a focused plan. There was a need to be differentiated in a marketplace that was quickly becoming commoditized. They fought and won, not using tradition price and promotional tools, but by understanding the customer, redefining the processes that touch the customer and setting up technology that could let them stay ahead of the wave.

About the Authors

MICHAEL HOBMEIER

Michael Hobmeier is a Partner in PricewaterhouseCoopers and Leader of the CRM practice in Switzerland.

URS BRINER

Urs Briner is a Principal Consultant in our CRM practice in Switzerland.

Part Five

Enabling the CRM Strategy: Overview

The CRM concept has a lot of potential, but it is still in its infancy. Having the proper strategies in place is important, but it is how you weave them together that is critical. To do that properly you must learn from the best practices of others, and that is the purpose of this part of the book.

We start off with CRM implementation issues, Chapter 15, "Implementing CRM: 20 Steps to Success." But how do we know that we are successful, that we are achieving improved customer satisfaction, and that we are adding value to both the organization and the customer relationship? Enter the balanced scorecard. While a balanced scorecard is an excellent tool for monitoring and tracking slow, steady growth and change, we contend that organizations also need a way of measuring their ability to respond to challenge in today's competitive, fast-changing business environment. The time has come to perhaps "unbalance" the scorecard. Organizations need catalytic measures to supplement their balanced scorecards. Chapter 16, "Using Catalytic Measures to Improve CRM," briefly describes the development and impact of balanced scorecards and then defines a catalytic measure and provides several examples of organizations applying some form of this. Finally, it outlines how an organization might implement its own catalytic measures.

But is CRM a core competency for every organization, and can this relationship with the customer be better enhanced though an outsourced third party that can also have a vested interest in the growth of the customer relationship? Chapter 17, "Best Practices in Outsourcing CRM and Lessons Learned," provides an overview of the CRM outsourcing industry and suggests best practices in planning and managing the outsourcing programs. Our authors argue that everything favors outsourcing: the rapid pace of change and high required investment in the state of the art, the real advantages of the state-of-the-art, economies of scale and several other factors. However, to get the full benefits of outsourcing, businesses must follow certain best practices in planning and managing vendor relationships. Best practices in

outsourcing begin with the selection of the most appropriate vendor for
the business: The functional and strategic alignment of vendor capabilities with company's needs, vendor experience, vendor technologies
and control environment. Best practices in managing outsourcing vendors include: clarity in establishing performance expectations, not
abdicating the "management" of the company's customers to the vendor, proactive measurement and feedback of vendor's performance,
sharing and propagating best practices among multiple vendors, and
maintaining the ability to switch to a new vendor with ease should it be
warranted by shifts in company's business needs.

Culture change must subsequently be addressed and thus we have
Chapter 18, "Learning and Knowledge Management Programs in the
Age of CRM." To build and sustain an effective CRM culture in the age
of e-business, organizations must revamp and significantly realign
their traditional learning and knowledge management programs. This
can mean a need to start with an analysis of required competencies
and run through development and delivery of continuous learning
systems and knowledge management programs and tools.

Ironically, the very cause of this change also may help solve the
learning and knowledge management challenge, at least in terms of
supporting infrastructure. Internet-based virtual universities open to
staff, suppliers and customers may address the need for quick and
integrated learning. Internet sites that facilitate the creation of personalized Web portals may be an ultimate answer, for they embody the
essence of a CRM culture from a learning and knowledge management
perspective—getting customers, suppliers and staff just what they
need when they need it. This chapter thus addresses the fundamental
shift in competencies and some of the resulting implications for learning and knowledge management.

We close with Chapter 19, "Implementing CRM: The Need for
Performance Alignment." Many organizations talk about performance
measurement and standards, but few take the next step toward performance management. The entire measurement system must be aligned
to the CRM strategy and a culture of continuous improvement must be
established. While the example provided relates to a public sector case
study, the principles provided have universal applicability—a structured and balanced approach to performance management must
exist. Without it, alignment will not be created, and sub optimization
of the CRM strategy will occur.

Thus we have five key best practices to consider on the road to a successful CRM strategy. Each practice is necessary to enable the over-arching CRM strategy and its core sub-strategies (customer strategy, product and channel strategy, and infrastructure strategy).

CHAPTER FIFTEEN

Implementing CRM:

20 STEPS TO SUCCESS

Henrik Andersen
Per Ø. Jacobsen

ALL TOO OFTEN, organizations believe the solution to their problem is new or better technology. Software and hardware vendors claim that their product is the most versatile and flexible CRM solution, one that will meet your current as well as future needs. Research, including a recent Gartner report, has shown that the "silver bullet" does not exist. To achieve a CRM strategy, an organization cannot rely exclusively on a system solution—software products that allow the organization to track and retrieve information on the customer, that track and prompt sales activity and allow the customer service representative to be informed while servicing and cross-selling the customer—by phone or Web.

And even if they have taken the time to think through their customer strategy and channel and product strategy, without a properly implemented infrastructure strategy success will not be achievable. There are many pitfalls in implementing CRM. Often, the benefits promised by systems suppliers are not realized in practice, even though one has chosen the "right" system. Why do things sometimes go wrong, and why are many companies not able to achieve the performance breakthrough that lives up to their investments in technology? There are many reasons, among them:

- Anchoring
- Resource needs
- Unrealistic expectations
- Lack of sufficient training

Anchoring—Ensuring that the initiative has a solid foundation and support system is extremely important. Too often, the implementation of IT systems is seen as an isolated process confined to the boundaries of the IT department alone. In practice the implementation projects are change projects that transform the affected part of the company into a new enterprise, one that is more focused on the customer and on improvement of the company's relationship with them. Therefore, it is of utmost importance that the implementation project is anchored within a high level of the organization and outside the IT department.

Resource needs—The internal and external resources required to customize and implement the software solution for a CRM implementation are usually underestimated. This applies to both the number and type of resources needed. Acceptance of the status quo, lack of will to change and an over-focus on the present situation rather than the desired future outcome result in huge extra costs, or in the worst case scenario failure to achieve the planned business improvement.

Unrealistic expectations—normally the purchase of a CRM system creates unrealistic expectation with regard to both the implementation project and the resulting business improvements. As a starting point a new system does not deliver any improvement advantages, if the business process and installation are redesigned simultaneously.

Lack of sufficient training—The importance of a thorough and detailed training program to the end users is often overlooked. In many cases, staff have not been sufficiently trained in the new CRM system and typically use less than 50 percent of the application's functionality. Organizations are so rushed to put in a new system that proper training is short cut. There is no time to train, the organization is behind schedule and typically over budget and starts to cut back. What a waste.

"If, a decade ago, we had had a greater understanding of the business and organizational dynamics of technology, I think we would now have an even greater payback from our investment in it. In my experience, the new systems that work best are those that are aligned not only with the business but also with the way people think and work."

Bob L. Martin, CEO of Wal-Mart Stores
Source: PricewaterhouseCoopers study 1997

Regardless of the extent of the system implementation, it is necessary to have a strong business focus to ensure the necessary change in processes, organization, people and culture. It is naive to believe that the introduction of a new CRM system will bring improvements if work conditions are left unchanged. The equation below illustrates the problem:

NT +OO = EOO
New Technology + Old Organization = Expensive Old Organization

Doing things the same way typically gives marginal improvements. New technology can take you only so far in creating fundamental change and improving CRM. Changes to processes, organization structure, people and culture are required. To be effective in implementing a CRM system solution, the 20 steps below can help. These will be examined under four main categories:

- Business-Oriented Solutions (1–3)
- Project Management (4–8)
- Change Management (9–14)
- Implementation Strategy and Planning (15–20)

BUSINESS-ORIENTED SOLUTIONS

1. Set Precise Goals

In this group of steps, the organization sets the stage—what processes are important, what goals will show success. But more than goals, it is a recognition that it takes people (middle, senior and front-line resources) to be involved to add value to the design and to support the initiative.

It is important that a CRM solution is business-oriented. This means that the solution should reflect the way the enterprise wishes to work in the future. To do this, it is necessary to start with the enterprise's CRM strategy and to ensure that once implemented the system will support the customer, channel and product strategies. The CRM strategy should be supplemented with concrete goals that can be used as reference points during the implementation process and can also function as critical success factors for the finished CRM solution. Don't be afraid to set some outrageous goals, as well as some realistic ones. These goals can be items such as "X% of new business attained, X% of increased sales through cross-selling opportunities; improvement in effectiveness of sales campaigns," and other similar objectives.

2. Involve all Departments Affected

The heads of the departments that are affected by the implementation should be involved. From the start they should understand the necessity of reaching an agreement concerning implementation goals. At the same time, it should be emphasised that the success of the process depends on the active involvement of the managers. This can be in the form of investing resources (e.g., business specialists to ensure that the processes and system are designed to meet their needs during the design stage) and in their willingness to "sell" the change internally in the organization. They must be advocates of this initiative.

3. Use the Best Employees in the Enterprise

It is necessary to involve the employees who best understand the business in this process. These business experts, in the role of process owners, must help define the business processes in conjunction with the CRM technicians. In other words, they must help define the CRM system's functionality—screen overviews, report formats, etc.

The advantage of involving employees as process owners is that the solution will almost certainly live up to the daily requirements of company users in terms of functionality—what will be tracked, what response time is required, what screen views will be needed, what reports must be produced. In addition, these process owners, in conjunction with the department heads, can act as front figures and help sell the change process to the organization.

PROJECT MANAGEMENT

The best of intentions is not enough. There must be rigor to the process and its key deliverables. This means that the effort must be well coordinated, follow a defined and agreed upon schedule with checkpoints and have active involvement from as many employees in the organization as is feasible.

4. Influence the Organization

Change management is a central element in project management. CRM software systems today build on new ways of thinking, which many organizations do not currently practice. "Team-based selling" is a good example because in this type of selling the sales representatives no longer act as individual hunters but rather as a team supported by the rest of the organization. Naturally this places new demands on how the sales force coordinates sales activities and shares information that previously was the individual sales representatives' responsibility and security (the salesperson, not the organization, owned the customer). If during the change process, this change in operating practice is not taken into consideration, implementation may meet resistance from employees and the business value of the implementation may be significantly reduced.

5. Coordinate with Other Enterprise Initiatives

Project managers are also responsible for coordinating the CRM project with other enterprise activities and projects. In the case of large projects or when several projects are being implemented at the same time, the project manager's main task is to coordinate the different projects, for example, ERP, e-business and/or CRM projects. The following Figure shows the organization of a project that includes both CRM and IT project implementations.

Figure 15.1: Typical Management Organization

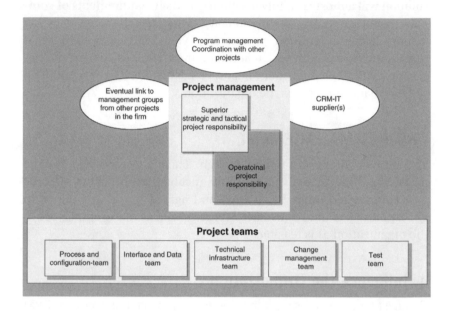

When putting together a project organization, one must include all the people in the enterprise who are involved in the project. As the Figure shows, this will require involvement of Information Technology (IT), process specialists and management, all knit and working together. External parties such as CRM-IT suppliers and external consultants should also be included in the project organization. However, the overall strategic management of the project must always be the responsibility of the enterprise itself.

6. Follow the Project's Progress Carefully

Despite the fact that good plans are initially put in place, a lack of diligence can result in sub-optimization when it comes to ensuring the success of a project, many mistakes are made. Often the enterprise discovers too late that the project plan is behind schedule. The project may seem to be moving forward because there is a lot of activity—but important deadlines are still far in the future. Miscalculations may arise but do not seem serious at the time. Gradually, as the project progresses past the various milestones, a picture begins to emerge of the tasks that have not been given sufficient attention (such as change management); but this does not cause management to pump more employees into the project either. Unfortunately in cases like this, the true CRM strategic goals will begin to fade and the solution will not be sufficiently anchored in the enterprise.

Time after time it has been demonstrated that the unexpected happens. That is why it is necessary to continually follow up and adjust the plan in relation to the original project goals. There are numerous reasons for project delays. Some are legitimate and acceptable, but others are a direct result of the lack of precise planning or no planning at all. But merely making a plan does not necessarily mean solving the problem. It is also important to follow up the plan with work. In other words, *"plan the work and work the plan."*

7. Respect Interfaces, Conversions and Data Transfer

The risk of insufficient planning is especially great when it comes to the development of interfaces, conversion and transfer of existing data. In some cases, these areas are themselves the project. If the converted data is not in order and the necessary interfaces do not have sufficient capacity, the system will not achieve its goals; in fact, it may not function at all. Quality assurance of data conversion as well as performance tests of the interfaces must therefore be undertaken as early as possible in the process.

The general performance of the system, including system tests, is another critical point that requires expert know-how. If a salesperson in the field is going to be able to obtain the maximum benefit from his or her laptop, the transfer of data must be fast and easy.

8. Involve Many Individuals

At an early stage of the project, it is necessary to involve a greater part of the organization than just the process owners. This is because it requires time to adjust to the changes brought about by CRM. Best practice shows that best results are achieved if about a third of the employees are somehow involved. This will then cause a great degree of buy-in and future positive word-of-mouth. Employees can participate in the development work, in meetings or in testing. In this way, they are able to learn about the system and hear how it will affect their daily work.

If employees are not involved, it is often difficult to ensure the necessary commitment to using the CRM software system. In the long term, this will affect the survival of the solution. Questions such as ownership of basic data, updating and so on may also cause many problems if employees do not understand the changes right from the start.

CHANGE MANAGEMENT

More than change in process and systems is required—a change in culture and practice must shadow this initiative. It is essential that senior management be on side. Communication cannot be ignored or given limited attention; it must play an active and supportive role. Training is a integral component of communication and must once again play a central role. Change causes fear, unrest and uncertainty for most people, so change management must address and neutralize these issues.

9. Find a Sponsor

The project needs a sponsor whose personal goals are directly linked to its success. The sponsor can help identify the resources and reduce the resistance of employees and can ensure that the system will survive once the consultants have left the enterprise. The best sponsors are often found in top management. Because of their positions, they have enough influence to find the necessary resources and accelerate the decision-making process. At the same time, they are able to coordinate the process with other change initiatives and make important decisions. Sponsors are especially effective when changes are to be communicated to employees. By participating actively in the process, they appear as project ambassadors, and when the changes are to be sold internally, these ambassadors can help employees understand the project vision, thus positively influencing employee perception of the project.

10. Speed Progress through a Sense of Urgency

It is the responsibility of management to create a sense of urgency and decisiveness to give the project the impetus necessary to ensure ongoing progress based on the project vision and guidelines. Management's direct involvement in the project and ongoing communication about the significance of the CRM initiative are decisive for the success of the project.

11. Make it Attractive to Participate in the Project

In large projects, the changes will require the full involvement of certain employees at various times. To create an effective work climate and to make it attractive to participate in the project, employees who are involved should know what their new positions in the organization would be after the changes. They should know that they will not be at risk by participating, rather that their value to the organization will increase. The project must not be used as a place to park "difficult" employees but as an opportunity for the best to shine.

12. Communicate Continually with Interested Parties

Communication is one of the most important ingredients when it comes to developing understanding for a CRM solution. From the start, change should be presented as aimed toward the business side and not the IT side. Employees must understand that the enterprise is initiating the project to achieve business benefits in the form of loyalty, cross-sales, improved customer service and such, and that all activities aim to maintain the competitiveness of the enterprise—and its ability to retain competent employees.

During the project, participants will come into contact with large parts of the organization and thus they are an important group when it comes to communications. All of these people should therefore have a good understanding of the whole project and be able to answer general questions such as: why is this necessary? and how is it going to benefit the company and me?

The following tips can help make a communication program a success:

- When choosing communicators, the enterprise should be selective. These people should be well-respected and perceived as reliable sources of information.
- One should avoid the enterprise "jungle drums" because they can be difficult to control.
- Employee understanding of the project must be kept up to date.
- There should be a steady stream of communication. Management should not be afraid to repeat key messages.
- Middle managers are good communicators and at the same time important supporters of the project.

- Employees should have the opportunity to come forward with feedback and ideas through "town hall" meetings.
- "Picture language" should be used to avoid too many details—a picture is worth a thousand words—use it to your advantage.
- All information about the project should be collected in a database and made available to all employees.

Communication does not come just from top management and the project team. Employee attitudes and thus their acceptance of the CRM solution are strongly influenced by other employees in the organization, in particular those that they respect, admire and follow. That is why at all times throughout the project, the project team should identify those influential people whose support is necessary for the success of the project. In situations where the person's support is not forthcoming, the team should try to find out what can be done to change the person's attitude.

In order to send the right messages to the right people, planning of communication must be guided by the individual's position in relation to the project. The model below can be used for this purpose.

Figure 15.2: Stakeholder Management

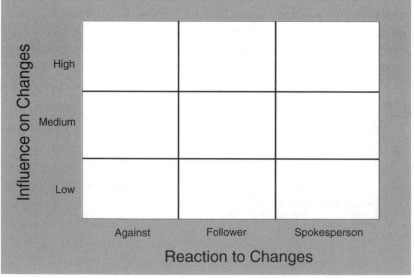

The model is based on the expected reactions to change. Advocates for the project should be identified as should individuals and groups who resist change in relation to the CRM project. The communications plan should be checked against the knowledge or power these individuals and groups have in relation to the changes. Individuals or organizational units that are found in the upper right-hand corner of the chart can be used to advantage as spokespersons. In this way, their position and attitudes can be used to influence other individuals and units in the right direction. At the same time, those who are high to the left on the chart are an important goal for communication and change management. If their resistance is ignored, it could affect the success of the project.

13. Keep a Steady Head (Stay Cool!)

Experience demonstrates that project managers typically go through several emotional phases, as shown in Figure 15.3 below. At the start of the project, participants will be optimistic and generally have great expectations. During this period, hopes should not be pumped up too much. It is important that management control employee anticipation and not over-sell the project. These great expectations typically disappear when the involved parties discover how much energy a CRM project demands. In addition, the complexity of the project increases as it gets under way and this causes a further loss of interest—and in the worst case a sense of defeat. During this phase, communication plays a decisive role. If the enterprise can reap so-called *quick-wins*, it is a good idea to save them until this phase of the project to keep up the momentum.

Figure 15.3: Employee Reactions to Change

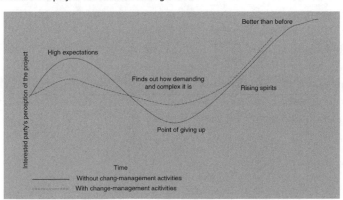

After this defeatist phase, the involved parties have usually passed the first midway stations on the journey. Then the level of expectations rises again as the CRM-IT solution begins to take shape. The dotted line in Figure 15.3 shows how a strong focus on change management can influence employee reactions throughout a project. It reduces the swings in the curves and makes implementation more effective.

14. Don't Skimp on Training and Education

Training both project participants and users is a prerequisite for a successful project. And only through training can the enterprise ensure that all involved parties know what to expect in terms of the solution of their particular tasks. All too often, the enterprise overlooks the fact that not all employees have the necessary general IT skills and that only a few understand the CRM technical or infrastructure concept. The first step of training should therefore give the target audience a business understanding of CRM.

Explain the overall strategy, the customer strategy and what it is based on: The desired end state of the channel and product strategy and how this will impact the success and future of the organization. After that, attention can be directed toward IT. In particular, lack of IT know-how often creates a situation in which employees feel insecure and unsure of themselves. Rumors about change increase this uncertainty and training becomes ineffective.

Only few people are able to absorb everything they hear during a traditional training session. Various teaching methods may be used to promote retention of information. Training could take place in the classroom, on the job, or it could be computer-based. The results of training programs improve when the teachers actively involve their students. This means that training programs should be as interactive as possible and preferably relate to the employees' everyday work situation. And if employees are allowed to test the new enterprise systems on their own PCs, their sense of familiarity can be increased. When employees learn new skills, their self-esteem increases; they feel more secure and have more self-confidence.

THE IMPLEMENTATION STRATEGY AND PLANNING

Now onto the work itself. A plan of action that will ensure success must be put in place. The home-run is not needed. A logical progression of small improvements leading to the full-scale CRM strategy is necessary, each with its own set of quick wins. And it is equally important not to overcomplicate the process and implementation so dramatically that change and currency cannot be maintained. The organization must continue to be nimble to address changing customer needs.

15. Consider Using Rapid Application Design (RAD)

Many things must be taken into consideration when defining an implementation strategy. The risks of the various strategies differ greatly, and this is often closely connected to the resources the enterprise has at its disposal. It is important, for example, that the project's ongoing design work is evaluated on the basis of how the finished solution will live up to the CRM strategy. Thus, it is important to focus on functional requirements (how must the salesperson use this to check the status of orders, credits or invoice payments) and seek a reasonable technical solution. This might not be the most advanced solution in the technician's eyes but a solution that offers a good return on investment.

16. The Profitability of Implementation

Choosing to implement a solution in every corner of the organization is not necessarily optimal. The acquisition of hardware, software, training programs, the development of local interfaces and so on requires significant investments. A good tactic is to choose those parts of the organization that will reap the greatest benefit from implementation and chose them for its first wave. A carefully selected pilot implementation will go a long way in giving confidence to those that must make the final decision on financing the roll-out throughout the organization.

17. Avoid Over-Specialized Solutions

When the enterprise tries to meet all the demands of functionality that the process owners want to introduce, it runs the risk of customizing the CRM software beyond its ability. Very few systems on the market are flexible enough to allow such a high degree of freedom. CRM systems that are highly customized can quickly become very costly and obsolete (the cost to maintain and support them will be prohibitive and changes of updates will be cumbersome).

It is therefore always a good idea to challenge the demands and specifications of the specialists to see if the same efficiency could be achieved using other methods or processes. As well, highly customized CRM systems cause particular difficulties when being upgraded to newer software versions. Special coded changes will typically be lost on an upgrade of a new version and it is therefore necessary to make a new code once more. Careful documentation of the configuration and changes in code are a vital element in every CRM-IT implementation.

18. Be Critical in Choice of Method

Experience with CRM implementation suggests that what is required is to a method for integrating IT with the business aspects of a solution. As shown in Figure 15.4, there must be a logical sequence of activities, from analysis through to implementation, together with a realistic timeline. The first stage is often the one that is too rushed—why look at something that will change? But without doing that, you will never be able to gauge success.

Figure 15.4: CRM System Management Method

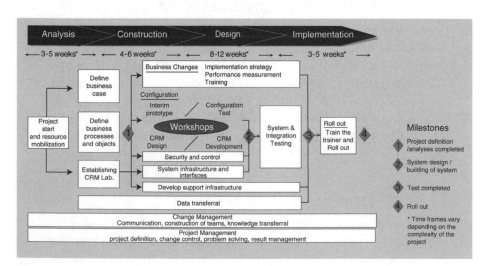

Each stop flows from the other to form a logical progression. And underpinning this is change management and project management.

19. Prepare Implementation Waves

In connection with dividing the implementation of CRM into different waves or progressions, the various parts of the organization have a right to know when it will be their turn. Before the start of a roll-out to a certain group or department, time must be set aside for installing the hardware and the enterprise should be sure that the employees have the necessary CRM and IT skills.

20. Focus on Quick Wins

To promote a willingness to change, top management normally needs to quickly show some quick wins to the organization to convince employees that the CRM efforts are worth the effort. Quick wins are convincing sales arguments for a CRM project to interested parties within the organization. Thus, management often tries to achieve several large quick wins at the start of a project to create the necessary momentum. In some cases, the improved earnings achieved by quick wins at the beginning of a project can almost pay for the rest of it. This highlights the importance of utilizing quick wins effectively.

With the above guidelines in mind, a CRM project is on the right track from the start. As Will Rogers once said "Being on the right track is not enough, you can still get run over by the train." The principles that have been explained in the 20 steps above, provide you with a route, a set of tracks to follow. You must keep on the track, speed up when required and change tracks when necessary—but always be in control.

QUESTIONS FOR THE READER:

- How many people from top management are part of the CRM project steering group?
- Has a visible connection between the enterprise's overall strategy and the CRM project been established?
- Has the company a clear feeling of the benefits the CRM implementation can create?

- Is it attractive to participate in the CRM project?
- Is the CRM project coordinated with other projects in your company?
- Has a training program with appropriate modules been developed with the project?
- Does the project group communicate regularly inside the company?
- Does the project make use of the participation of recognized and competent business-oriented employees?
- Does the project try to minimize the extent of company-specific customization?
- Does the project use a well-proven method and do the project participants understand it?
- How much money is there in the budget for internal communications?

About the Authors

HENRIK ANDERSEN

Henrik Andersen is a Partner in PricewaterhouseCoopers Management Consulting and Nordic Group Leader of its CRM consulting practice.

PER Ø. JACOBSEN

Per O. Jacobsen is a Principal Consultant with PricewaterhouseCoopers Management Consultants, based in Copenhagen, Denmark. His primary focus has been CRM consulting encompassing Sales and Marketing.

CHAPTER SIXTEEN

Using Catalytic Measures to Improve CRM

Dr. Nancy Staisey
Cathy M. Stanmeyer

W HAT GETS MEASURED gets done is a business truism, but while most would agree with this point, actually defining measures that can effectively drive performance and behavior is very difficult. In a recent survey, senior executives in the US and Europe reported that customer focus and innovation (in particular product innovation) would be the key engines of future performance improvement for their companies. Yet, the majority said that they are failing to measure these important strategic drivers effectively.[1]

During the past decade, many corporations have worked to improve their processes and performance by developing a balanced scorecard approach to self-measurement. This highlights the importance of tracking performance in a number of different areas, rather than relying purely on sales figures, revenue results or other purely bottom-line related measures. Numerous organizations have improved performance and more effectively linked it to strategy by using a balanced scorecard.

---

[1] PricewaterhouseCoopers, *Managing Corporate Performance Today and Tomorrow*, 1999.

Indeed, the scorecard has become an integral part of many organizations' customer relationship management, for it contains a "customer perspective" designed to ensure effective market segmentation, customer profitability and retention management. However, by its very balance, the scorecard can impede necessary quick changes and fail to effect the type of change in focus required.

THE BALANCED SCORECARD

In the early 1990s, Robert Kaplan and David Norton introduced the then-revolutionary concept of the balanced scorecard performance measurement.[2] They argued that organizations and managers were not effectively capturing their true performance when they tracked only financial measures. While financial measures are unambiguous, they do not show other less-quantifiable but still critical measures of performance, and firms need to assess their performance by looking forward as well as backward.

Kaplan and Norton pointed out that a balanced scorecard could be used to not only measure past performance but also model future strategy and build a cohesive approach for future competitive success. The scorecard becomes a strategic management system for achieving long-term goals, allowing organization leaders to set future performance standards even while guiding current activity. Accordingly, they suggested companies create unique scorecards reflective of their own businesses that contained four key perspectives:

- Financial Objectives—How do we look at our shareholders?
- Customer Outcomes—How do our customers perceive us?
- Internal Business Processes—In what areas must we excel?
- Learning and Growth—How can we continue to grow and develop?[3]

Considering performance, past and future, through these lenses allows organizations to answer questions and develop a cause and effect business strategy for the organization. By focusing on "lead" indicators (not those measured in time lags), management could truly

---

[2] Robert S. Kaplan and David P. Norton, "The Balanced Scorecard—Measures That Drive Performance," *Harvard Business Review*, January-February 1992, pp. 71–79.
[3] Kaplan and Norton, "The Balanced Scorecard—Measures That Drive Performance," p. 72.

understand the organization's performance drivers and could thus artic-ulate the business' strategy, communicate that strategy effectively and align initiatives toward that common goal.

The balanced scorecard approach has become commonplace in the past decade. Organizations use some form of it for everything from product and program performance to staff internal review and evalua-tion processes. Firms such as Rockwater, Apple Computer, Sears, FMC Corporation and PricewaterhouseCoopers all use a balanced scorecard to set and track performance goals. In fact, several niche firms have developed software and other scorecard support materials that they actively market.

Initially the balanced scorecard was welcomed by many who were focused on customer relationship management, because it put cus-tomer-based measures front and center for executives, many of whom had previously focused almost exclusively on financial performance measures.

Clearly, the balanced scorecard performance measurement has been an excellent tool for monitoring and tracking slow and steady growth and change in a more comprehensive way. In addition, repeated strong performance in a number of scorecard perspectives demon-strates stability. But does a balanced scorecard provide an organization a means to effect positive change quickly? In today's fast-paced market, competition has increased and customers are better informed than ever before. A balanced scorecard can provide some indication of corporate success, but firms are even better served if they supplement the score-card with catalytic measures as well.

WHAT IS A CATALYTIC MEASURE?

A catalytic measure by its very nature catalyzes—creates conditions necessary for—change. Catalytic measures focus an organization's effort on an identifiable change. Their implementation motivates and speeds change to a new way of approaching a particular problem, ser-vice, customer segment or even line of business.

The best catalytic measures are those that have face validity to customers and staff. All can agree that the organization would be bet-ter could it implement this approach, and the public nature of the ini-tiative allows clients/customers to judge performance based on clear, obvious criteria. For example, drivers frequently see signs on the back

---

Catalytic Measure 1: PricewaterhouseCoopers Includes "Cooperativeness" in Partner Evaluations

When PricewaterhouseCoopers began integrating its European practices, it initially had problems getting its partners to cooperate. Each country's practice, and even each partner within those practices, was used to controlling their own organization and making unilateral decisions. They had never had to consider the "greater good" before and were culturally ill-prepared to do so.

So firm leadership decided to take action. It identified a way to draw attention to each partner's willingness to pull together. The European leadership instituted a quarterly partner survey that required each partner to answer two questions about any other partner they'd worked with during the part quarter:

1. How much contact have you had with this individual?
2. How helpful was this individual?

Information collected in the survey was used in the firm's annual partner evaluation process (which is important in determining partner compensation.) The survey was a clear catalytic measure. Its goal: To start people talking. Leadership realized that once a dialog began, the various players would realize they could help each other and would begin working together. The hard part was getting them to the first conversation. The measure was successful becasue it had a clearly defined objective, it was public and it was transparent.

---

of trucks that announce: "Safe driving is my priority. How am I doing? Call 1-800-xxx-xxxx." This program is a public statement of a service goal that can be easily judged by the general public. This type of measure can stimulate an almost immediate change in behavior on the part of a driver the day the sign goes on the truck. It is clear to the driver that feedback can be immediate and specific—i.e., traceable to the individual driver.

Further, catalytic measures empower and convince staff that they can achieve some result without offering those employees any actual monetary incentive or formal personal recognition. The way the measure is defined engages and includes the employees so that their own pride ensures they will attempt to meet whatever requests are made of them.

ROAD MAP FOR IMPLEMENTING A CATALYTIC MEASURE PROGRAM

While all will agree that implementing a catalytic measures program makes sense, more than lip service is required. Steps must be put in place to ensure that the right measures are created, to support the required change or practice, and that it be done quickly and effectively. There are four primary steps to implementing a catalytic measure:

- Identify the Area Needing Change
- Identify a Relevant Milestone
- Create a Measurement Approach
- Announce and Implement the Program Quickly

These steps vary in complexity and detail.

Identify the Area Needing Change

The first step to successfully introducing a catalytic measure is to identify the part of the organization that is truly facing some challenge that is ultimately affecting the service it provides and therefore requires change. This area might be broad. "Customers are writing letters to the CEO indicating our customer service is poor," or it might be narrow—"Our phone response times at our call center are not satisfactory." The goal is to clearly delineate what the customer needs from the organization and where the organization is failing to meet these needs. Often this step seems simple: The organization is very aware of a particular problem and executives feel strongly about the need for new behavior. However, it is important to truly focus on the source of the problem and choose one area to target, rather than trying to fix a host of problems with one catalytic program.

Identify a Relevant Milestone

Identifying a relevant milestone for the type of change sought is perhaps the most critical step in the process. This milestone should be directly linked to the desired change, and it should definitively change when the area changes. For instance, the US Postal Service knew that it needed to improve the speed at which it served its customers. So leadership in North Carolina identified a clear marker linked directly to the necessary improvement: USPS clerk speed as compared to clerk speed at the local fast-food restaurants.

Catalytic Measure #2:
The US Postal Service Issues a Service Guarantee

Customer feedback on postal service in the southeastern postal region indicated that consumers were most frustrated with the time they spent waiting in line at postal stations. Once they were served, they believed the clerks were generally friendly and knowledgeable, but the line wait had them so aggravated that they generally left the office with bad tastes in their mouths.

To resolve this customer perception in a clear, easily verifiable way, a North Carolina division manager issued a challenge to his employees, customers and the media. He claimed that post offices in the part of North Carolina were meeting the same service standards as the local McDonald's restaurants (which were offering "Service in XXX minutes, or it is free.") The manager challenged customers and the press to test his claim.

This catalytic measure was immediately effective. Postal clerks were quickly engaged and began a sort of competition to improve service time. They could understand and identify their success or failure on a personal level on a daily basis. On average, the postal clerks did provide faster service than the McDonalds' against which they were being compared.

In addition, the milestone or trigger should be tied to the customer interface/experience and chosen to be readily judged by both the customer and the service provider. As a result, the marker will show an immediate response. For example, a European airport has attempted to improve its performance in passenger security by announcing its results directly to its customers. Passengers walking through the security checkpoint see a sign informing them that the airport is moving passengers through security on time between hours X to Y, Z% of the time. This provides the customer with some information, but it is not directly linked to any one passenger's experience, nor can any passenger identify success or failure. On the other hand, a catalytic measure the airport might implement would be to post a similar sign that guaranteed on-time performance or the passenger would be given something, like being moved to the front of the security line on the next trip or given a voucher for a free drink in the airport lounge. While the existing program measures performance, the catalytic program would motivate change. Moreover, the customer could judge its success. Customers want consequences; they don't care what happens overall if they personally have poor experiences.

Key Questions to Ask When Creating a Catalytic Measure

- Is this measure unique and directly linked to the area I want to improve?
- Can my employees understand this measure with minimal explanation?
- Would my customers agree that the change I'm seeking is good?
- Do my customers value the measure I'm proposing?
- Is the measure tangible?
- Can the measure be implemented quickly (in a day or a week?)
- Will feedback be fast?

Finally, the marker should be simple enough to implement quickly. For instance, many retail firms use mystery shopping programs to develop data on how clerks respond to customer needs. But these programs measure current behavior; the test is not obvious to real customers and does not contribute to change—at least not at the time of implementation. Moreover, a mystery shopping program requires the firm to make up a sample, develop a scoring method, arrange and conduct shopping visits and finally report the data—results that can take months to develop. By contrast, the $5 program at the major bank was easily implemented and showed an immediate response—customers and employees could look at the clock and see whether the bank's line-wait promise was being met. Measurement was actually conducted by the consumers themselves, who directly understood the impact on their experience.

Catalytic Measure #3: The $5 Program at a Major Bank

The CEO of a major bank was facing change in his industry. Recognizing that competition was increasing and the organization needed to improve customer service to develop and retain customers, he invested in a program to improve the customer service and customer-facing processes in his banks. The program was designed to enhance customers' experience at the branch level. Using information gathered at local focus groups on transforming the customer experience, the improvement program provided training for clerks and other branch officials and it was accompanied by a significant marketing campaign.

After the improvement program had been fully implemented, the bank asked customers to evaluate it. Surprisingly, customers could not identify much that had changed. At the same time, the bank headquarters was also trying to improve service by providing more ATMs to improve customer access. Although headquarters pressed for installation of additional ATMs, the local branches pushed back, arguing they lacked space for the ATM terminal and that cramping already busy branch lobbies was not the way to increase customer satisfaction.

Faced with this resistance as well as the unimpressive customer response to the service improvement program, the CEO decided they needed a bolder stroke. He redefined the bank's measure of customer service to line wait. The bank then began a major ad campaign to inform customers, "If you wait in line for longer than five minutes, we will give you $5."

Introduction of this one catalytic measure produced two dramatic and surprising results:

1. The branches giving away the most $5 wait fees were those that had been seen by headquarters as strong, effective performers. Why? Branches that made things easier for headquarters were perceived as good. They were meeting centralized reporting deadlines, responding to higher level requests in a timely fashion and so on, but they were servicing headquarters, not their customers. By contrast, the branches headquarters had identified as poor or failing performers actually focused on the customer, had shorter line waits and paid fewer fees.

2. A few days after implementing the new performance program, headquarters experienced a sudden surge in requests for ATM terminals. Space had not suddenly opened up in those branches. Rather, employees had actually learned and benefited from the customer service training program and were realizing that to effectively use what they'd learned, they needed time to devote to customers with actual service problems. ATMs would not cramp already busy lobbies, they would actually reduce congestion, for lines would decrease if some customers served themselves.

By using a catalytic measure to supplement its existing performance measurement system, the bank brought about immediate change and improvement in customer statisfaction. Creating a visible measure branch employees could see (and understand the implications of failing to carry out) changed handquarters' perspective on branch performance. In addition, it stimulated clerks to implement techniques they'd learned in the retraining program but had previously ignored.

Create a Measurement Approach

An effective measurement approach will make normally intangible results such as improved customer satisfaction more tangible. It is a means of quantifying the link between the area needing change and the relevant milestone discussed above. Specifically, the measurement approach needs to be simple enough to implement quickly and identifiable to employees and customers alike.

Specificity is key. For instance, one airline developed an employee thank-you program through which frequent travelers were given thank-you coupons to award to employees they felt were providing good service. Supervisors noted that certain employees received many of these coupons and took that result into consideration during evaluations. This program was specific to the successful action—the "good" employee received the customer's and ultimately the supervisor's direct notice. By contrast, restaurant comment cards that invite guests to critique the service they received do not necessarily provide a direct, measurable link to good service that the customer and the employee can see and quickly identify.

Announce and Implement the Program Quickly

The final step is to announce and quickly implement the catalytic program. An organization should first clearly explain the program's goals and underlying strategy to its employees. By informing and empowering them, the organization is ensuring a clear "direction or focus." Staff will buy into the program and be motivated to meet its requirements if they understand both why their performance is being measured and how their efforts relate to strategic goals.

Catalytic Measure #4:
Canada's Training Program for Unemployed Fishermen

Due to depleted stocks of cod fish, the Canadian government was forced to place a moratorium on fishing, putting 40,000 fisherment out of work. To proactively address this problem, Canada funded a special employment-training program for those affected. In the past, Canada used a balanced scorecard to measure the success of such programs. They focused on metrics such as:

- number of program entrants
- number of individuals completing program
- cost per participant
- number of counseling sessions scheduled
- number of participants placed in new jobs

But Canada decided to try something new for this program. They chose to judge success on only two measures: 1) number of program participants who found long-term employment (measured as employment for more than XX months) and 2) monetary savings to the Canadian Employment Insurance Fund.

These requirements forced the employment counselors running the program to reassess the value of the training they provided and tailor it more carefully to the likely needs of the individual participants. The program was refocused away from quick placement (which often resulted in only short-term employment) to preparing participants for long-term employment in a position paying enough to avoid the need for unemployment benefits.

The Canadian government tracked the program using a database and several surveys. Results showed significant improvement over previous programs because the performance metrics were limited and transparent. By utilizing catalytic measures, Canada quickly effected a true cultural change in employment counselors' behavior.

After explaining the program to employees, the organization should announce it to the public and begin it as quickly as possible. By definition, a major goal of any catalytic program is to quickly stimulate change. Accordingly, rapid announcement or advertisement of the program is critical. In addition, it goes without saying that the organization must hold to its commitment—PricewaterhouseCoopers, for example (see Catalytic Measure #1), had to use the feedback it received as part of its future evaluation criteria. Similarly, the major bank (see Catalytic Measure #3) would have lost all credibility if it refused to pay a customer who contended she'd waited longer than five minutes. By creating a measure that engages the customer, the organization becomes that much more accountable to that customer.

CONCLUSION

This chapter has described the relevance and significance of catalytic measures for firms seeking to improve their customer relationships. We have described the common balanced scorecard method of performance measurement and identified situations in which an organization needs to effect immediate radical change and must therefore rely on a different approach to measuring and improving its performance. After describing catalytic measures, we have detailed how an organization might implement them. Sidebars highlighting successful catalytic programs provide additional examples demonstrating how some organizations use these measures to effect change and improve customer service and customer relationships.

Leading organizations are responding to the increasing challenges in the today's changing business environment by focusing on developing and implementing the appropriate strategy to meet their customers' needs. As technology provides customers with access to more information and more alternatives, firms can no longer rely on customer loyalty. They must continuously seek to better manage and improve their performance so as to retain and even gain customers.

The first step for any such improvement program is to recognize that the current situation is unsatisfactory but change is achievable. Each of the organizational leaders in the examples contained in this chapter took that first step. They identified a problem area that demanded change and recognized that externally focused measures could lead them to that change. The heads of the highlighted organizations understood that to improve their customer relationships, they needed quick, immediate action that was easy to measure. They implemented programs accordingly and focused not on leading indicators but on those that themselves lead change. The result: catalytic programs producing empowered employees better serving more satisfied customers.

About the Authors

DR. NANCY STAISEY

Dr. Nancy Staisey is a Partner in PricewaterhouseCoopers' America's CRM management consulting practice. She currently serves as leader of PWC's Global Postal Industry Team.

CATHY M. STANMEYER

Cathy M. Stanmeyer is a Principal Consultant in the above mentioned group.

CHAPTER SEVENTEEN

Best Practices in Outsourcing CRM and Lessons Learned

Gina Boulton
Suresh Gupta
Brad Benton

I F CUSTOMER RELATIONSHIP Management (CRM) is not a project or a product, but a strategy to understand, anticipate and manage customer needs, who must deliver against this strategy? Must it be the employees of the organization, or can CRM be delivered through a third-party supplier of call center services? That has been a question that has puzzled business for years, but with new advances and investment in the CRM field, some dramatic changes are occurring.

America is quietly changing the way it does business. CEOs and boards of directors are focusing on core competencies as the most reliable way to deliver shareholder value and capture market share. Anything that does not contribute directly to these goals is a candidate for divestiture or outsourcing. Legal, advertising, human resources, marketing and even payroll departments are disappearing and the call center is being closely studied. While the CRM activities are still largely performed by in-house departments, outsourcing is increasingly the new focus of world-class organizations, including blue-chip companies like American Express, Citicorp, GE and others.

The amount spent on call centers—both captive and outsourced— routinely outstrips growth projections. In 1996, industry experts predicted that North American companies would spend $100 billion by the year 2000, but that benchmark was reached the very next year (1997). And outsourcing, while still a small component of the market, was projected to grow at nearly four times the rate of captive call centers between 1996 and 2000. The economics of outsourcing trends of the future will continue to drive this growth in outsourcing.

DOLLARS AND CENTS

Skeptical executives may still take the view that reputable vendors with well-trained staff are more expensive than in-house call centers, but this is a myth. It is not uncommon to save up to 30 percent by outsourcing the call center, whether it be inbound call handling or outbound telemarketing services. Why? First, state-of-the-art call centers are prohibitively expensive to set up. Bricks and mortar, well-trained staff, interactive voice response units, automatic call distributors (ACD), e-mail response systems and other technological tools of the trade—all of which are rapidly evolving and just as rapidly outdated—add tremendously to both start-up and operating costs, not to mention capital allocation. Well-capitalized outsourced vendors/suppliers with the necessary technological bench strength can amortize these expenses across a broad range of clients.

Second, 24-hour call centers are expensive to staff in light of fluctuating call volume. A direct-mail apparel retailer may not get many calls at 3 a.m., but someone has to be there to answer the phone just in case. Vendors handling a number of clients can control staff expenses by identifying each company's call patterns and deploying call center agents accordingly. They can use more sophisticated computer telephony integration (CTI) tools, automatic call distributors, and client/server technology to deploy agents more effectively by switching them between tasks and between inbound and outbound calls during high call-volume periods.

Third, this is their business. Successful teleservices/call center vendors do more than work the telephone—they identify trends, anticipate problems, keep up with industry changes and, perhaps most important of all, are often better equipped to capture and process the wide variety of data that come pouring in.

TELESERVICE TRENDS

In the next century, only technology and imagination limit the tasks that cutting-edge call centers will be able to accomplish. The major trends will be:

- Globalization
- Consolidation of Call Centers (Captive or Outsourced)
- Integrated Delivery Channels
- Partnering

Globalization

Today's world was almost impossible to imagine just 10 years ago. The dismantling of the Soviet Union and the aggressive economic development of China have opened vast markets. The advent of the euro in January 1999 has begun to knock down residual trade barriers across much of the European market. Deregulation has facilitated cross-border commerce, and technology now links countries as far apart as Nigeria and Peru. Telephone use is penetrating even the most isolated areas. And as reported by the *Financial Times*[1], it is not so far-fetched to envision physicians in Washington, DC dictating memos to typists in India or kitchenware shoppers in the UK placing orders with sales reps in Utah. Soon Italians calling a US airline in Rome will be connected to Italian speakers in north London.

Decreasing international phone rates will provide further impetus to globalize call centers. According to the World Bank, the cost of a transatlantic call in the year 2000 is only one percent of what it was in 1987, and by 2010 it will be a mere three cents an hour. More multinational companies will utilize teleservices to extend their cross-border reach, improve service to existing customers and support their sales forces more effectively.

---

[1] Financial Times Survey, "Reporting Britain," *Financial Times*, April 23, 1998.

Consolidation of Call Centers (Captive or Outsourced)

If geography no longer matters, then there is not much point in having call centers scattered across the country, each with its own staff and database. An integrated call center with a single customer database is a far more effective customer relationship management tool because it accumulates comprehensive market intelligence that can be analyzed and made available to everyone in the organization who can benefit from it.

The growing popularity of shared services—that is, consolidation across business units of support functions such as accounting, human resources and information technology—will provide a further impetus to consolidate in-house call centers. The resulting improvements in customer service and savings in operating cost are reflected directly in the bottom line. For example, Delta Airlines established a shared European reservations sales center in London a couple of years ago. The airline expects to save almost $50 million as a result of consolidating activities previously handled in 13 separate cities from Amsterdam to Zurich.

This opportunity has not been lost on teleservices vendors, which have been consolidating at a rapid clip over the past five years. This trend will accelerate over the next decade, leading to an integrated, mature industry dominated by a few large players. The largest agency today by far is the former MATRIXX Marketing, which was a wholly owned subsidiary of Cincinnati Bell until it was spun off into a new entity in 1997. Called Convergys, the company has grown steadily through an acquisition program that dates back to the 1970s. In December 1997, it acquired AT&T Customer Solutions, which nearly doubled its size. While Convergys leads the field, a number of other vendors already enjoy revenues of $200 million or more.

Over the next decade, professionally managed, well-capitalized organizations with revenues of $50 million or more will solidify their positions as the industry's dominant players. The smallest vendors, those that rely on a few large clients, and the undercapitalized will be acquired or otherwise disappear. To improve its image and protect its investments, the industry will continue to develop standards and practices above and beyond any state or federal regulation. A handful of vendors dominate the outsourced segment. However, they now face growing competition from technologically sophisticated and well-capitalized new entrants seeking a foothold in an already overpopulated field.

Integrated Delivery Channels

In their pursuit of excellence and competitive advantage, a number of companies have taken the next step and combined teleservicing with non-voice delivery channels—the Internet, fax, video and direct mail. Many are finding that Web teleservicing, partially driven by the growth of e-business, is developing into a singularly cost-effective way to serve consumers. Dell Computer may have invented (and certainly has mastered) the process. A consumer visits Dell's home page, selects a computer and then customizes it from a list of options. Dell immediately furnishes the price and offers a number of ways to complete the purchase—by computer, telephone or mail.

Other industries are catching on. Insurance companies are bypassing agents by offering policies and reviewing eligibility through the Internet. Brokerage houses routinely offer clients access to Web trading, thus reducing the number of brokers and customer service representatives they need.

Partnering

Some companies are finding it beneficial to enter into a "co-sourcing" arrangement. This is, in effect, a partnership in which the vendor and the organization share responsibilities for teleservicing processes. The terms of partnership vary depending upon the needs of the client, and the partners themselves decide who is responsible for the physical plant as well as equipment, staff, control systems and day-to-day management. The negotiations may also include a flexible plan for reimbursement. Many organizations will continue to experiment with a mix of outsourced and captive call centers until they strike the balance that works best for them. These client-driven changes will play an increasingly important role in shaping the industry's future.

CRM OUTSOURCING

Best practices in outsourcing begin with selection of the most appropriate vendor for the business: the functional and strategic alignment of vendor capabilities with company's needs, vendor experience, vendor technologies and operating environment.

How to Choose a Vendor/Supplier

How can a company that has decided to outsource its call centers make an informed decision? Those considering outsourcing for the first time, as well as those reviewing existing relationships with suppliers, should base their decision on the following criteria:

- **Functional alignment.** Does the vendor do what you need it to do? Those who wish to engage in Web-enabled customer service, for example, should not consider a firm whose core competence is limited to outbound sales.

- **Experience.** How long has this vendor worked with similar programs and with what success?

- **Cross-functional needs.** Do you want your call center data analyzed to extract strategic intelligence? If so, there may be only a limited number of experienced vendors to choose from.

- **Vendor technologies.** Will the technological marriage work? Determine whether or not the vendor's technologies are compatible with your specific needs and how easy or difficult it would be to integrate your business work flows with vendor processes.

- **Internal controls.** Does the vendor deliver consistently complete and accurate data in a timely manner? Does it have the controls necessary to promptly substantiate its billing practices and work?

Focus on Controls

For good reason, internal controls have become an additional defining criterion in vendor selection. Without adequate controls and accounting systems, it is impossible to capture accurate billing data and without those controls, it is impossible to maintain the necessary separation between competing clients. As well, systems already working at peak capacity may collapse under the weight of added volume or program changes.

Knowing this to be so, companies have expanded the traditional selection criteria of price, service, flexibility and reputation to include the quality and sophistication of the vendor's internal management control systems. Both customer care outsourced vendors and those that use their services are adopting control reviews to evaluate how well the vendors manage their business and their process risks.

A case in point is the experience of a company that outsourced several million dollars worth of telemarketing services to a well-respected vendor. In one fateful monthly invoice, the company noticed an apparent overbilling of several hundred thousand dollars and asked for justification. The vendor could not provide it because of poor record keeping and inadequate internal controls. The company promptly fired the vendor and instituted a policy of reviewing prospective vendors' operational and financial controls before awarding customer care contracts.

How to Manage an Outsourcing Vendor

In order to determine how leading companies manage their outsourced customer care activities, PricewaterhouseCoopers recently (1999) compared business practices of four large corporations that were among the largest users of outsourced customer care.

Figure 17.1: Outsourced Customer Care in Four Leading Corporations

	Company A	Company B	Company C	Company D
Organization model	Insourced and outsourced programs managed separately	Insourced and outsourced programs managed together	Facilities management model – vendor supplies CSRS and their support, company provides facilities and technologies	Inbound and outbound programs separately
Number of Teleservices programs outsourced	Over 100 programs	Over 150 programs	20 programs	15 programs
Inbound or outbound	Inbound and outbound	Inbound and outbound	Primarily inbound	Primarily inbound

The comparison of the companies' business practices focused on eight key management activities undertaken by the outsourced vendor:

- Establish organizational policies and strategies in the amount of time and effort in the creation of new or revision of existing internal policies and procedures related to the outsourced vendors

- Implement new services and major service changes: the design, development and implementation of new service charges within the vendor/supplier

- Increase organizational effectiveness: the allocation of time to the implementation of new programs and initiatives to increase the effectiveness of the organizational alignment

- Manage contracts and invoices: the time involved in reviewing the existing performance of the vendor and the accuracy and appropriateness of the invoices

- Manage ongoing services: day-to-day management activities related to the vendor

- Manage systems development: the day-to-day management of changes to existing systems that affect the interface between the customer and the vendor as well as the vendor and the organization

- Monitor performance: time involved in actual monitoring of the quality of service delivery as well as performance against standard

- Provide clerical/secretarial services: the administrative support required for the above items

Varying levels of effort, as measured by the amount of time senior management dedicated to these activities, were devoted to these processes. For example, the number of dedicated professionals performing these activities varied from just a handful of employees to over 200 among the benchmarked companies. Not surprisingly, the majority of the work effort in each case is concentrated in managing ongoing service and monitoring performance.

Cost Efficiency of Vendor Management

Key questions in looking at how well various companies manage their outsourcing relationships are the amount of money devoted to vendor management and how much effort is required to oversee the operations of the vendor, which includes time on site, managing and reviewing reports. Unfortunately, a high level of staff devoted to the eight process-es outlined above does not necessarily ensure superior performance by a vendor.

Effectiveness of Vendor Management

A significant proportion of the analysis focused on comparing specific practices employed by world-class companies in managing their ven-dors. Best-practice process definitions were developed for each of the eight process categories listed above. This involved two steps: First, each process category was decomposed into a number of activities. For example, a key activity in Monitor Performance included tracking cus-tomer complaints. Second for each of the activities, lagging, leading or best practice definitions were defined. For the complaints-tracking activity this resulted in the following definitions:

- Lagging companies typically have anecdotal information about complaints and may have developed informal tracking mecha-nisms.
- Leading companies formally report and categorize complaints, perform root-cause analysis and conduct customer follow-up.
- Best practices involve ensuring customers know how to complain, engaging vendors that use a complaint tracking system and pro-duce monthly reports. Specific targets are established (e.g., less than five complaints per 100,000 contacts) and are usually built into performance incentives

LESSONS LEARNED

These lessons are reflected in the best practices culled from the survey results. Underlying these are five common themes that, according to every-one interviewed, form the foundation of sound vendor management.

1. Clarity in Establishing Performance Expectations
2. Do not Abdicate the CRM to the Vendor
3. Proactive Measurement and Feedback of Vendor's Performance
4. Sharing and Propagating Best Practices Among Multiple Vendors
5. Maintaining the Ability to Switch to a New Vendor with Ease

1. Clarity in Establishing Performance Expectations

Most disputes between customers and vendors stem from unclear performance expectations. Time and again, disappointed customers have realized that they did a poor job of communicating their expectations to the vendors. Part of the difficulty lies in the fact that many customers have had false expectations that once they outsource their customer care activities, they can essentially wipe their hands and leave it to the vendor to field customer calls. And in those cases where they did stay involved, some did not devote sufficient effort to achieving a meeting of minds with regard to specific cost and service performance metrics. The best-practice companies had formal service level agreements (SLAs) with their vendors that were updated at least every year. In addition to having these, one of the survey participants went as far as establishing a formal agreement between the vendor management department and the user departments (e.g., marketing, customer service etc.), which was outsourcing their programs. This practice was very helpful in minimizing gaps between what was expected versus what was delivered.

2. Do Not Abdicate the CRM to the Vendor

World-class companies have realistic expectations from outsourcing. They know that even though a vendor may be sufficiently capable of handling their day-to-day customer care activities, they cannot and should not abdicate customer relationship management to that vendor. They have to maintain a close watch on their customers' needs and expectations and monitor how effective the vendor is in fulfilling those expectations. Moreover, in a dynamic business environment, customer needs are apt to change frequently as new products—and hence, new customer care programs—are introduced in the marketplace. Such changes are best managed by vendor in-house management staff.

3. Proactive Measurement and Feedback of Vendor's Performance

The old adage "what gets measured gets done," is particularly true in the customer care outsourcing arena. The outsourcing market is in the middle of a transformation. A fragmented industry with over a thousand providers, it is poised for massive consolidation, which has already begun with a slew of mergers and acquisitions in the last couple of years. However, the process has barely begun and there is a lot more to come. In such an environment, it is imperative for organizations to monitor vendor performance proactively. Best-practice companies achieve this, not by quarterly or half-yearly staged reviews of vendor performance but rather by instituting continuous monitoring programs to measure performance against pre-defined metrics and continually adjusting those to make them consistent with changes in their customers' needs.

4. Sharing and Propagating Best Practices Among Multiple Vendors

It is an open secret that the most productive client-vendor relationship is one of true partnership between the two. However, in practice this lofty goal is rarely achieved. The leading users of outsourcing have approached the ideal of a true partnership by instituting formal sharing of best practices among their vendors, particularly when a customer care program is serviced by multiple vendors. In fact, it is a best practice among these companies to distribute a customer care program to more than one vendor to facilitate apple-to-apple comparisons between various vendors. Such a practice is extremely effective in promoting world-class performance by the outsourcing vendors.

5. Maintaining the Ability to Switch to a New Vendor with Ease

This is an obvious need though hard to fulfill. Apart from the usual operational disruptions in switching vendors, often it requires building new systems interfaces with the new vendor thus contributing to delays in switching. Best-practice companies minimize these disruptions by spreading the work among multiple vendors. One survey participant had a policy of placing almost every outsourced program with more than one vendor. Of course, for a small program with, say, less than 50 seats, it is often not economical to employ multiple vendors. In those cases there is no substitute to maintaining a particularly close partnership with the vendor to minimize the need to switch.

CONCLUSION

Outsourcing of the customer care function, typically the call center, promises rich dividends in the pursuit of CRM. However, to make the most of this promise, users of outsourcing must keep their eyes on the ball. As stated earlier, CRM is a strategy that has to be clearly defined with action plans and standards. When these are in-house functions, they can be monitored easily, and corrective action can be taken quickly and decisively. When this becomes an outsourced function, the vendor chosen must also be monitored closely, but you are dependent on the vendor to emulate you not only in care of the customer but also in corrective action and continuous improvement as well. Only by thorough, strong standards, monitoring and sharing of best practices will success be a reality.

About the Authors

GINA BOULTON

Gina Boulton is Vice President of External Enterprises Management at American Express.

SURESH GUPTA

Suresh Gupta is a Partner in PricewaterhouseCoopers' America's CRM practice. His primary focus is within the Financial Services industry sector and the outsourcing of Customer Care.

BRAD BENTON

Brad Benton is a Director in PricewaterhouseCoopers' America's CRM practice.

Learning and Knowledge Management Programs in the Age of CRM

Hemant Minocha

T O BUILD AND sustain an effective customer relationship management (CRM) culture in the age of e-business, organizations must revamp and significantly realign their traditional learning and knowledge management programs. This can mean a need to start with an analysis of required competencies and run through development and delivery of continuous learning systems and knowledge management programs and tools. Not too long ago this may have resulted in someone from the human resources (HR) department conducting a training assessment, developing a learning program (most likely in an instructor-led format), and delivering formal training to organization staff. Furthermore, organizations that were at the leading edge may have collected the materials and made them available in some relatively simple (by today's standards) electronic format such as a static Web site or electronic document repository.

So what is different for organizations operating in today's CRM climate? Plenty! First, the rush to implement enterprise-wide resource planning (ERP) information systems has often resulted in better data and operational integration at all levels of the organization. While initially lauded for integrating backoffice functions, ERP today serves as the basic building block for fully integrated relationships not just inside the organization but with suppliers and customers as well. This means that traditional HR departments must broaden their scope to look at the learning and knowledge management needs of customers and suppliers as well as internal staff, if the organization wants to be competitive. Secondly, the speed of the Internet means that new suppliers that need to be trained are just a click away while conversely, customers are just a click away from checking out the competition. So to be competitive not only do organizations need to address much broader learning and knowledge management requirements, they must do so more quickly and seamlessly than the competition.

Ironically, the very cause of this change may also help solve the learning and knowledge management challenge, at least in terms of supporting infrastructure. Internet-based virtual universities open to staff, suppliers and customers may address the need for quick and integrated learning. Internet sites that facilitate the creation of personalized Web portals may be an ultimate answer, for they embody the essence of a CRM culture from a learning and knowledge management perspective—getting customers, suppliers and staff just what they need when they need it.

The following sections describe the fundamental shift in competencies and some of the resulting implications for learning and knowledge management. Specifically, they will examine the:

- Impact of a CRM Culture on Sales and Marketing Organizations
- Impact of a CRM Culture on Customers
- Impact of a CRM Culture on Suppliers
- Road map to Developing Required Competencies

IMPACT OF A CRM CULTURE ON SALES AND MARKETING ORGANIZATIONS

The sales world of today is in a tremendous state of flux in attempting to respond to the highly dynamic and volatile marketplace. As the pace of worldwide change accelerates, cycles that used to take years or even decades now are measured in months in many industries. This reality of a culture of "instantaneous responsiveness" may mandate fundamental changes in the way business is conducted. To operate successfully in the global marketplace, organizations have been moving to a customer-centric focus and are being challenged to quickly and accurately discern what customers are demanding—and provide it efficiently. The customer relationship management (CRM) model, with its customer-centric focus, places the customer's needs first and involves three fundamental steps:

1. Understanding customers completely

2. Aligning organizational capabilities in order to better deliver what its customers may perceive as heightened value

3. Facilitating the immediacy of information availability both inside and outside of the organization.

In the evolution to this customer-driven culture, major organizational changes may be necessary. Organizations can no longer afford to be internally focused or composed of functional silos, if indeed they ever could. Real-time information flow and communication across the entire organization are operational necessities. Strategy is driven by marketplace demands and organizations are striving to appear seamless to customers; in other words, although there are multiple touch points where the customer touches the organization, all parts of the organization must have access to every piece of information relevant to each customer. Customers today demand that they be effectively and efficiently serviced and will not tolerate being told "that's not my department" or "I don't have that information, let me transfer you to someone who does."

Organizations strive to achieve a "closed-loop" sales and marketing process where all customer issues are "closed" by those who make first contact with the customer to maximize customer satisfaction and retention, increase revenues and decrease costs. Other desired outcomes of the closed-loop process include: improved internal and external communications, longer-term relationships with clients, elimination of multiple systems and conflicting data, improved productivity and, most importantly, improved customer service. The entire sales process, from strategy, branding and campaign management, through the effective servicing of customers after the sale needs to be flawlessly planned and executed.

In this new and dynamic marketplace, information flow needs to be assured not only among internal resources but also to every part of the organization's value chain. This value chain consists of an extended supply chain encompassing partners and contractors coupled with a well-linked delivery chain to customers.

Impact On Organizational Competencies

The realization of this customer-centric vision may necessitate fundamental changes in the competencies of an organization's resources, particularly for those involved in the sales process even indirectly. While always important, interpersonal skills now become critical to an organization's success. The ability to attract and retain customers is directly correlated to customer perception, and perception is managed through the broad spectrum of communication. This new reality presents unique new communication challenges. Where salespeople once could rely on gauging customer reaction easily in face-to-face encounters, they are now challenged by the very technology that facilitates contact—that is often remote—with greater numbers of prospects and customers.

In contrast with the sales world of just a few years ago, today's salespeople find themselves in a continuous search for information. Leads must be generated and handed off to appropriate individuals. Competitors must be identified and strategies developed to effectively compete for sales. In reality, selling is a complex and information-intensive process, often requiring the salesperson to act as an expert consultant and problem solver. Consultative selling skills coupled with highly effective problem solving and negotiating competencies are requisites for effectiveness in the sales arena of today. There was a time when sales and service people could rely on predictable questions and had ready answers reflecting the organization line, but in the new world of e-business unpredictability is the norm. Anyone touching the customer must be able to think on his or her feet. This is not to say that they are expected to tell the customer anything simply to defuse a volatile situation, but rather that the employee must possess the ability to rationally handle the situation without unnecessarily escalating it. Critical thinking skills are intrinsic to this process.

Salespeople more than ever rely upon a wide array of technology to keep abreast of changes in the marketplace and identify trends leading to new business opportunities. This, in turn, demands that they be technologically proficient and supplied with up-to-date hardware systems and applications. The training and retraining of this sales force is no longer something confined to employee orientation but a continuous, ongoing process. To facilitate this, new technologies must be adopted, embraced and put into place. Given the rate at which technologies are superseded, the constant retraining of the sales force presents a significant ongoing challenge.

Sales professionals need to possess a comprehensive knowledge of the organization's strategic initiatives and be absolutely clear on how their functions fit into the strategy. No longer can they afford to operate as individuals. They are now part of sales teams, which possess a wide range of skills and knowledge to handle increasingly complex sales situations. This shift represents a fundamental change in the sales paradigm and, predictably, engenders significant resistance from the people involved. Contacts and leads, long the lifeblood of a salesperson (and jealously guarded), must now be in the public domain to facilitate team and supply chain communication and interaction. This shift may challenge organizations and their HR function to develop innovative new compensation systems to retain and motivate sales professionals operating in CRM cultures. In this new paradigm, sales team members each provide timely and accurate information that, when effectively combined, presents all with a more comprehensive view of the customer. The successful adoption of a CRM culture can result in the ability to foster and maintain a collaborative, trusting relationship that converts opportunities into sales.

Organizations moving to different sales methodologies need to align with the technologies they have chosen to employ. Salespeople once had the luxury of functioning in any way they saw fit, so long as they closed sales and met quotas. With a shift to team selling, everyone involved in the sales process through the entire value chain needs to be thoroughly versed in the chosen sales process and clearly understand their unique role. Each member of the team needs to know what to expect along the continuum of the sales process.

Where does marketing fit into this new equation? Marketing's single most important objective has always been the generation of leads. Historically, it viewed operationalizing this objective by getting the sales pipeline filled with new potential sales opportunities at the least possible cost. It was then up to salespeople to qualify those leads and turn them into sales. This process is fundamentally flawed in that it relies on quantity and sacrifices quality and is a very inefficient way to conduct business. The onus for qualifying leads cannot rest solely upon the sales force if they are to be expected to perform at heightened levels. For marketing to function it needs to provide highly accurate information on potential customers and on potential opportunities with existing ones; in other words, it needs to prequalify leads prior to sending them to the sales force. In this way, salespeople can spend less time in ancillary tasks and activities and maximize the time building and maintaining long-term customer relationships. Therefore, marketing not only needs to change the way it fits into the sales process, but it needs to provide its resources with better data analysis tools and skills. It must, in fact, become a conduit passing information back and forth both internally and externally and continuously learning and refining its approach.

The service function likewise needs to undergo a significant transformation with corresponding implications on competencies. Service personnel must be a part of the same system as other members of the closed-loop sales process. Customers demand that questions be answered and problems solved with the initial contact and often won't hang around while you transfer their call. This necessitates not only up-to-date information at customer service representatives' fingers but also a host of soft skills such as effective interpersonal communications and problem solving. CSRs need to see themselves as a totally integrated part of the enterprise and have a true commitment to the customer.

All of this boils down to two things: knowledge must be available across multiple customer touch points, and the closed-loop sales process rests upon a foundation of data. The ability to access the exact information needed from a sea of information will provide a competitive advantage to an organization. Knowledge has always been power, but in the ever-changing global economy it is power that successful organizations must bestow on the entire enterprise.

IMPACT OF A CRM CULTURE ON CUSTOMERS

How has CRM changed the way customers act? The cultural transformation we have been discussing has been taking place concurrently in organizations worldwide. Some have been early adopters, while others are accepting CRM culture more gradually. But all organizations are developing CRM cultural norms and eventually all sales and customer service representatives will see team selling, closed-loop sales, knowledge-based sales and service and pipeline management as the only way to do business.

And here is where an interesting phenomenon happens. The CRM norms that organizations are beginning to live by as sellers are the same expectations they have as buyers. In other words, as organizations become more educated and more adept sellers, they also become more competent customers. Customer competency may become a competitive advantage, especially for value-added resellers. Let's talk about two of these customer competencies: pushing information and investigating.

Pushing Information

As customers in the new CRM culture we expect our vendors to use their technology to understand our needs. As customers, we can gain an advantage by becoming adept at pushing information from our organization to our suppliers. The more information that our suppliers know about our organization contacts, the products we have purchased from them in the past, our sales process and the like, the better they will be able to provide products and services that meet our needs.

As an example, the more sales pipeline information we can push to our suppliers, the better chance we have of reducing inventory and building our just-in-time production. Similarly, the more a supplier knows about the way we have configured and utilized their products and those from other suppliers, the better opportunity they will have to suggest solutions for cost savings or service enhancement, and the better the supplier will be able to help the customer internally sell the solutions they propose.

The challenge is in changing the individual and collective behaviors of the organization. We hesitate to share information about ourselves and our organization when a salesperson calls. Yet we wonder why they propose solutions that miss the mark. This is a direct customer impact of the new sales paradigm mentioned earlier and may significantly affect not only organizations and their sales forces but also customers in the way information is utilized in sales processes.

Investigating

With the advent of eCRM customers have the ability to look inside their suppliers like never before. Customers who are able to effectively and systematically investigate what their suppliers offer and then use the suppliers' Web-based self-service capabilities may be able to purchase products and services at a lower price, have greater control over product configuration and access to a wider array of customer service options.

The challenge is for customers to overcome their existing ways of doing things—that interaction with a "real person" is better, that sales representatives should "tell me what I need," and that "the supplier should sell to me." Like the guerilla sales and marketers armed with customer knowledge, customers can gain competitive advantage by becoming guerilla purchasers—able to locate and utilize the information that suppliers are providing en masse via eCRM on the World Wide Web.

One of the areas where Web self-service is taking hold early is in human resources. A major motion picture studio is moving to Web self-service for employee benefits enrollment. This will give employees access to more information about their benefits providers than ever before at the click of a mouse and greater flexibility in selecting and making changes to the benefits packages they purchase. The challenge is to help the employees change their thinking from, "Why am I doing this? This is HR's job," to "This is great. I can now purchase services that better meet my needs and expectations."

IMPACT OF A CRM CULTURE ON SUPPLIERS

In an environment where truly the customer is king, the demands on suppliers of goods and services will increase. We will be seeing fewer independent suppliers but numerous complex supply chains and groups of suppliers clustering their products and services together to provide a seamless-cost competitive service available whenever demanded, wherever desired. The Internet is changing everything, ensuring that supply and demand will never be the same. Adjusting to these new realities will require businesses to radically modify their business processes, develop new technological solutions, and build products and services that are dictated by fast-changing markets and customer preferences. Many businesses and job roles will disappear, and the nature of work itself is likely to change. What competencies will be required for this customer-driven environment?

Create New Demand Chains

A key competency of customer-driven economy will be to create new demand chains, to develop new business and customer relationships, to combine the best of a breed and change all this periodically. This will be manifested in a keen understanding of marketplace dynamics and evolving new business structures and relationships: Knowledge of every aspect of a given industry and other facets of the economy will become critical. For a manufacturing company, it will be just as important to develop efficient manufacturing processes as it would be to track best practices in distribution and logistics or new developments in the customer-facing software to allow customers to directly order products. This culture of constant change will lead to new demands for skills and agility in establishing alliances and redesign processes. Long term will be redefined as two to five years.

You Are Nothing if You Cannot Communicate

The lifeblood of the new world will likely be communications between demand chain links, customers, employees, contractors, technologists, new customers, new channels, different new customers, new markets, new suppliers, new customers who are suppliers and new suppliers who are customers. With whom will we communicate? Who is listening? What is the attention span? Who will communicate? How will they communicate? What will they communicate? The ability to successfully communicate has become another critical competency and will be a significant factor in corporate and individual success in the future.

You Cannot Escape Technology

Tying the new suppliers to customers will be technology and the Internet, and the ability to deploy these catalysts of change will be another essential skill set. A core competency will be to build technology-based distribution and e-tailoring capability to tailor services to customer needs on the fly will be an engine for growth. This will likely involve the ability to adapt to new technologies, "integrate" with a community of technology-based "malls" and trade outlets and be wired into customers. The role of a distribution manager may well be one of tying into virtual distribution centers and will therefore dictate a new set of skills and competencies.

A ROAD MAP TO DEVELOPING REQUIRED COMPETENCIES

With all the changes in required competencies in organizations, customers and suppliers to stay competitive, combined with major technology advances, we are at the beginning of a major paradigm shift in the field of learning and knowledge management. This includes two major premises:

- Learning and knowledge management may be driven by the people who need it. At least that's how it may be for competitive organizations. Gone is the day of commodity-oriented training and the HR department trainer who told the staff what they needed to learn. Here is the advent of truly services-oriented internal and external consultants who specialize in learning and knowledge management. They may treat all learners—whether they are organization customers, suppliers or organization staff—as unique.

- Learning and knowledge management activities primarily will be integrated with business transactions so that they occur as simultaneously as possible. Formal learning opportunities, i.e., those bounded by time and/or space, will decline in prevalence as learners demand just-in-time solutions any time, any place. All will demand as few clicks of the mouse as possible to get what they need. Too many clicks and customers will form a relationship with a new organization with fewer clicks. Too many clicks and suppliers will find new business partners who make it easier to do business and run more efficiently. Too many clicks and employees will move to competitors with fewer clicks to improve the quality of their work life.

Given this paradigm shift, the challenge for internal and external learning and knowledge management consultants may be to design programs that are far more flexible, responsive and effective than ever before. Learners may determine objectives, content, delivery methods and timing. Those responsible for developing solutions may find themselves using methods they've never used before and revising traditional thinking about effective instructional systems design.

Below we describe a five-stop road map for developing required competencies. This is consistent with the paradigm shift described above.

Step 1: e-Business and Customer Relationship Management Training

The first stop on the road map is a formal training session on the implications of e-business and a CRM culture from the perspective of HR staff. The purpose of the session is to provide participants with a conceptual understanding of these major changes in the business world. It should describe how those changes lead to the transformation in the field of learning and knowledge management.

This stop is the first one because it's absolutely critical that the human resources department understand that its entire way of operating is about to change. HR is used to being an internal function. Now it is emerging as a critical customer and supplier interface on top of its traditional audience.

Step 2: Establish an Advisory Board

The second stop on the road map is the establishment of an advisory board of staff, customers and suppliers to help identify and assess learning and knowledge management needs and priorities. The scope of their charge shouldn't be constrained to their respective roles. In other words, advisory board members should be able to comment on the needs of customers, suppliers and organization staff, not just on whichever "side" they sit on.

The advisory board should meet regularly to help the internal learning and knowledge management consultants interpret whatever hard data they are reviewing as well as provide unstructured feedback. This may help the internal consultants determine the extent to which the hard data and trends they are examining (e.g., operational and marketing/sales reports previously the exclusive domain of other departments) suggest areas for improvement in learning and knowledge management or reflect on other issues.

Step 3: Develop E-Education Systems

The third stop is the creation of an intranet-based virtual university and personalized learning and knowledge management portal. The virtual university should house more of the formal learning programs.

The personal portal should provide a customized window (unique to each person) into the virtual university and other sources of knowledge.

The best virtual universities are set up as computerized management instruction (CMI) systems. CMI is an enterprise-class training delivery and management system that enables any time/any place learning, manages virtually any type of content (e.g., systems, processes, soft skills, new product offerings) and performs training administration tasks (e.g., registration, testing, tracking, reporting). When building a virtual university with CMI in mind, select tools that are:

- based on open systems architecture
- Web-based
- compliant with required standards and regulations
- capable of robust reporting and testing capabilities
- capable of handling synchronous and asynchronous learning activities
- scaleable

These criteria may help mitigate any risk that the solution won't be as accessible and long-lived as desired. Among the larger organizations that have been actively involved for a while, there's a push to integrate competency assessment, career development, staff planning and virtual universities on-line. It's important to keep options open to facilitate integration with other organization functions.

Personal learning and knowledge management portals may help reduce the number of mouse clicks customers, suppliers and organization staff need to make. They may do this because they may sift through all the possible "content" available and bring out only that which is of most use by the owner of the portal. Thus, the learner is clearly the one in control.

Step 4: Design, Develop and Launch Content

Perhaps the largest technical issue internal learning and knowledge management consultants will face is the design of learning materials. After many years of preparing participant and instructor guides, computer-based training programs with multiple lessons and even satellite broadcast training, today's trainers have learned how to chunk materials effectively. The problem is that what has been successful up to now won't be going forward.

Customers, suppliers and organization staff may drive toward getting their learning and information in smaller chunks, much smaller than currently offered. In fact, much of the chunking may create such small nuggets of information that many probably won't even consider it a learning program. That's why learning and knowledge management are really converging. A good example of this today can be seen in many call centers. Service representatives who answer calls have scripted walk-throughs to guide them on customer calls. These are good examples of how learning may occur on demand and at the same time as a transaction is occurring.

Additionally, content must be chunked smaller than it is today because it must be more reusable. Since customers, suppliers and organization staff may all need learning and knowledge management services from the organization, efficiencies must be found. By chunking content into very small nuggets, it is much easier to reuse it for different audiences. For example, content designed for sales and marketing staff may have components that are accessed by suppliers and customers. It's the personal learning portals that assemble the pieces into person-specific packages.

Of course, all this content then has to be linked to the business and capable of being combined with other materials dynamically to offer learners what they need. This may take a combination of instructional design and Web-publishing competencies.

Step 5: Evaluate Results and Facilitate Continuous Learning

The last stop on this road map involves evaluating results and developing action plans to facilitate continuous learning. Unless there is learning, there will be no improvement. Organizations must learn from their mistakes and these and the best practices of others. In other words, this is a feedback loop that helps the organization stay competitive.

Traditional means of evaluating effectiveness will virtually disappear. Organizations will be able to get far better information than ever before. By looking at hard data related to sales and customer trends, as well as inventory and financial reports, and using the advisory board to help interpret the data, organizations will have a far better measure of the effectiveness of training (in terms of bottom-line impact) than ever before.

CONCLUSION

The paradigm shift is starting, but only a few will be successful. Those successful organizations will recognize the importance of learning and knowledge management and the need to integrate this with actual business transactions—the learning organization must be created. e-business has created change, and those that embrace change and learning will survive.

About the Author

HEMANT MINOCHA

Hemant Minocha is a Partner in PricewaterhouseCoopers' management consulting practice. He was assisted in this article by Karen Ball, Stephen Browne, Paul Drnevich, Randall Hawn, Daniel Murphy, and Robert Thomas.

CHAPTER NINETEEN

Implementing CRM:

THE NEED FOR PERFORMANCE ALIGNMENT

Moosha Gulycz

C RM DOESN'T JUST happen. While an organization may have the desire to improve its customer focus, without a proper CRM vision, strategy, action plan and mechanism to measure, monitor and manage that plan, success may be fleeting. That mechanism is a strategic performance alignment (SPA) program, and it must be based on three critical measures, or success factors; the organization's understanding of its customer, its understanding of its own organization, and its commitment to continuous improvement in quality service. Essentially, it is a framework that enables the CRM vision and fosters a cycle of continuous improvement.

What follows is a case study of a government agency involved in a dramatic change, from an internally focused, non responsive organization to one successfully focused on CRM.

THE ORGANIZATION

PDS (a fictitious name) is a government agency with a high degree of contact with its constituents. In the course of any day the organization takes approximately 42,000 calls, across six different locations, including calls around general enquiries to disputes, fraud identification and eligibility questions. Calls come from the general public, media and politicians.

THE CALL TO ACTION

By presidential order, and through Vice President Gore's announcement, *Conversations with America*, federal government workers were directed to engage in a two-way conversations with their customers on how to improve customer service and create customer service standards. This was bolstered when the president issued another directive stating, "It is time to increase efforts to engage customers in conversations about further improving government service."

PDS faced a significant challenge. Customer complaints were on the rise, performance standards did not exist, employees were not aware of what they were expected to do and there was no process in place to ensure continuous improvement in quality service.

Action Taken

The agency underwent a four-step process, which began with its endorsement of the CRM vision articulated by the president and vice president. Figure 19.1 illustrates the cascading steps followed to address and sustain CRM in this case.

Figure 19.1: Performance Alignment: The Four Step Process

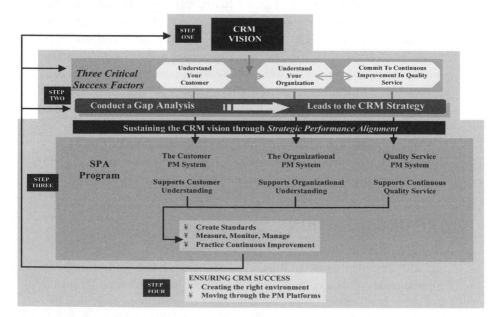

' PricewaterhouseCoopers, 2000. All rights of use and reproduction reserved

Step One: Determining and Aligning the CRM Vision

Before the right SPA program could be designed, the desired end state, which is the CRM vision, had to be confirmed. While there was little doubt that the presidential directive would be accepted, buy-in at all levels of the organization was still required. Discussions were held with the agency's senior management group and a selection of staff at various levels to validate the direction and intent of the vision and begin to solicit buy-in. Following that, confirmation of the CRM vision was communicated throughout the organization. As with any vision, this one had to then be aligned within the organization—enter Step Two.

> Alignment means ensuring that in order to realize the vision, a strategy existed. All components of the CRM strategy must, of course, be focused in the same direction and working together to achieve the CRM vision. All components and divisions of the organization must also move in the same direction, which has to be clear enough, so that without doubt, every individual knows where they are going and how they fit in.

Step Two: Developing The CRM Strategy

> If you know the enemy and know yourself, you need not fear the result of a hundred battles. If you know yourself but not the enemy, for every victory gained, you will also suffer a defeat. If you know neither the enemy nor yourself, you will succumb in every battle.
>
> Sun Tzu, *The Art of War*

The CRM vision set the stage—the goal of battle. It described the purpose of the battle, where the CRM road was eventually to lead, where the battle was to be fought and pointed the organization in that direction. But the CRM vision did not give sufficient context to win. It did not necessarily reflect the unique needs of its customer base (the enemy) or an assessment of the strengths and weaknesses of the organization (Sun Tzu's reference to yourself) and its capabilities to deliver against its customer needs. The vision therefore had had to be translated into a

CRM strategy that encompassed customer needs, organizational competencies and commitment to quality service.

A vision is a statement of high-level purpose that answers the question of what will ultimately be accomplished. A strategy is a detailed breakdown of the vision. It is the steps and activities that implement and operationalize the vision.

The strategy was developed through an assessment of where the organization was with respect to three areas that are critical success factors:

1. **Understand the Customer** To what extent did the organization understand the needs of its customers and those needs that were unique to certain market segments? To gain an understanding of the customer, their habits and their likes and dislikes, information was acquired on:

   - who the customers were and their needs
   - customer purchasing patterns
   - the impact of marketing and/or communication efforts
   - the match between services and products and customer need
   - current levels of customer satisfaction

     This information was then used to:

   - plot the current customer needs, wants and expectations
   - predict where customer needs, wants and expectations were growing
   - predict future customer needs, wants and expectations

2. **Understand the Organization** Was the organization prepared to deliver to customer needs, did it have the required human and physical resources, and was the organization committed to deliver to these needs? As shown in Figure 19.2, to gain an understanding of the organization, the agency reviewed if they had the:

Figure 19.2: Key Organizational Requirements

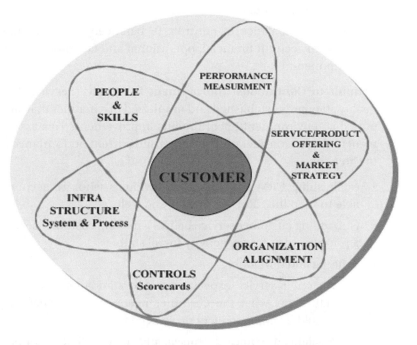

' PricewaterhouseCoopers, 2000. All rights of use and reproduction reserved

- People and skills to make it happen (Did it have the right complement of resources, and did the right skill set exist?)

- Organization aligned (Did silos exist? Also, were the goals and objectives of the organization understood and was the organization moving toward a single service view?)

- Infrastructure that allowed it to happen (Was the right technology in place to allow the organization to deliver against these goals?)

- The required systems and processes that paved the way to being more customer responsive

- Services and products customers wanted

- Market strategy that captured customer attention (Was the organization's marketing message supportive to the current offering and aligned with customer needs?)

- A performance measurement system that monitored all required components
- The proper balance of controls (a balanced scorecard that took into account financial, operational and customer service components)

3. **Commit to Continuous Improvement in Quality Service** Were quality standards established and monitored in a manner that supported an environment of continuous improvement? This assessment took into consideration progress and current performance in the areas of:

- establishing CRM champions—individuals who are accountable to keep the CRM vision alive and well
- embedding customer service beliefs—making customer service a priority, a day-to-day activity for all staff
- defining and developing:
  - customer service expectations and standards—letting all staff know what the customer needs are and what they should be doing to meet these needs
  - a balanced scorecard—measuring all areas that are important to the customer, not just focusing on one (e.g., cost of service)
  - customer service surveys—asking customers what they thought of the service and what they want from the service in the future
  - a complaint management process—inviting customers to voice all of their concerns and then doing something with this information

By conducting a gap analysis within each of the three critical success factors the required detailed steps to reach the vision were determined. (Were these three critical factors sufficiently focused and have progressed enough to support and achieve the CRM vision?) Together these steps represented the CRM strategy.

Step Three: Building the SPA Program

By completing Step Two the CRM strategy was developed. The next step, Step Three, was to build a robust SPA program to ensure the three critical success factors were knitted together and continued to support moving the organization towards its vision. The program included a performance measurement system for each of the three critical success factors that aligned with, and directly supported, the CRM vision. The performance information from the program:

- promoted and demonstrated CRM accountability by assigning performance owners (those responsible for various aspects of performance)

- assisted the organization in making better decisions by providing them with information that pointed them to informed changes

- improved allocation of CRM resources by demonstrating where more people, money and time were needed

- invited continuous improvement by advising where they could do better and where they were meeting best in class

During the course of completing Step Three, the agency learned that to be successful the SPA program had to include the following objectives:

- a continuous desire to improve management practices—there had to be a commitment to use the performance information

- to focus organizational efforts on customer needs, wants and expectations—the customer performance information pinpointed these needs, wants and expectations

- assess progress in meeting need, want and expectation—ongoing customer measurement and monitoring demonstrated where improvements were being made or where there were performance gaps and action was required

- ensure the information to make necessary and best customer change decisions was available—performance information had to be timely and relevant, not just a stack of data reports and statistics

- drive positive change by
    - focusing attention on the organization's CRM vision—reminding the organization where it wanted to go and where it was heading

— providing a positive way to direct efforts of management and staff to meet new goals and new ways of doing business— showing where a good job was done and where this could continue and where it could be improved

— continually improving performance, at both the organizational and individual level—involving staff and assisting them to see how they could improve and, in turn, the direct impacts of their improvements on the organization

Through the introduction of SPA an organizational-wide dynamic and interactive process was implemented that involved:

- setting the optimal CRM outcome that was directed by the CRM vision—taking the vision and determining what the agency ultimately wanted to accomplish for itself and with its customers

- setting priorities that together would achieve the outcome—implementing the most important steps of the strategy first

- identifying the goals and objectives required within each critical success factor to meet CRM priorities—putting an action plan against these most important steps

- defining and tracking performance measures related to each of the goals and objectives—determining what had to be tracked and analyzed to determine if progress was being made

- implementing a system of measurement, a balanced scorecard approach was used—ensuring that all important areas are measured, not just the obvious ones

- reporting performance and using performance information to improve management and drive change for continuous improvement—being accountable by putting it in writing and using the information to make required changes

- revisiting the CRM vision for refinement—taking all the information and analyzing whether the vision is still relevant and achievable

The program included three systems of performance measurement.

A. The Customer Performance Measurement System

B. The Organizational Performance Measurement System

C. The Quality Service Performance Measurement System

A: The Customer Performance Measurement System

In carrying out the customer component of the CRM strategy, an understanding of customer requirements was determined. The questions what does the customer need, want and expect were answered, but this was not as simple as just asking the customer. The information showed that at times the customer didn't know what they needed or wanted, and their expectations were built around past experience only. Customers expected what they were used to. In this situation, it was determined that customer needs and expectations should continuously be driven upwards by anticipating and providing the customer with what they wanted even before they knew it. This was accomplished by providing the next group of service offerings even before the customer demanded them. However, this could be accomplished only by acquiring a comprehensive customer database, using that information to first predict future customer needs and then by meeting these needs before they became current.

It was obvious that a fundamental shift in thinking had to occur. Customers had to be viewed from the *outside in* rather than the *inside out*.

Viewing the customers from the outside in means listening to them periodically and from the perspective of what the agency needed and wanted to hear. Viewing from the inside out means continuous listening to the customer. The voice of the customer is taken into account every day and integrated into the day-to-day activities of the agency. The customer is not just surveyed once a year. There is a mechanism in place to voice their opinion at any time, any day.

The customer performance measurement system provided readily available and ongoing customer performance data. Data measured customer behavior patterns including purchasing, complaints and participation in reward programs. The customer performance data flagged necessary changes to the CRM strategy. Further, it indicated future customer need, want and expectation by predicting patterns of behavior that, in turn, were investigated and acted on proactively.

As previously noted, the customer performance data identified where required changes were necessary and helped to identify emerging customer needs. For example, identifying and acting on patterns of requests for new information early on can result in the launch of new staff training and consumer education programs for this agency.

B: The Organizational Performance Measurement System

In carrying out the organizational component of the CRM strategy, an understanding of organizational requirements was determined. It answered the questions what is the organization capable of now and in the future, how could the organization be mobilized to achieve the CRM vision, what was required and how would they get there? For PDS, this meant the CRM strategy had to ensure that by filling the gaps identified through answering those questions, the organization would be fit and ready to optimize CRM. The agency found that the following areas, listed in Figure 19.3, must be part of its organizational performance measurement system to ensure that the CRM vision could be addressed and sustained. Each time there was a significant change in customer need, an assessment took place to determine if it was in a position to continue to meet those changing needs.

Figure 19. 3: Organizational Performance Evaluation Criteria

Providing and sustaining quality CRM requires the appropriate level and mix of:

- *People and skills*—Are your people ready to attain the CRM vision? Do they understand and align with CRM? Are they equipped with the right skills and capacity? Can they do it?

- *Structure*—Does your structure support the appropriate roles, responsibilities and authority? Is accountability clearly defined by position and does this contribute to and enable the CRM vision?

- *Service and product offering*—Is your organization in the right business? Does the business need expansion or significant change? Do your current products and services meet customer needs, wants and expectations? Can they sustain emerging trends?

- *Market strategy*—Does your market strategy target correctly? Is your strategy innovative and creative? Will it capture attention?

- *Process*—Are your processes enabling or inhibiting? Do they promote creativity, ownership and accountability? Or do they stifle?

- *Infrastructure and enabling supports*—Can your organization accomplish your CRM vision? Does it have the necessary and required technology, training programs, culture and environment? Is the leadership appropriate? Do you have CRM champions not only at the top but also across the organization?

' PricewaterhouseCoopers, 2000. All rights of use and reproduction reserved

By measuring areas related to the above, the agency then had the required performance data to guide it in determining the ongoing organizational strategy. It was then able to:

- hire the right people
- provide the necessary training to improve current people
- define the roles appropriately
- determine the business it should be in to meet customer need
- target communications to ensure most impact
- implement processes that move it forward
- ensure that it could accomplish its CRM vision

C: The Quality Service Performance Measurement System

Commitment to continuous improvement in quality service did not automatically happen because there existed a CRM vision or a good understanding of the customer and organization. To ensure this commitment was sustained, a quality service performance measurement system was designed and implemented. This system was developed from the CRM vision itself. First, service beliefs were developed and secured into the organization. In developing service beliefs, answers were determined to questions such as:

- What does my workforce and organization have to believe in order to reach and sustain our CRM vision?
- What values and principles must be championed throughout the organization?
- What type of organizational philosophy is required to translate the CRM vision into practical everyday reality?

Next, expectations (the minimum that has to be done), targets (where you want to get to soon) and stretch targets (where there is a possibility of getting to over a longer period of time) were developed for each of the service beliefs. However, expectations, targets and stretch targets could not be developed without first defining quality service. That was done through a series of customer focus groups and then validated though internal service provider focus groups.

Many organizations would have stopped here. However, without also developing and implementing a three-pronged sub-measurement process to ensure continuous improvement, PDS would not have known what they had achieved and to what degree. There would be no means to enable continuous improvement or to ensure appropriate information to refine expectations, targets and stretch targets.

This three-pronged measurement process included a balanced performance scorecard, a corresponding customer service survey and a proactive customer issue management process. The scorecard encompassed all areas of measurement that were relevant to quality service, but it was discovered that not all areas held equal value in the quality equation. Therefore each of the measurement areas within the scorecard was weighted according to priority and importance, some areas counting for more than others.

The corresponding customer service survey supported and enhanced the performance data obtained through the scorecard. When developing the customer service survey, care was taken to ensure that the information obtained would be compatible and comparable to the scorecard information. Finally, a proactive customer issue management process was developed. It took all customer problems, categorized them into relevant information groupings, and ensured enough detail to make the information useful without overloading the system with insignificant details. Balance was sought and obtained between what would be too much information and what would be too little.

Step Four: Ensuring CRM Success

In the last step, two final components were implemented to ensure success. The right environment had to be created, and a staged progression from setting a foundation for performance measurement to one where performance information was used for continuous improvement was required. If this evolution did not occur the agency would not have the performance information it needed and could not use it to ensure success.

CREATING THE RIGHT ENVIRONMENT

To ensure optimal CRM success the right environment had to be created to get maximum benefit from the organization and its people. The environment had to shift from an organization where top management directed, controlled and instructed staff to one where staff participated, became proactive and were actively encouraged to contribute to the achievement of the CRM vision. In this new CRM-focused organization, staff were brought in and encouraged to buy into the CRM vision from the beginning. This shift was essential to ensure the organization was fit and ready to achieve the vision. Figure 19.4 documents some of the fundamental shifts that had to occur to create the right environment.

Figure 19.4: The Shift Required

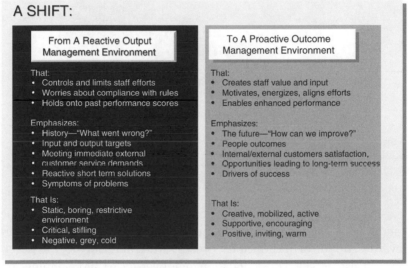

A SHIFT:

From A Reactive Output Management Environment	To A Proactive Outcome Management Environment
That:	That:
• Controls and limits staff efforts	• Creates staff value and input
• Worries about compliance with rules	• Motivates, energizes, aligns efforts
• Holds onto past performance scores	• Enables enhanced performance
Emphasizes:	Emphasizes:
• History—"What went wrong?"	• The future—"How can we improve?"
• Input and output targets	• People outcomes
• Meeting immediate external	• Internal/external customers satisfaction,
customer service demands	• Opportunities leading to long-term success
• Reactive short term solutions	• Drivers of success
• Symptoms of problems	
That Is:	That Is:
• Static, boring, restrictive	• Creative, mobilized, active
environment	• Supportive, encouraging
• Critical, stifling	• Positive, inviting, warm
• Negative, grey, cold	

© PricewaterhouseCoopers, 2000. All rights of use and reproduction reserved

A STAGED EVOLUTION: MOVING FROM PLATFORM TO PLATFORM

Once the three performance measurement systems—the customer performance measurement system, the organizational performance measurement system, and the quality service performance measurement system—were successfully implemented, it was necessary to ensure that the systems would lead the organization toward the CRM vision.

PDS, like many other organizations, had instituted performance measurement systems before, but these systems did not achieve the results desired. The systems were too focused on the metrics themselves and not on the measurement of outcomes and using that for continuous improvement. Organizations must evolve through three stages, known as platforms, as shown below.

Figure 19.5: Performance Platforms to Success

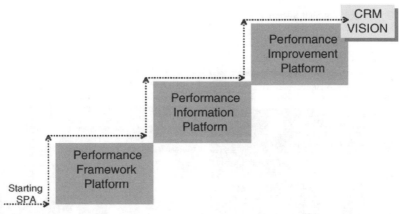

' PricewaterhouseCoopers, 2000. All rights of use and reproduction reserved

In starting this initiative, PDS recognized that a foundation had to be established—the performance framework platform. After that, a high-level description of the principles, process and criteria for SPA was developed. It also provided the foundation for longer-term CRM planning and acted as a communication tool for discussing CRM performance. The performance framework platform did not provide any performance information to assist the agency in moving toward its CRM vision, rather it provided a common means or language for discussing performance issues and their needs, in support of the CRM vision.

The performance information platform was the second platform. With buy-in to the need for performance measurement and an agreed set of metrics, the next goal was to track performance against these. The metrics were aligned with the CRM strategy and the organization was collecting performance data with full knowledge of its purpose. To collect this data, a combination of monitoring activities had been implemented:

- traditional audits—an independent review of performance
- self assessments—assessments administered by staff on their individual performance against these metrics
- client surveys—questionnaires provided to customers that measured satisfaction levels and requested information on additional needs
- remote monitoring—an independent measurement of performance conducted by an objective third party from a remote location

With a sufficient history of information—typically six months of performance data—PDS was then able to move to the third stage, the performance improvement platform. At this stage, the organization was ready to use performance information to manage the CRM strategy. A clear picture of CRM performance was being painted and there was a commitment to, and excitement around, performance improvement. More specifically, measures became focused on CRM outcomes.

After an initial review of the existing process for performance data collection and a validation of the performance measures, it was determined that the right data was now being collected, but some further refinement was necessary. To establish which of the performance measures should be kept and which should be eliminated, the measures were checked for:

- validity—was the measure appropriate for the CRM program?
- controllability—did it relate to factors that management could directly affect?
- clarity—was the measure clear and understandable?
- accuracy—was it reliable and able to be confirmed?
- cost—did the benefit of collecting the data outweigh the cost to collect it?
- timeliness—could it be collected and processed within a useful time frame?
- consistency—did it relate to the same factors in all cases, at all times?
- accessibility—how easy was it to collect the information?

In addition, the agency ensured that:

- Consistent terminology was being used.
- Only information that was needed to paint a picture of CRM performance was being collected, not unnecessary information.
- A regular reporting process enhancing accountability was implemented.
- Success was being demonstrated by providing examples of how performance information was being used.

Upon completion, the agency eliminated unnecessary measures and simplified their SPA efforts. This reduced the feeling of being overwhelmed. The collection of performance information began to be viewed as positive.

LESSON LEARNED

By implementing performance measurement systems that were strategically aligned against the three CRM critical success factors, the agency had great success. The CRM vision was kept relevant and alive by using the performance information to cycle back to the vision each year and either validating it or changing it to reflect new customer needs. The organization maintained a focus on key areas required to achieve the overall CRM vision by analyzing the performance information and identifying if they were getting closer to the vision.

The information required to align the organization against its CRM vision was available, and the information showed changes in staff levels were required. Internal organizational commitment was built by showing staff the improvements that were made. Customer loyalty was built and sustained by contributing information that assisted in managing customer, business and internal organizational relationships. Requirements for change levers such as change management workshops, customer service training, and new technology solutions were defined.

FINAL THOUGHTS ON WHAT'S NEEDED TO SUCCEED

In addition to the above achievements it is recommend that:

- Early efforts should be kept as simple as possible.
- A good understanding of your customer comes first—find out what is important to them.
- A gap analysis should be conducted early on in the process. The gap analysis described in Step Two as a critical starting point.
- Performance measures that are aligned with each of the critical success factors should be defined. Together, the performance measures should paint a picture that advises if movement toward the CRM vision is being made.
- An environment where people are mobilized must be created—without them your efforts will be lost.
- Early efforts should be targeted for early wins—to gain momentum and enthusiasm.
- Movement from platform to platform is a must.
- Cycling back to the CRM vision for refinement, strategic adjustments and continuous CRM improvement must be made.

Successfully implementing CRM can be achieved only through dedication, focus and a determination not to sway from the SPA route. Remember, any route will take you there if you don't know where you are going.

About the Author

MOOSHA GULYCZ

Moosha Gulycz is a Principal Consultant in PricewaterhouseCoopers' America's CRM consulting practice. She specializes in the area of Performance Management and Quality Service.

Conclusion

I'VE SAID IT before, and I'll say it once again, the only sure road to success is to be innovative. But innovation is not about creativity and originality, it is about stealing—we must steal (or more realistically, learn) from the best practices of others. Constantly ask yourself, what can I learn from the best practices of organizations that probably do not operate within my industry sector? And that is what we have set out to do in this book. To start, we provided you with a framework—a framework to develop a CRM strategy and the substrategies that must be articulated. Let's recap:

Customer Relationship Management (CRM) is neither a concept nor a project. Instead, it's a business strategy that aims to

- understand
- anticipate
- manage the needs of an organization's current and potential customers

CRM is a strategy that must be tailored to each market segment and therein is the challenge and the opportunity. To be effective in managing the customer relationship, an organization must:

- define its customer strategy
- create a channel and product strategy
- understand the importance of a robust and integrated infrastructure strategy

Part One of our book set the stage. It provided an end state for a CRM strategy. What is it that organizations will be capable of when as they evolve through the stages of CRM? As promised, we have provided examples from across a number of industry sectors, telecommunications (Chapter One), distribution and business services (Chapter Two) and financial services (Chapter Three). All have relevance as you begin to frame your strategy.

In Part Two, we set out to provide context around customer strategy, our first CRM substrategy. Three customer strategies were explored in detail and the necessary evolution from Stage I: customer acquisition (Chapter Six), to Stage II: customer retention and loyalty (Chapter Four) and ultimately to Stage III: strategic customer care (Chapter Five) were discussed in detail.

Part Three focused on the hard choices of product and channel strategy. Not all customers are the same, and all may not deserve (or require) the same level of service. At the same time, all customers should not have access to the same products or channels reserved for your most profitable customers. This section of the book led you through the need for more structure in new product development (Chapter Seven), and its role within CRM. It also brought to the forefront channel issues and hurdles that must be overcome to succeed (Chapter Eight). Here, the e-channel received considerable attention (Chapter Nine and Ten) together with the channel management and conflicts that must be addressed. While the Internet has and will continue to have a huge impact on the way we do business, it is not the only issue that has to be addressed related to which products and services will be offered to which customers through which channels (Chapter Eleven).

In Part Four, we dealt with the last of our CRM substrategies—the infrastructure strategy. The infrastructure consists of an interlinking of the processes that touch the customer (making it easy to do business with), the technology that enables those processes, and the organizational structure and people competencies that are required to ensure that maximum benefit is achieved. We started with an overview of the benefits that can be achieved if all are aligned (Chapter Twelve). A case study from within the publishing industry (Chapter Thirteen) provided a context for power of technology and the key tools that will be required, followed by a second case study in the telecommunications industry (Chapter Fourteen). The message is clear—investment and discipline is required in developing the infrastructure. It is not the most expensive technology that is required, rather the right technology for the right reasons. And if all three components are molded together properly, the benefits and rewards to both the organization and the customer can be significant.

Our last section, Part Five, provides a series of best practices in implementing CRM. There are many lessons to be learned (Chapter Fifteen), but without a measurement system in place and a balanced approach, success may be fleeting (Chapter Sixteen). Sometimes it is worthwhile to step back and assess if, in fact, your organization has the core competence to deliver effective CRM, or should this be outsource to organizations that have greater competence in this field. It's not heresy, as you have found out in Chapter Seventeen. Regardless, you must create a learning organization—one that supports continuous improvement and an unrelenting focus on improved customer relations (Chapter Eighteen). In closing, to quote the Mad Hatter in *Alice's Adventures in Wonderland* "Any road will take you there if you don't know where you are going." A vision of the future must be considered, goals must be established and performance measurement must be aligned to ensure that you are following the path to optimal CRM (Chapter Nineteen).

There you have the road map and the keys to success as seen through the eyes of those that have followed the path and been successful. As you read through these case studies, and the learnings provided, consider the next big enterprise CRM changes and challenges that organizations will face over the next five to 10 years. We hope that these examples may steer you in the right direction. The winners as you will note, are focused on CRM—and enhancing their ability to understand, anticipate and manage the needs of their current and potential customers. They target specific customers and add value to their businesses by providing tailored, differentiated service. Not only does this increase the profitability of their customers but also enhances customer loyalty and dependency—and increases their own profitability as well. Continuously executing this circle of cause and effect is key to achieving sustainable and profitable growth.

As an organization, we at PricewaterhouseCoopers are committed to help organizations achieve sustainable and profitable growth, and that is the purpose of this book. We have created a global management consulting service known as *Customer Relationship Management (CRM)*. Our goal is to help organizations understand and anticipate the needs of an enterprise's current and potential customers through proper deployment of skilled customer-facing personnel, optimal process and enabling technologies.

CRM: A Strategic Imperative in the World of e-Business is a practical book based on examples and best-practices case studies, but it is much more than a collection of anecdotes. It provides a foundation to help you achieve Customer Relationship Management (CRM)—and the long-term and profitable growth that results. It is an important cornerstone for organizations truly seeking success in a highly competitive and rapidly changing marketplace.

Appendix I

Foreword
Denis Collart
Paris, FRANCE
(33) 1 56 57 4303
denis.collart@fr.pwcglobal.com

Chapter One
Putting CRM to Work: The Rise
   of the Relationship
Lawrence Handen
San Francisco, California,
USA
(415) 657 6142
lawrence.handen@us.pwcglobal.com

Chapter Two
The Need for a Market-Intelligent Enter-
   prise (MIE): Laying the Foundation
Harris Gordon
Boston, Mass.
USA
(617) 428 8683
harris.gordon@us.pwcglobal.com
Steven Roth
Boston, Mass.
USA
(617) 428 8683

Chapter Three
A Case Study CRM and Mass
   Customization: Capital One
Stanley A. Brown
Toronto, CANADA
(416) 869 2990
stan.a.brown@ca.pwcglobal.com

Chapter Four
Creating Loyalty: Its Strategic
   Importance in Formulating Your
   Customer Strategy
Henrik Andersen
Copenhagen, DENMARK
(45) 39 45 9383
henrik.andersen@dk.pwcglobal.com
Per Ø. Jacobsen
Copenhagen, DENMARK
(45) 39 45 3945
per.ø.jacobsen@dk.pwcglobal.com

Chapter Five
From Customer Loyalty to Customer
   Dependency: A Case for Strategic
   Customer Care

Stanley A. Brown
Toronto, CANADA
(416) 869 2990
stan.a.brown@ca.pwcglobal.com

Chapter Six
Customer Acquisition and CRM:
    A Financial Services Perspective
Christopher Formant
New York, New York
USA
(212) 596 5382
christopher.formant@us.pwcglobal.com

Chapter Seven
CRM through New Product Development
William M. Takis
Arlington, Virginia
USA
(703) 741 2488
bill.takis@us.pwcglobal.com
Lorraine M. Cote
Arlington, Virginia
USA
(703) 741 1868
lorraine.cote@us.pwclobal.com
Catherine M. Stanmeyer
Arlington, Virginia
USA
(703) 741 2476
cathy.stanmeyer@us.pwcglobal.com

Chapter Eight
Channel Management and CRM
Stanley A. Brown
Toronto, CANADA
(416) 869 2990
stan.a.brown@ca.pwcglobal.com

Chapter Nine
Embracing the e-Channel
The above Chapter is extracted in part
    from PricewaterhouseCoopers'
    1999 publication entitled
    "Electronic Business Outlook."

Chapter Ten
e-Channel Management
Andy Pritchard
London, ENGLAND
44 (0) 207 804 0847
andrew.f.pritchard@uk.pwcglobal.com
Peter Cantor
London ENGLAND
44 (0) 207 804 0847
peter.cantor@uk.pwcglobal.com

Chapter Eleven
The Customer-Centric Organization
    in the Automotive Industry
J. Ferron
Detroit, Michigan
USA
(313) 446 7174
j.ferron@us.pwcglobal.com

Chapter Twelve
The Tools for CRM: The Three Ws
    of Technology
Lawrence Handen
San Franicsco, California
USA
(415) 657 6142
lawrence.handen@us.pwcglobal.com

Chapter Thirteen
Using the Tools: Database Marketing,
    Data Warehousing and Data Mining
Eric Falque
Paris, FRANCE
(33) 1 5657 4384
erik.falque@fr.pwcglobal.com

Chapter Fourteen
CRM in the Telecommunication
    Industry: Case Study of Swisscom
Michael Hobmeier
Zurich, SWITZERLAND
(41) 1 630 3250
michael.hobmeier@ch.pwcglobal.com
Urs Briner
Zurich, SWITZERLAND
(41) 1 630 3256
urs.briner@ch.pwcglobal.com

Chapter Fifteen
Implementing CRM: 20 Steps to Success
Henrik Andersen
Copenhagen, DENMARK
(45) 39 45 9383
henrik.andersen@dk.pwcglobal.com
Per Ø. Jacobsen
Copenhagen, DENMARK
(45) 39 45 3945
per.ø.jacobsen@dk.pwcglobal.com

Chapter Sixteen
Using Catalytic Measures to Improve CRM
Nancy Staisey
Arlington, Virginia
USA
(703) 741 1983
nancy.staisey@us.pwcglobal.com
Catherine M. Stanmeyer
Arlington, Virginia
USA
(703) 741 2476
cathy.stanmeyer@us.pwcglobal.com

Chapter Seventeen
Best Practices in Outsourcing CRM
Gina Boulton,
Suresh Gupta
New York, New York
USA
(212) 259 2036
suresh.gupta@us.pwcglobal.com
Brad Benton
New York, New York
USA
(212) 259 2036
brad.benton@us.pwcglobal.com

Chapter Eighteen
Learning and Knowledge Management
Programs in the Age of CRM
Hemant Minocha
Arlington, Virginia
USA
(703) 741 2597
hemant.minocha@us.pwcglobal.com
Daniel Murphy
Arlington, Virginia
USA
(703) 741 1000
Robert Thomas
Arlington, Virginia
USA
(703) 741 1000
robert.m.thomas@us.pwcglobal.com
Karen Ball
Arlington, Virginia
USA
(703) 741 1648
karen.ball@us.pwcglobal.com
Paul Drnevich
Arlington, Virginia
USA
(703) 741 1000
Randall Hawn
Arlington, Virginia
USA
(703) 741 1000
randall.f.hawn@us.pwcglobal.com
Stephen Browne
Arlington, Virginia
USA
(703) 741 1000
stephen.browne@us.pwcglobal.com

Chapter Nineteen
Implementing CRM: The Need for
Performance Alignment
Moosha Gulycz
Toronto, CANADA
(416) 815 5014
moosha.gulycz@ca.pwcglobal.com